The
EVERYTHING®
Cooking for Two
Cookbook

Dear Reader:

In today's fast-paced world, cooking can be a hassle. It seems as though food plays a minor role in the everyday life of most Americans. People race through their day to get home and reward themselves with fast food or frozen dinners, completely forgetting what their immigrant ancestors relished most—a great meal spent with someone they cared about.

Realizing that cooking is a labor of love, not a chore, can perhaps change this trend. Hopefully this book will inspire the reader to cook not only for someone besides themselves, but to try new flavors and ingredients, and to look at food as a reflection of foreign cultures and as a way to view history.

I truly hope that this book acts as an inspiration to aspiring cooks as well as seasoned veterans of the kitchen. Cooking for two can be immensely rewarding without demanding an all-day commitment, and cooking in general can be therapeutic and relaxing if one makes it so. Use this book as a guideline. Omit or substitute ingredients if you have an aversion to them, experiment and play in the kitchen, and most of all, have fun feeding others.

Best of luck,

The EVERYTHING Series

Editorial

Publishing Director	Gary M. Krebs
Associate Managing Editor	Laura M. Daly
Associate Copy Chief	Brett Palana-Shanahan
Acquisitions Editor	Kate Burgo
Development Editor	Karen Johnson Jacot
Associate Production Editor	Casey Ebert

Production

Director of Manufacturing	Susan Beale
Associate Director of Production	Michelle Roy Kelly
Cover Design	Paul Beatrice
	Erick DaCosta
	Matt LeBlanc
Design and Layout	Colleen Cunningham
	Holly Curtis
	Erin Dawson
	Sorae Lee
Series Cover Artist	Barry Littmann

THE
EVERYTHING®
COOKING
FOR TWO
COOKBOOK

300 creative ideas for making
relaxing meals at home

David Poran

Adams Media
Avon, Massachusetts

I would like to dedicate this book to Chef Mauro, who cooked for the Danielle Villa in Grado, Italy, and who inspired my lifelong love affair with food and cooking. Wherever you are Mauro, gràzie!

An Everything® Series Book.
Everything® and everything.com® are registered trademarks of F+W Publications, Inc.

Published by Adams Media, an F+W Publications Company
57 Littlefield Street, Avon, MA 02322 U.S.A.
www.adamsmedia.com

ISBN: 1-59337-370-8
Printed in the United States of America.

J   I   H   G   F   E   D   C   B   A

Library of Congress Cataloging-in-Publication Data
Poran, David.
The everything cooking for two cookbook / author: David Poran.
p.   cm.   --   (An everything series book)
ISBN 1-59337-370-8
1. Cookery for two. I. Title. II. Series: Everything series.

TX652.P667 2005
641.52'612--dc22
2005011008

This book is available at quantity discounts for bulk purchases.
For information, please call 1-800-872-5627.

Contents

acknowledgments

I would like to thank all of the following people for their help, support, and friendship: my agent, June Clark, and my patient editor, Kate Burgo. Thanks to my sister, Maya, and my parents, Ela and Michael Poran, who have always given me unconditional love and support, even when I didn't deserve it. I would also like to thank the Culinary Institute of America and all of the fine instructors who helped me find my way in this challenging career and who helped keep me grounded. Special thanks to Julia Child, Jacques Pépin, and Madeline Kamman for their early influence on my life through the magic of food television.

Introduction

Face it, cooking for a crowd is tough. Lots of work, many different tastes, and tons of dirty dishes make this task a bit of a chore even for the most enthusiastic cooks. Cooking for one, on the other hand, often kills inspiration and creativity as the solo diner prepares the meal alone and eats alone.

However, the addition of another person transforms the dining experience. Cooking for two is just the right-sized task. Whether the second diner is a spouse, lover, family member, or friend, the cook can easily express his or her love for that person by creating something special, quickly.

Set the mood. If romance is the goal and a meal is one of the vehicles to get there, be aware that the food is just one component of the meal. Flowers speak volumes. Some carefully placed blooms on the table can prove quite the mood enhancer. Avoid a huge arrangement in the middle of the table—this tends to obstruct your view of your sweetheart. Perhaps sprinkle some rose petals on the table, or put a few large flower tops in glass bowls with floating candles. Also, nasturtiums and other edible flowers can adorn salads and plates and be eaten as a fragrant aphrodisiac. Light the fire of love. Candles are important. Everyone looks more beautiful and sensual in candlelight. Some small votive candles on the table, or even scattered about the room, will provide the mood you want.

Champagne is the sexiest drink. Don't confuse the issue. No need to change wines with each course. Drink champagne throughout the meal for an easy and sensual choice. The magic of champagne is that it goes well with everything.

Eating at the table is optional. Instead, consider serving appetizers on the terrace or by the fireplace. Or serve the entire meal on the roof or even in the bedroom. Variety truly is the spice of life. Have chocolates in the bedroom with scented candles burning for a real dessert.

Certain foods, such as oysters, figs, asparagus, and chocolate, are known for their aphrodisiac qualities. Additionally, the act of cooking for, or being cooked for, has its health benefits. Remember when you were sick as a child? Just knowing that Mom was putting on a pot of her chicken soup could make you feel a little bit better even before you ate it. Knowing that someone cares enough for you to spend time preparing something to make you feel better is medicine for the heart and soul. Conversely, giving of yourself by preparing something special for a loved one to soothe either her mind or body feels great, too. Remember, though, that the foods that comfort you do not necessarily comfort others. Keep the other person's tastes in mind when you plan the menu, much like you would when picking out a gift for that person.

Every recipe in this book serves two. Therefore, there are no "serving sizes" given for individual recipes, though occasionally there are tips on how to prepare dishes in larger quantities. This book provides not only a list of recipes pared down to serve just two people but also creative solutions for preparation, service, and cleanup, so the two of you can enjoy each other's company over a fabulous meal. So please, come in and sit down. Your table for two is ready.

chapter 1
the basics

To cook for two, you need a few kitchen tools, a tasty menu, and a second person. That's it. There are lots of ways you can make cooking for two a simple and fun endeavor that results in delicious meals you'll both enjoy. This chapter includes some tips for how to make your dinner for two more enjoyable and less work.

The Right Tools for the Job

Put away Grandma's giant stockpot and that huge skillet. Cooking for two allows the cook to use smaller tools, which facilitate more efficient cooking time, easier cleanup, and less clutter in the kitchen. Following is a list of helpful tools and gadgets that will make your adventures in cooking for two a pleasure.

pots and pans

The heavier the pot or pan, the more efficient it is at conducting heat. Search the Internet for bargains and closeouts, as well as blemished items from factory stores. Also, go to wholesale restaurant supply stores and ask around. You don't have to own a restaurant to shop at these stores. Look for items that are entirely made of metal. Wooden and plastic handles cannot be placed into the oven and tend to wear out or break before the pan does. Some recommended brands include All-Clad, KitchenAid, Cuisinart, and Calphalon. Here is a list of the essentials:

- 2-quart saucepan (for sauces and small batches of soup)
- 5-quart saucepan (for pastas and larger batches of soup and stew)
- 9-inch sauté pan
- 12-inch sauté pan
- 12-inch straight-sided skillet with lid
- 12-inch cast-iron pan
- ½ standard sheet pan
- 12-inch strainer with handle
- Small stovetop wok

knives

Do not go out and buy the twenty-piece knife kit with wooden block. Choose your knives from a reputable source; avoid any mail-order knives or knives that promise you the world. Choose knives that fit comfortably in your hand, aren't too heavy, and have a *full tang* (this means the blade extends all the way through the handle of the knife, making for a very sturdy tool). Buy the best that you can afford. Higher-quality knives will last longer, and using them will give you much more satisfaction when cooking. Look online, browse factory store closeouts, or check out auctions for blemished knives, which will save you money but still provide you with the best-quality tools. Who cares if the handle color is off or there is a scratch on the surface of the blade? These surface blemishes do not affect the function of the knife. Some good brands to choose are Global, Dexter-Russell, and Sabatier.

Following is a list of basic knives that are essential to the modern kitchen:

- 8-inch chef's knife with a wide blade
- 8-inch offset serrated knife
- A long, thin, and flexible slicing knife
- 4-inch utility knife

This small collection of wares will cover just about every dish in this book. Many kitchens are cluttered with seldom or never-used pots, pans, and junk that do nothing but take up space. Avoid the urge to buy large sets of pots and pans; the small collection listed here is all that you need. And you can get many of these items on sale, at closeouts, or from flea markets!

tools

Again, this small collection of essentials can unclutter your kitchen drawers and get you working like a pro. Get these tools from a restaurant supply house—you will save money and have the tools the pros use.

- Large kitchen spoon
- Large kitchen spoon with slots or holes to allow liquid to pass through
- Heatproof rubber spatula
- 2-ounce ladle
- 8-ounce ladle (also makes a handy measure for 1 cup of liquid)
- Fish spatula

- 8-inch tongs
- 12-inch balloon whisk
- Standard wooden spoon
- Wooden spoon with a flat end (for scraping pan bottoms easily)
- A cylindrical stainless steel vessel to store your tools on the countertop
- A set of three stainless steel mixing bowls (small, medium, and large)

All of these tools are available either in retail or restaurant supply houses. They are inexpensive, highly versatile, and just about all you will need.

gadgets

You can certainly get by without any of these gadgets, but if your goal is to be an accomplished cook, or even just to make your time in the kitchen run smoother, you should consider them.

- Food processor with mini-bowl attachment (The mini-bowl will make cooking for two easier. With less food to prep, the small bowl comes in very handy.)
- A good blender (Get this at the restaurant supply store. Ask for a "bar blender.")
- Immersion blender, such as the Braun (This allows you to purée soups and sauces directly in the pot they were made in and avoids unnecessary burns or spills.)
- Bamboo steamer (These can be purchased in any restaurant supply store or Asian specialty store. They are cheap and make steaming anything a breeze.)
- Clamshell grill, such as the George Foreman (Hey, they just work.)

Do not be intimidated by this list. These are merely suggestions, taken from my own kitchen. Get what you can, but most importantly, have fun and enjoy!

How the Pros Prep Ahead Without Sacrificing Quality

Ever wonder how that roast chicken you ordered arrived so quickly and seemed perfect? Or how the risotto appetizer took only ten minutes but was al dente? Knowing a few basic techniques not only saves time, but also allows the cook to spend more time enjoying the cooking process and less time panicking.

do it a day ahead

Many items can be partially cooked or even fully prepared at least one day ahead. This will give you more time to plan menus and concentrate on the details. You can also prep several days ahead so that daily cooking does not take over your busy life. Here are some items that you can cook ahead:

- Make all soups a day ahead if possible. This allows the flavors another day to blend.
- Most sauces can and should be made a day ahead. However, avoid making things like cream sauces or cornstarch-thickened sauces a day ahead. They are not as easy to reheat from stone cold and tend to scorch.
- Anything cured, pickled, or marinated can be made up to a week in advance.
- Pasta can be cooked a day ahead. Just make sure the pasta is cooked quite al dente, cooled rapidly under cold running water, drained, and tossed with a light coat of olive oil. The pasta can then be reheated in boiling water just before serving. This takes the guesswork out of timing the pasta to the sauce.
- Large cuts of braised meats may be prepared the day before. The cooling allows the meat to soak up some pan juices, and with them, more flavor. (Mom's pot roast always tasted better the next day.)
- Most vegetables can be boiled, shocked in ice water, drained well, and placed in airtight containers lined with dry paper towels for up to four days. Simply reheat them in boiling water or in a sauté pan with some butter or oil when needed. You can cook and shock your vegetables for the week on Sunday, keep them in the fridge, and have them handy whenever you need them.

make in bulk, portion, and freeze

If you find a recipe you like, make it in bulk the next time around and freeze it in portions. Here are some helpful tips to make your storing and freezing easier and more efficient.

When buying meat, look for deals in bulk and place single servings in freezer paper, then freezer bags. Label and date the bags, and freeze them for use another day. Most meats last well for up to 4 months in the freezer. When needed, move portions directly from the freezer to the fridge for use the next day. Or, if needed the same day, place the meat in a bowl, still in the freezer bag, and run cold water over the portions until defrosted. This usually takes about ten to fifteen minutes.

Never defrost items on the counter or out of the fridge unless using cold running water. This is a recipe for bacterial growth. Conversely, never cool food for hours on the counter. Foods must be cooled rapidly to avoid bacterial growth. Place uncovered in the fridge until cold, then wrap tight.

Vinaigrettes and pesto last for weeks. Make enough to have some on hand for salads and sandwiches. Pesto also freezes very well. Broths and sauces can be poured into ice cube trays, frozen, and put into zip bags. This is a convenient time-saver. Whenever you need broth or sauce for a dish, the cubes can go directly from freezer to pan in the exact amount you need.

general tricks and hints

Remember, chefs are constantly challenged with the task of creating consistent results from inconsistent ingredients. Here are some tricks the pros use to keep it simple.

Remember to use fruits and vegetables in season. Not only are they cheaper and more abundant, they also taste better and have more nutritional value than produce that is out of season. Use fresh herbs whenever possible as opposed to dry. If an ingredient in a recipe is unavailable, do not abandon your quest; simply try a substitute or omit the ingredient. It is the only way to become a confident cook. Let the market determine your menu. See what produce looks great and is in season, and then build your menu around those items by adding protein of your choice and garnishes.

Food Safety Guidelines

Although these rules vary slightly state to state, if you follow these guidelines you will greatly decrease the possibility of food-borne illness.

the danger zone

The danger zone is when potentially hazardous foods are between 40 and 140°F. (These foods are almost any that contain water. These include cooked and raw meats, cooked vegetables, pastas, and grains, among other things.) The basic idea is to try to keep foods out of this temperature zone as much as possible. This means keeping cold foods cold and hot foods hot. Letting foods cool for hours on the counter before putting them in the fridge is a major no-no. On the same note, letting a turkey defrost on the counter overnight is also a recipe for disaster. Also, if you need to keep a pot of stew or soup on until someone comes home, keep it on a low flame and monitor the temperature to ensure that it is above 140°F.

use an instant-read thermometer

Also called a *meat thermometer*, these are available at any kitchen store or restaurant supply house. Digital models are now available and are inexpensive. I recommend these over standard thermometers because the digital thermometers never need to be recalibrated and are always accurate. The safe temperatures for most meats, fish, and poultry are as follows:

- **Beef/lamb**—Steaks and roasts should be cooked to 145°F for medium rare; ground meat should be cooked to 160°F.
- **Pork**—There is virtually no threat of trichinosis from pork in the United States, but pork should be cooked to 160°F to avoid other bacteria.
- **Poultry**—Poultry and any stuffing inside poultry should be cooked to 165°F to kill salmonella bacteria.
- **Fish**—Fish should be cooked to 140°F. If eating sushi or sashimi, the fish should be prefrozen for at least twenty-four hours at below 0°F.
- **Any leftover meat or fish**—Cook to 165°F.

If in doubt, go a bit over rather than a bit under. Also remember that large cuts of meat such as roasts and birds continue to cook after being removed from the oven—usually about 5 degrees higher.

don't cross-contaminate!

Professional kitchens use color-coded cutting boards: red for raw meats, yellow for raw poultry, green for raw vegetables, and so on. Although you do not need to go this far in your personal kitchen, the importance of using clean and sanitized boards and knives for raw meats and then resanitizing for foods or vegetables that are not going to be cooked cannot be overemphasized. For example, *do not* cut your salad on the same board you just used to cut raw chicken without first properly cleaning and sanitizing the board.

ALERT!

A simple sanitizing solution is a teaspoon of bleach per quart of cold water. Wipe down your tools, boards, and knives between uses after washing to ensure properly sanitized surfaces. Change this solution whenever it appears murky or every 2 hours.

Working Cleanly and Efficiently

Always plan your work area. When I train my cooks, I always make sure they plan their task before they start cutting or chopping. Do you have enough containers or bowls for the finished product? Is there a place for the garbage or scraps handy? Asking yourself these questions will streamline your work and help keep you focused.

Organize your cabinets. If you haven't used it in a year, you probably never will. Get rid of unnecessary items. If you are a pack rat and have trouble throwing things out, place your seldom-used kitchenware in a box, tape an inventory list on it, and store it in the cellar or attic. Organize you fridge by keeping raw foods and foods that are more sensitive to heat in the bottom of the fridge. Check to see that all the condiments in the fridge really need to be there. Inventory and organize your pantry. Take a hard look at what you have. Throw away spices and flour that is older than two years. Check to see if any oils have gone rancid. (Smell them, don't taste!) When in doubt, throw it out. Do this once a year and either cook or discard items that you have forgotten about. Then, organize your pantry and cabinets in a way that makes it easy for you to see what is on hand. This will make creating shopping lists much easier. Keep all cans in one area, pastas and grains in another, and ethnic ingredients in a separate section. Do what works for you, but keep it consistent. Your life will be much easier.

Set up a scrap or garbage container on the counter. This will stop the endless moving across the kitchen to throw out an onion skin or plastic wrapper. If your garbage container can be placed on the floor next to you without inconveniencing you, this is also a good option. Work in an "assembly line" method. If you have to peel and dice carrots for example, peel them all at once, then cut them. Do not peel one, trim one, and then cut one. This is an inefficient use of time. Envision yourself in a factory, and think of how things would run there.

Try to use a single pot or pan for multiple tasks. For instance, if the recipe calls for a piece of fish to be browned before braising but also has a vegetable component, cook the veggies first, cool them, wipe the pan, and brown the fish. I tried to be specific when writing recipes in the book to mention such techniques, but use common sense and think ahead. Have enough bowls and containers. Keeping you prepped veggies and other foods in small containers on your countertop in a ready-to-go position saves time. The new disposable "Tupperware" type containers are very useful and can be stacked up to save counter space.

Clean as you go. Taking a minute to wash a bowl or pan between cooking tasks is a very efficient way to work. You can easily wash a pot while your chicken is browning in the pan. Keep your countertop organized. Have a spot for finished product, prepped product, and untouched product. This avoids needless shuffling about.

Have fun with it! Pretend you are setting up your own little restaurant. You can organize things however you want. Remember, just because things have been one way forever doesn't mean they have to stay that way. Mix things up a bit. Start a new culinary life for yourself. Cook!

chapter 2
cold appetizers

Quick-Cured Salmon with Dilled Sour Cream Sauce

This is a twist on the classic Scandinavian gravlax.
If you like smoked salmon, you'll love this.

½ pound salmon fillet, as thick as possible
1 teaspoon good-quality vodka
1 tablespoon kosher salt
1 tablespoon brown sugar
Grated zest of ½ lemon
Dash brandy
½ cup sour cream
2 teaspoons chopped fresh dill
Salt and freshly ground black pepper, to taste
1 small head butter lettuce separated into leaves or 2 cups mixed baby greens, washed and dried
2 teaspoons capers
4 tablespoons olive oil

1. Chill the salmon in the freezer for about 20 minutes. (This will make it possible to slice the salmon more thinly.) Cut the salmon into 1/8 inch or thinner slices across the fillet. The slices should be roughly rectangular in shape. (Do not worry if they are not perfect.) Lay the slices of salmon on a dinner plate and splash with the vodka.

2. Mix together the salt, sugar, and lemon zest; sprinkle over the slices of salmon, turning the slices over to season both sides. Cover with plastic wrap and refrigerate for 20 minutes.

3. Discard the liquid that has collected on the plate. (This is water from the salmon, which is pulled out during the curing process.) Rinse the slices of fish under cold water and dry on paper towels.

4. To make the sauce, combine the lemon juice, brandy, sour cream, dill, and salt and pepper. Let stand at room temperature for 30 minutes before serving.

5. To serve, arrange the greens in the center of a large plate. Drape the slices of salmon gently over the greens. Drizzle the sauce around the plate and over the fish and greens.

6. Fry the capers in the olive oil in a small skillet until they open and become crisp (about 1 minute), Drain and sprinkle over the salmon and serve.

Lox, Lachs, or Lax?

Gravlax is a classic Scandinavian preparation of salmon. The words lax, lox, or lachs refer to salmon, and grav means "grave." This dish's name literally translates as "salmon from the grave," so named because traditionally the fish was buried in the earth to cure.

Lime and Cilantro Scented Crab Salad

Buy the best crabmeat that you can afford. Do not hesitate to ask your fishmonger to open a container of crabmeat and show you the contents for a thorough inspection.

1. In a small skillet, heat about 1 tablespoon of the olive oil until barely smoking. Add the avocado and season with salt and pepper. Sauté over high heat for about 1½ minutes, tossing gently. Transfer the avocado to paper towels and let cool to room temperature.

2. Roughly chop 1 tablespoon of the fresh cilantro leaves. Gently toss the chopped cilantro with the crabmeat, the remaining 1 tablespoon olive oil, the lime juice, jalapeño, and salt and pepper.

3. Firmly pack half of the crab salad into a ring mold placed in the center of a serving plate. (If you don't have a ring mold, you can use a tuna can with both the top and bottom removed.) Remove the mold and repeat with the remaining crab salad on another serving plate.

4. Arrange the radish slices on top of the crab salad. Place the tomatoes around the crab salad in a "starburst" fashion, cut side down. Arrange the avocado chunks on the plates in a random fashion. Drizzle the plates with olive oil and sprinkle with the whole cilantro leaves.

Buyer Beware
Don't be afraid to ask to inspect the crab before buying it. Some unscrupulous packers fill the crabmeat tubs with shredded crab and place the nice big lumps on the top of the container to fool the consumer.

---

2 tablespoons extra-virgin olive oil, plus extra for garnish
1 unripe Haas avocado, peeled and cut into chunks
2 tablespoons fresh cilantro leaves, washed and dried
½ pound jumbo lump crabmeat, picked through for bits of shells, but left as large as possible
Juice of 1 lime
About ½ teaspoon seeded and finely chopped jalapeño pepper
Kosher salt and pepper, to taste
2 medium-sized red radishes, sliced
3 grape or cherry tomatoes, sliced in half lengthwise

Shrimp Cocktail 101

12 uncooked U-12 shrimp,
shell-on
Juice of 1 lemon
½ peeled small white onion
1 bay leaf
2 tablespoons kosher salt
½ cup ketchup
1 teaspoon Worcestershire
sauce
2 tablespoons prepared
horseradish
Dash Tabasco sauce
Salt and pepper, to taste
2 cups shredded iceberg
lettuce

The key to this dish is the method used for cooking the shrimp. Just watch the clock and have your ice water bath ready to go when the shrimp are done.

1. Fill a saucepan with 3 quarts of cold water. Add the shrimp, half of the lemon juice, the onion, bay leaf, and kosher salt. Bring to a boil over high heat. As soon as the water boils, turn off the heat and let the shrimp sit in the water for exactly 4 minutes, uncovered. Remove the shrimp and cool quickly in ice water for about 5 minutes or until very cold. Drain.

2. To clean the shrimp, peel off the shell and legs and run a shallow incision along the top of the shrimp to remove the vein. (This is gray or black in color and is the digestive tract of the shrimp.) You can rinse the cut area of the shrimp under cold running water to make this process easier.

3. To make the sauce, mix together the remaining lemon juice, the ketchup, Worcestershire sauce, horseradish, Tabasco, and a bit of salt and pepper.

4. Mound 1 cup of lettuce in the center of each serving plate. Fan out the shrimp on top of the lettuce beds, and spoon the sauce in an attractive pattern around the beds.

Size Matters
Shrimp are sorted by size and species. For instance, if the box is labeled "16-20," this means that there are roughly 16 to 20 shrimp per pound. The letter U is also used as a code, which means "under." So if the box reads U-12, this means there are less than 12 shrimp per pound.

Japanese Spicy Tuna Tartar

A tartar is typically a preparation of raw meat, aggressively seasoned, and served cold. The classic tartar is steak tartar, which includes capers, onions, garlic, Worcestershire sauce, and raw eggs.

1. Heat the vegetable oil in a small skillet until barely smoking. Fry the wonton skins until they are golden brown and crispy, about 1 minute. Transfer to paper towels to drain.

2. Combine all the remaining ingredients except the shiso leaves (or basil) and let marinate in the refrigerator for 30 minutes to 1 hour.

3. When ready to serve, top each won ton skin with a shiso leaf and place a healthy-sized spoonful of tartar on top of each. Place 10 on each plate and serve with cold sake. Eat with your fingers, like you would a fancy canapé. These are also great for parties.

You Don't Have to Go to China
You can find pickled ginger, won ton skins, and siracha sauce in most ethnic sections of large supermarkets. Another place to look is in Asian-owned fish markets.

1 cup vegetable oil
20 wonton wrappers
¾ pound sushi-grade tuna cut into the smallest dice possible
2 scallions, sliced as thinly as possible
1 tablespoon soy sauce
Juice of ½ lime
1 teaspoon Asian chili sauce (such as siracha, or substitute your favorite hot sauce)
1 teaspoon sesame oil
1 teaspoon finely chopped pickled ginger
20 large shiso leaves or basil leaves

Oysters in the Nude with Three Sauces

*One of the most luxurious and simple foods on earth,
raw oysters have that magical blend of briny seawater, slippery texture,
and earthy flavor that makes them unique unto themselves.*

1 pound coarse sea salt
2 dozen shucked raw oysters
   on the half shell
¼ cup red wine vinegar
1 shallot, finely minced
1 teaspoon freshly cracked
   black peppercorns
½ cup white vinegar
¼ Granny Smith apple,
   peeled and cored
¼ loosely packed cup cilantro
   leaves
1 small garlic clove
1 recipe Shrimp Cocktail 101
   sauce (page 14)

1. Spread out the sea salt on 2 plates and arrange the oyster shells in the salt so the oysters do not tip and spill their "liquor." Refrigerate.

2. Mix together the red vinegar, shallots, and pepper. Set aside.

3. Combine the white vinegar, apple, cilantro, and garlic in a blender and purée until smooth.

4. To serve, arrange 12 oysters on each serving plate. Drizzle the red vinegar sauce over 4 of the oysters on each plate. Place a small dollop of the cilantro-apple sauce on 4 of the oysters on each plate, and spoon cocktail sauce on the remaining 4 oysters on each plate. Serve cold with champagne or a crisp white wine.

Remember the "R Rule"
If the current month does not have an r in it, avoid eating raw shellfish. June, July, and August are associated with warm waters and higher bacteria counts in shellfish.

Luxurious Mango-Lobster Salad

Lobsters were once considered trash. The fields of New England were fertilized with lobsters, and legend has it that a law was passed in Maine that prohibited prisoners from being fed lobster more than twice a week.

½ pound cooked lobster meat, diced, or 1½ pounds whole, fresh lobster
1 ripe avocado, cut in half lengthwise and pitted (leave the skin on)
Salt and pepper, to taste
Grated zest of ½ lemon
1 ripe mango, peeled and cut into thin, quarter-sized pieces
1 small shallot, finely minced
1 teaspoon chopped fresh tarragon leaves
2 tablespoons extra-virgin olive oil

1. If you are using a fresh lobster, fill a pot with enough water to cover the lobster. Bring to a boil and add a pinch of salt. Gently place the lobster in the water and let boil for 7 minutes, uncovered. Transfer the lobster to a bowl of ice water to cool. Remove the meat from the shell, and dice the meat.

2. Season the avocado with salt and pepper, and rub the flesh with the lemon half to keep it from browning.

3. Toss the lobster meat with the lemon zest, mango, shallot, tarragon, oil, and salt and pepper.

4. Stuff the lobster mixture inside the cavity of the avocado, allowing it to spill over slightly for an abundant presentation. Serve immediately.

The Pits
To remove the pit from an avocado, simply cut the avocado in half lengthwise, twist the halves apart, and gently drive the blade of your knife into the pit. Twist the pit slightly, and knock the pit off of the knife into the garbage. Your fingers never even need to touch the pit.

Scallop, Corn, and Oyster Mushroom Salad

This sounds like an odd combination, but corn and mushrooms have very similar flavor profiles, and the natural sweetness of scallops pairs magnificently with these ingredients.

Extra-virgin olive oil, as needed
½ pound scallops, patted dry
Salt and pepper, to taste
½ pound oyster mushrooms, tough stems removed and caps torn into strips
3 ears corn, shucked and kernels cut off the cob
½ medium-sized red onion, finely minced
2 small plum tomatoes, seeded and diced
¼ cup roughly chopped flat-leaf parsley
2 cups endive lettuce or baby spinach, washed and dried
1 tablespoon red wine vinegar, plus extra for dressing

1. Add enough of the oil to a heavy sauté pan to just coat the bottom. Heat until barely smoking.

2. Add the scallops in a single layer, being sure not to crowd the pan. Season with salt and pepper. Cook the scallops for about 2 minutes, turning them only once when browned on the first side. Transfer to a plate immediately and place in the refrigerator to cool, uncovered.

3. Wipe out the pan and add enough oil to just coat the bottom of the pan. Heat until barely smoking, then add the oyster mushrooms. Cook the mushrooms for about 4 minutes or until the water that is released from the mushrooms evaporates. Remove from heat and let cool.

4. Toss together the cooled scallops, along with any accumulated juices, the cooled mushrooms, the raw corn, onion, tomatoes, parsley, and vinegar. Season to taste with salt and pepper.

5. Lightly dress the greens with a dash of oil and vinegar and sprinkle with salt and pepper. Arrange the greens in the center of large serving plates. Equally divide the scallop salad over the greens, and enjoy.

No Need to Cook!!
Raw corn is an amazing treat when the corn is in peak season. Do not hesitate to take a nibble at the market to assure that your corn is sweet, tender, and juicy. To remove the kernels from the cob, cut the ear in half, stand each half on your cutting board one at a time, and simply run your knife between the cob and the kernels. The kernels will fall right off.

Grilled and Chilled Asparagus in Vinaigrette

Grilling asparagus yields incredible-tasting results. The skin caramelizes and the asparagus takes on a smoky sweetness that is indescribable.

1 bunch (about ¾ pound) asparagus (the largest you can find)
¼ cup extra-virgin olive oil
1 large red bell pepper
2 tablespoons balsamic vinegar
2 teaspoons chopped fresh dill
Salt and pepper, to taste

1. Take 1 asparagus spear and bend it until it snaps. The point at which it breaks delineates where the tough part meets the tender part. Use this asparagus as a measure for the rest, and cut them all to the same length.

2. Toss the asparagus with a small amount of the oil just to coat them, and season with salt and pepper.

3. Grill the asparagus on a hot grill or in a dry cast-iron pan set over high heat until the skin is blackened and blistered and the spears soften. (It's okay if they appear almost burned.) Let cool, then cut into thirds.

4. Place the red pepper directly over the flame of your grill or burner and use tongs to turn it until the entire skin is completely black. Wrap in plastic wrap and let steam for 10 minutes. Peel off the skin under cool water. Remove the seeds and ribs, and cut the pepper into julienne strips.

5. Mix together the remaining oil, the vinegar, dill, and salt and pepper. Toss with the asparagus and the red pepper.

Flavors of Spring
Dill and asparagus are a natural combination. Each has a unique sweetness and freshness, which makes them ideal partners. Many Mediterranean cultures, especially the Greeks, have used this combination for centuries.

Barbecued Pork Shoulder Terrine

4 pounds boneless pork
    shoulder, cut into 4-inch
    chunks
1 tablespoon brown sugar
1 tablespoon ground paprika
2 teaspoons garlic powder
2 teaspoons onion powder
1 teaspoon dry mustard
½ teaspoon mesquite
    seasoning or 1 dash
    liquid smoke
3 tablespoons salt
1 (12-ounce) bottle dark beer
1 cup water
2 tablespoons Worcestershire
    sauce
2 dill pickles, medium diced
3 cups shredded green
    cabbage
¼ cup peeled and shredded
    carrot
1 cup white vinegar
1 tablespoon vegetable oil
2 tablespoons granulated
    sugar
1 teaspoon celery seeds

Not a true terrine because it is not packed into a terrine mold, this innovative dish has a multitude of uses. The recipe will make enough for several servings. Freeze the remainder for another use.

1. Preheat oven to 350°F. Toss the pork with the brown sugar, paprika, onion and garlic powders, dry mustard, mesquite seasoning, and 2 tablespoons of the salt. Place in an ovenproof casserole dish and pour the beer, water, and Worcestershire sauce over the meat.

2. Cover and place in the oven for about 4 hours or until the meat literally falls apart to the touch.

3. Carefully remove the meat from the liquid and place in a large mixing bowl. With a wooden spoon, gently mix the meat to achieve a shredded consistency. Add the pickles and mix again.

4. Lay out 2 pieces of plastic wrap, each about 16 inches long. While the meat is still warm, divide it into 2 equal piles and place one pile in the center of each piece of plastic wrap. Wrap up each in a cylindrical fashion. Fold the sides of the wrap over the meat and roll into loose sausage shapes about 8 to 10 inches long.

5. Lay out each "sausage" on a piece of aluminum foil about 8 inches longer than the wrapped meat. Tightly roll up each sausage, twisting the end of the aluminum foil in opposite directions at the same time to tighten the roll as much as you can without breaking the "sausage" open. Chill in the refrigerator overnight.

6. To make the slaw, mix together the cabbage, carrots, and the remaining 1 tablespoon salt. Allow to wilt for 20 minutes, then squeeze the cabbage dry. Discard the liquid.

7. In a saucepan, combine the vinegar, oil, sugar, and celery seeds. Bring to a boil. Remove from heat and pour over the cabbage. Let cool on the counter until cool enough to handle, then drain the liquid from the slaw.

8. When ready to serve, unwrap the pork terrine and cut into ½-inch slices. Place a small pile of slaw in the center of serving plates and arrange the pork around the slaw.

Versatility Is Key
You can also use this pork for taco filling, or add it to baked beans. It also makes a great shredded meat sandwich, or it can be sliced cold and eaten as a snack. Try some grilled with melted cheese and onions.

Watermelon and Feta Cheese Nuggets

It's okay to be skeptical when first presented with this pairing, which was inspired by a street snack in Israel, but be prepared to be blown away by its complexity and simultaneous simplicity.

10 (2-inch) cubes seedless watermelon
¼ cup finely minced red onion
5 Moroccan oil-cured olives, pitted and finely minced
1 tablespoon extra-virgin olive oil
½ cup crumbled feta cheese
10 small mint leaves

1. Dig a small hole in each watermelon cube about ¾ of the way down into the flesh. A melon baller works great for this. (Basically you want to create a cavity to fill.)

2. Mix together the onions, olives, and oil. Place a small amount in each watermelon cube, filling them about halfway.

3. Fill the cavities the rest of the way with the crumbled feta and top each cube with a mint leaf. Serve as a finger food.

"Smoked" Eggplant Dip

1 cup plain, whole yogurt
Salt and pepper, to taste
1 large purple eggplant
    (about 1½ pounds)
¼ cup finely minced red
    onion
3 garlic cloves, smashed
¼ cup mayonnaise
Juice of 1 lemon
2 pita bread rounds
1 tablespoon extra-virgin
    olive oil
1 teaspoon ground cumin
2 tablespoons chopped fresh
    parsley

Also an inspiration from the Middle East, this recipe is a twist on the classic "baba ganoush." The key to this dish is the "smoking" of the eggplant.

1. Spoon the yogurt into a strainer lined with a coffee filter, and position the strainer over a bowl to catch the liquid. Place in the refrigerator and let drain overnight. The next day, discard the liquid whey and season the remaining "yogurt cheese" with salt and pepper. Reserve in an airtight container in the refrigerator.

2. Place the eggplant directly over the open flame of a grill or a gas burner, or place in a dry cast-iron pan set over high heat. "Smoke" the eggplant all over until the skin is completely charred and the flesh has softened. A knife inserted into the deepest part of the eggplant should slide out with no resistance. (This may take up to 15 minutes.)

3. Place the eggplant in a bowl, cover with plastic wrap, and let sit in the refrigerator until cool enough to handle. Scrape the meat out of the skin, being careful to pick out and discard any small pieces of charred skin.

4. In a food processor, blend the eggplant, garlic, mayonnaise, lemon juice, and salt and pepper into a smooth purée. Then add the onion.

5. Brush each pita with a small amount of the olive oil and dust with the cumin and a bit of salt. Toast on the grill or under the broiler until the cumin starts to become fragrant and the edges of the pita begin to char slightly. Cut into triangular wedges.

6. Serve the eggplant dip and the yogurt cheese in small crocks, garnish with the parsley, and use the pita chips to scoop up both dips. Serve this with cold mint tea for a true taste of the Middle East.

Grilled Peaches with Blue Cheese

Here the traditional fruit and cheese combination is modernized by grilling the peaches. This accents their natural sweetness and adds another dimension from the light charring of their flesh.

ஃ

¼ cup pecan halves
2 medium peaches, slightly
    firmer than perfectly ripe
2 teaspoons vegetable oil
Salt and pepper, to taste
¼ cup crumbled domestic
    blue cheese

1. Preheat grill on high, brush the slats clean, and coat them with a light film of oil. Preheat oven to 350°F.

2. Spread out the pecans on a baking sheet and toast in the oven for about 5 minutes, until lightly browned. Remove from oven and let cool.

3. Cut the peaches in half and remove the stones. Toss the peach halves with the oil and salt and pepper.

4. Grill the peaches cut-side down until the flesh begins to char and they start to soften, about 3 minutes. Turn the peaches over and spoon an equal amount of the blue cheese into the pit cavity of each half. Continue to grill until the cheese starts to melt, about 3 more minutes.

5. Divide the peaches between 2 serving plates and toss the toasted pecans in and around the peaches. Let cool to room temperature before serving.

You Can Grill More Than Peaches
Experiment with other fruits on the grill. Generally speaking, firmer fruits work well. Try pears, pineapples, apples, apricots, and of course, peaches. Treat them all the same by tossing the pieces in a light coat of oil and giving them a slight seasoning with salt and pepper. Do not grill melons or berries.

The Ultimate Tomato

*This dish was inspired by an appetizer on the menu of the famous
New York restaurant Daniel in the early 1990s.
Make this dish only when tomatoes are at their peak.*

2 medium to large beefsteak
    or heirloom tomatoes
2 shallots, finely minced
2 tablespoons shredded basil
    leaves
4 tablespoons extra-virgin
    olive oil
2 tablespoons sherry wine
    vinegar
Salt and pepper, to taste

1. Peel the tomatoes by cutting the core out, scoring the opposite side of the skin with a small X, and immersing the tomatoes in boiling water for about 30 seconds. After 30 seconds, immerse the tomatoes in ice water for about 2 minutes. Peel the tomatoes gently with a paring knife and your fingers.

2. Have a large baking sheet handy. Slice the tomatoes as thinly as possible. When slicing, lay the slices out on the baking sheet in the same order in which they were sliced. (The idea is that you will be reassembling the tomato back into its original shape.)

3. Sprinkle each slice with the shallots, basil, oil, and vinegar. Just as you are ready to serve, season with salt and pepper and reassemble your tomatoes into their original shape. Place each in the center of a plate and sprinkle with more basil and a bit more olive oil.

Poison Fruit
The tomato is a member of the nightshade family of plants. Many members in this family are poisonous to humans. In the 1700s tomatoes were reputed to be poisonous and were not eaten in the United States. It took awhile, but the virtues of this fruit were eventually discovered and it became a popular addition to many dishes.

Baby Potatoes with Sour Cream and Caviar

Serve these tidbits on New Year's Eve or birthday parties when the expense of caviar is forgiven. If Russian sturgeon caviar is too expensive, there are some great domestic caviars available made from both sturgeon and American paddlefish.

10 red bliss potatoes (about 2 to 3 inches in diameter)
1 tablespoon extra-virgin olive oil
Salt and pepper, to taste
½ cup sour cream
2 tablespoons minced fresh chives
1–2 ounces caviar

1. Preheat oven to 400°F. Slice the potatoes in half lengthwise. Toss the potatoes with the oil and salt and pepper. Place the potatoes, cut-side down, in a single layer directly on the oven rack. Roast for about 15 minutes or until a knife inserted in the center comes out with no resistance. Remove with a spatula and let cool to room temperature.

2. Mix together the sour cream and 1 tablespoon of the chives.

3. When the potatoes are cool, make a slight cut down the center of the cut side of each and dig out a small cavity with a small spoon.

4. Fill each potato half with the sour cream, top with as much caviar as you can, and sprinkle with chives. It is okay for these to overflow, as the opulence of the caviar should be emphasized.

Sturgeon Caviar Comrade?
Since the fall of the Iron Curtain, the export and illegal trade of caviar from Russia has brought this mighty fish—which can reach over 1,000 pounds—to the verge of extinction. Try using the American caviars that are now readily available, or salmon roe, which is in plentiful supply. Please avoid using supermarket "caviar," which is usually lumpfish roe that has been died either red or black. It is inferior to the point of being just plain bad.

Seared Southwestern Beef Carpaccio

A carpaccio is typically very thin slices of raw meat or fish served with flavorful accompaniments. The twist on this Italian classic is the Southwestern seasonings, which evoke the flavors of Texas and Mexico.

8 ounces center-cut filet
    mignon
1 teaspoon ground cumin
1 teaspoon ground coriander
1 teaspoon ground chili
    powder
1 teaspoon kosher salt
½ loosely packed cup cilantro
    leaves, washed and dried
4 grape tomatoes, cut into
    fourths lengthwise
1 shallot, minced
2 teaspoons capers, rinsed
3 tablespoons extra-virgin
    olive oil
Juice of ½ lime
Salt and pepper, to taste
2 ounces aged jack cheese

1. Preheat a heavy skillet, preferably cast iron, over medium-high heat. Mix together the cumin, coriander, chili powder, and kosher salt. Rub the beef with the spice mixture, coating it completely on all sides.

2. Sear the beef on all sides in the dry skillet so the spice mix blackens. The entire procedure should take no more than 2 minutes. (You just want to sear the outside, leaving the beef basically raw on the inside.) Place the beef in the freezer for about 30 minutes to firm up the meat. (This will allow you to slice the meat very thinly with ease.)

3. When the meat has chilled, slice the beef so you have disks of beef about ¼ inch in thickness. Place each slice between 2 layers of plastic wrap and pound with a rolling pin until the beef is paper-thin. Leave in the plastic wrap and store in the refrigerator until ready to serve.

4. When ready to serve, peel off 1 layer of plastic and press the slices onto 2 serving plates, then peel off the other layer. Assemble the salad by tossing together the cilantro, tomatoes, shallot, capers, 1 tablespoon of the olive oil, the lime juice, and salt and pepper. Arrange this salad in the center of the plate on top of the carpaccio.

5. To finish, use a vegetable peeler to peel off long strips of the cheese and let them fall randomly about the plate. Drizzle with the remaining oil.

Hey Jack

Aged jack cheese is a uniquely American product. Manufactured in a similar style to the famous Parmigiano-Reggiano, this cheese is aged for months to achieve an intense nutty and sharp flavor. Seek it out—it is worth the effort.

Portobello and Goat Cheese Sandwiches

The popular portobello mushroom didn't start off with such an illustrious pedigree. Actually overmature cremini mushrooms, these giants were discarded by the mushroom farms for years until someone gave them a name.

1. Preheat oven to 450°F. Remove the stem from each mushroom. Brush the caps with a damp paper towel to remove any dirt particles. Turn the mushrooms upside down and scrape out the black "gills" with a spoon.

2. Mix together the olive oil, vinegar, honey, half the garlic, and salt and pepper. Brush evenly over both sides of the mushrooms. Place the mushrooms, stem side down, on a baking sheet treated with nonstick cooking spray. Roast for 10 minutes. Remove from oven and chill in the refrigerator.

3. To make the cheese filling, whisk together the goat cheese, milk, chives, lemon zest, Parmesan cheese, and the remaining garlic. Blend together until smooth and spreadable.

4. When the mushrooms are cold, press them between paper towels to absorb excess water.

5. Spread a thin layer of goat cheese in the hollow of each mushroom, leaving a 1/8-inch ring around the outside edge. (This allows the filling to spread out and not spill over the edges when the "sandwiches" are assembled.)

6. Arrange a layer of basil leaves across the entire surface of 2 of the mushrooms so the basil covers the cheese filling and hangs over the edges by about ¼ inch. Cap each with another mushroom. Place the sandwiches in the center of serving plates. Sprinkle a few torn basil leaves on each plate, place a lemon wedge alongside, and drizzle with extra-virgin olive oil.

---

4 medium portobello mushrooms (about 5 inches in diameter)
¼ cup extra-virgin olive oil, plus extra for drizzling
3 tablespoons balsamic vinegar
1 teaspoon honey
2 garlic cloves, smashed
Salt and pepper, to taste
6 ounces soft goat cheese, at room temperature
1 tablespoon milk
2 teaspoons chopped fresh chives
½ teaspoon grated lemon zest
1 tablespoon grated Parmesan cheese
1 loosely packed cup basil leaves
2 lemon wedges

Chicken and Lettuce Wraps

½ pound skinless, boneless
  chicken breast
1 tablespoon salt
1 bay leaf
2 tablespoons high-quality
  mayonnaise
1 tablespoon roughly
  chopped toasted walnuts
2 teaspoons chopped fresh
  dill
Salt and pepper, to taste
6 large leaves red leaf lettuce
¼ lemon
2 teaspoons extra-virgin
  olive oil

The key to this preparation is to poach the chicken breasts perfectly and very gently. Because chicken breasts contain almost no fat, they are in constant danger of becoming dry and overcooked.

1. Fill a small pot with 1 quart of cold water. Add the chicken breast, the 1 tablespoon salt, and the bay leaf. Bring to a boil. As soon as the water boils, turn off the heat and allow the chicken to poach until a thermometer inserted in the thickest part of the chicken reads 165°F, about 6 minutes.

2. Remove the chicken from the pot and place on a plate in the refrigerator. Let cool for at least 30 minutes. When the chicken is cool, dice into very small pieces, about the same size as the walnut pieces.

3. Mix together the chicken, mayonnaise, walnuts, and dill. Season to taste with salt and pepper.

4. Divide the chicken mixture equally between the 6 leaves and roll the leaves into little "spring rolls." Trim the lettuce leaves so there is no excess. Arrange 3 rolls on each plate, squeeze the lemon over them, and drizzle the oil over the top.

Pink Chicken
Sometimes chicken appears pinkish even after it has been cooked to 165°F. This is due to the hemoglobin in the chicken, and sometimes has to do with the feed that the chickens are given. As long as an accurate thermometer reads 165°F, the chicken is safe.

Duck Breast "Sushi" with Plum Sauce

This dish is a play on the presentation of nigiri sushi, which is raw fish draped over rice. Here we season the rice with pickled ginger and use the rosy red slices of medium-rare duck breast to simulate the appearance of tuna.

1 cup uncooked short-grain rice
2 cups cold water
2 tablespoons rice vinegar or apple cider vinegar
2 tablespoons granulated sugar
1 tablespoon minced Japanese pickled ginger
2 scallions, cut as thinly as possible on a bias
1 (6- to 8-ounce) duck breast
4 tablespoons prepared Chinese plum sauce or hoisin sauce

1. Place the rice and the water in the smallest pot available. Bring to a boil, then immediately turn down to the lowest simmer possible. Cover and cook for exactly 18 minutes. When cooked, place in a large mixing bowl and break up with chopsticks or a fork.

2. Add the vinegar, sugar, and ginger to the rice and mix gently until the rice reaches room temperature (about 15 minutes). Stir in half the scallions and keep the rice at room temperature.

3. Score the skin of the duck breast in an X pattern. Place the duck breast, skin-side down, in a sauté pan with ¼ inch of water. Bring to a gentle simmer and cook until the water boils off completely. Continue to cook the duck breast skin-side down over medium heat until the skin is golden brown and it begins to crisp.

4. When the skin is an attractive brown color, flip the duck breast over and cook the flesh side for approximately 2 minutes. Remove the duck from the pan and let cool in the refrigerator for about 15 minutes.

5. Take small bunches of rice (about the size of a small egg) and gently form them into rectangles about 2 inches long, 1 inch wide, and 1 inch high (sushi shape). The rice should hold together but not be too firmly packed. Lay the rice bunches on a platter as you go, or divide between 2 serving plates.

6. Slice the duck breast straight across so the slices are about 1/8 of an inch thick and about the same size as the rice rectangles. Place a small dollop of plum sauce on the top of each rice rectangle, drape the duck over the top, and top with another dollop of plum sauce. Sprinkle the remaining scallions over the top.

Chilled Lamb Medallions

½ pound boneless loin of lamb, trimmed of all sinew and fat
Salt and pepper, to taste
1 cup canned cannellini beans, drained and rinsed
½ cup extra-virgin olive oil, divided
Juice of ½ lemon
1 garlic clove, smashed
1 sprig fresh rosemary
¼ cup finely chopped pimiento
1 tablespoon minced fresh chives

Sheep often grazed in the rugged hills of the Mediterranean region where wild rosemary is abundant. The sheep often ate so much rosemary that their flesh became perfumed with its scent from within.

1. Season the lamb with salt and pepper and sear on all sides in a dry skillet over high heat. Reduce heat to medium and cook slowly, turning occasionally, until the meat reaches an internal temperature of 135°F. Remove from the pan and cool in the refrigerator for 1 hour.

2. With an immersion blender or in a food processor, make the hummus by puréeing the beans with half the olive oil, the lemon juice, garlic, and salt and pepper. Purée until very smooth.

3. Pull off the leaves from the rosemary sprig. Combine with the remaining olive oil in a microwave-safe container. Microwave on low for 1 minute. (You can also gently heat the oil in a pan with the rosemary. Do not fry the rosemary.) This infuses the oil with the rosemary flavor. Strain the oil and let cool to room temperature.

4. Mix the pimiento with the chives and add about 1 teaspoon of the rosemary oil. Cut the lamb into 6 medallions and arrange on a plate, splaying out the slices from the center like a flower. Season the top of each piece of lamb with salt and pepper. Top each medallion with a spoonful of the hummus, then a spoonful of the pimiento mixture. Drizzle the lamb and the plate with some rosemary oil.

USA or New Zealand?
Although perfectly fine and flavorful, be aware that New Zealand lamb is always frozen for transport to the United States, and it loses some of its texture, moisture, and flavor as a result. Seek out domestic lamb, especially Colorado lamb. It is readily available—just ask your butcher where the lamb is from and if it has been frozen.

Prosciutto and Avocado with Hazelnut Vinaigrette

Made in the Parma region of Italy, prosciutto is ham that is salted and hung for almost a year to achieve its amazing, silky texture and nutty flavor. It is never cooked or smoked in any way.

1/3 pound thinly sliced prosciutto ham
1 ripe Haas avocado
Freshly ground black pepper, to taste
2 tablespoons toasted and crushed hazelnuts
1 tablespoon extra-virgin olive oil
1 tablespoon hazelnut or walnut oil
2 tablespoons red wine vinegar
2 tablespoons chopped fresh parsley
Salt and pepper, to taste
1 loosely packed cup arugula leaves, washed and dried

1. Cut the avocado in half lengthwise and remove the seed with a knife. Peel the skin gently away and cut out any bruised portions. Cut the avocado into ½-inch slices, lengthwise, and season with pepper. Loosely wrap each avocado slice in a slice of prosciutto.

2. Make the dressing by mixing together the nuts, oils, vinegar, parsley, and salt and pepper. Arrange the arugula leaves on two plates as a bed. Arrange the ham-wrapped avocado across the plates in a neat row and spoon the sauce over each piece of avocado.

Differences in Avocados

In the market there are usually 2 kinds of avocados offered in the United States: bacon and Haas. The bacon avocados are much larger, are light green in color, and have a smooth skin. They also have less fat and more water. The Haas avocados are smaller, darker in color, have a pebbly skin sometimes with a purplish hue, and have a much richer, less watery flesh. They are Mexican in origin.

North African Lamb Loin Tartar

This dish is a combination of the classic steak tartar
and an Arabian raw lamb preparation.

6 ounces trimmed lamb loin,
cut into 1/8-inch dice
1 shallot, minced
6 Moroccan oil-cured olives,
pitted and minced
1 teaspoon capers, rinsed
½ teaspoon ground cumin
2 scallions, minced
Juice of 1 lemon
3 tablespoons extra-virgin
olive oil
Salt and pepper, to taste
Pita chips or good-quality
bread toast

Mix together all of the ingredients except the bread. Season with salt
and pepper and serve on pita chips or toast.

Fluke New Sashimi Style

This is sort of a cross between Japanese sashimi and Peruvian ceviche.

½ pound fresh fluke fillet
1 shallot, minced
½ teaspoon minced jalapeño
pepper
1 teaspoon chopped fresh
cilantro
2 tablespoons citrus soy
sauce
1 tablespoon lime juice
½ teaspoon sesame oil

1. Cut the fish across the fillet into very thin slices and arrange the slices
   on a plate in an attractive way, slightly overlapping each other.

2. Mix together the remaining ingredients and spoon over the raw fish.
   Serve immediately.

Choosing Fish for Sashimi

*The most important factor in choosing fish to eat raw is that the fish has
been kept cold for its entire time out of the water. Go to busy fish markets that have high product turnover to find the best fish.*

chapter 3
hot appetizers

Molten Brie with Sautéed Pears

The rind of Brie is not only edible, but also delicious. It has a very different character than the smooth cheese within.

2 teaspoons butter
1 firm pear (such as Anjou), peeled, cored, and sliced ¼ inch thick
Salt and pepper, to taste
2 (3-ounce) wedges Brie
¼ cup toasted whole cashews
2 lemon wedges

1. Preheat oven to 400°F.

2. In a small sauté pan, heat the butter on medium until it stops bubbling.

3. Add the pears, increase heat slightly, and season with salt and pepper. Sauté for about 1 minute just to soften the pears slightly and give them a little golden color. Squeeze the lemon in the pan and transfer the pears to a plate and keep warm.

4. Place the Brie on an ovenproof plate and bake for about 2 to 3 minutes or until the cheese starts to ooze a bit.

5. Carefully transfer the Brie to a serving plate using a spatula. Arrange a small pile of pears next to the cheese and sprinkle with the cashews. The idea is to have a little bite of everything at the same time to let the flavors merge in your mouth.

Brie 101
Brie is a soft-ripened, double-cream, or even triple-cream cheese from France. The longer the cheese ages, the softer and stronger in flavor it becomes. Eventually the cheese will smell of ammonia and be unpalatable, but some folks really love it when it gets super old and stinky. For this recipe, use a slightly firmer Brie, which will probably be the only type you can find in a supermarket.

Easy Spinach Soufflés with Smoked Gouda

The smoked cheese adds an aggressive and distinct flavor. You can also substitute regular Gouda or any semisoft cheese such as Cheddar, fontina, or Edam.

4 tablespoons butter, divided
1 cup frozen chopped
    spinach, thawed and
    squeezed very dry
1 small garlic clove, smashed
Pinch nutmeg
Salt and pepper, to taste
¾ cup heavy cream
2 eggs, beaten
¼ cup all-purpose flour
¾ cup grated smoked Gouda
2 tablespoons grated
    Parmesan cheese

1. Preheat oven to 375°F. In a small sauté pan, heat half the butter on medium until it stops bubbling. Add the spinach, garlic, nutmeg, and salt and pepper. Sauté for about 3 minutes. Remove from heat and let cool slightly.

2. Mix together the cream, eggs, flour, Gouda, and Parmesan until well incorporated. Fold in the spinach.

3. Use 1 tablespoon of the butter to grease 2 cups of a standard muffin tin or two 6-ounce ovenproof ramekins. Divide the mixture between the tins or ramekins. If there is a bit too much, make a smaller soufflé in another tin.

4. Place in the oven and cook until the tops are brown and a toothpick inserted in the center of each soufflé comes out clean, about 15 minutes. Carefully tip them out of the pan and top each with the remaining butter. Let cool for about 3 minutes. Serve warm.

True Soufflé
This is not a true soufflé because there are no whipped egg whites folded into the mixture. The term is loosely used today to accommodate many new preparations.

"Nontraditional" Fondue with Pear William Liquor

The classic fondue has a splash of Kirsch or cherry liqueur. Here, pear brandy sliced pears are used instead.

1 pound Emmentaler or other high-quality Swiss cheese, grated
3 roasted garlic cloves, smashed into a paste
¼ cup all-purpose flour
1½ cups dry white wine
2 tablespoons Pear William brandy or other high-quality pear brandy
Ground nutmeg, to taste
Salt and pepper, to taste
Crusty bread
Sliced apples and pears

1. Toss the cheese, garlic, and flour together in a bowl.

2. In a small, heavy saucepan, bring the wine to a boil. When the wine begins to boil, add the cheese mixture and cook over medium heat, stirring constantly until the mixture is very smooth. Add the brandy, nutmeg, and salt and pepper.

3. Transfer to a fondue set and serve with the bread, apples, and pears to dip.

Roasting Garlic

Roasted garlic has had a sweeping impact on the culinary scene for a good many years. The easiest way to make it is to take an entire bulb of garlic and brush off any loose skins. Coat the entire bulb with 1 teaspoon of extra-virgin olive oil, wrap it in foil, and place in a preheated 350°F oven for 1 hour. When the garlic cools off, slice off the top of the bulb, leaving each clove "headless." You can then squeeze the soft and sweet garlic out like toothpaste from a tube.

Broiled Boursin and Tomato Bruschetta

Oven-dried tomatoes will not be as dry as sun-dried tomatoes and will have a much fresher flavor. They keep in the refrigerator for about 10 days.

6 plum tomatoes
3 tablespoons extra-virgin olive oil
Salt and pepper, to taste
6 slices (about 1 inch thick) baguette or other crusty bread
2 garlic cloves
1 package (5.2 ounces) Boursin Garlic & Fine Herbs Cheese
1 tablespoon chopped fresh parsley

1. Preheat oven to 275°F. Cut the tomatoes in half lengthwise. Drizzle with 1 tablespoon of the oil and season with salt and pepper. Place the tomatoes directly on an oven rack positioned in the center of the oven. Set a sheet pan on the rack below to catch any drippings. Bake for about 6 hours or until the tomatoes are about one-third their original size.

2. Preheat broiler. Brush each piece of bread on both sides with the remaining olive oil and broil on a baking sheet on both sides until just golden. Remove from broiler, and rub each slice of toasted bread with the garlic cloves. (The bread will act as an abrasive, and the garlic will disintegrate.)

3. Top each piece of bread with a few slices of the tomato and then an equal amount of the cheese. Return to the broiler on a baking sheet until the cheese begins to brown, about 2 minutes.

4. Remove the bruschetta and sprinkle with the parsley. Serve hot.

Try Different Goat Cheeses

Boursin is a soft, herb-infused goat cheese that comes from France. It is available in almost all supermarkets and comes in a small green and white box. The texture is both rich and slightly crumbly. Seek it out; it is worth it.

Puff Pastry Pizzettas Puttanesca

Puff pastry is available in the freezer section of the supermarket and is a breeze to work with.

2 (6-inch) sheets puff pastry, thawed and trimmed into rounds
2 tablespoons capers, rinsed
2 tablespoons roughly chopped black olives (preferably kalamata)
1 small red onion, minced
3 garlic cloves, smashed
4 anchovy fillets, minced
1 teaspoon dried red pepper flakes
3 tablespoons grated Parmesan cheese
2 tablespoons extra-virgin olive oil
2 ounces fresh mozzarella cheese, finely diced
¼ cup shredded basil leaves

1. Preheat oven to 425°F. Place the rounds of puff pastry on a cookie sheet lined with parchment paper. Poke each piece of puff pastry all over with a fork. (This keeps the dough from rising too high while baking.)

2. Mix together all the ingredients except the basil and mozzarella cheese. Spread the mixture onto the pastry rounds, leaving a small edge of "crust." Sprinkle the mozzarella on top, dividing it equally between the 2 pizzettas.

3. Bake for about 12 minutes, until the edges of the crust are very golden brown and the mozzarella is melted and gooey.

4. Remove from the oven, cut into fourths, and divide between 2 plates. Sprinkle the basil over the top and serve.

A Dirty Word
The term puttanesca is the Italian word for "prostitute." This mixture of capers, garlic, anchovy, and red pepper flakes is attributed to the ladies of the evening because it is spicy and fast. Those poetic Italians!

"Frico" Cheese Crisps with Onions and Mushrooms

A frico is a cheese crisp from the northeastern region of Italy known as Friuli. Traditionally filled with a mixture of potatoes, this recipe uses mushrooms to lighten this dish for a suitable first course.

5 tablespoons extra-virgin olive oil, divided
1 (10-ounce) package white mushrooms, sliced
Salt and pepper, to taste
1 tablespoon balsamic vinegar
2 tablespoons butter
1 large Spanish or white onion, thinly sliced
1 cup grated Montasio cheese
1 tablespoon chopped fresh parsley

1. Heat a 10- to 12-inch sauté pan over medium-high heat, add 2 tablespoons of the olive oil, and heat until barely smoking.

2. Add the mushrooms and increase heat. Sauté the mushrooms over high heat until any water that releases from them has evaporated. Season with salt and pepper, then add the balsamic vinegar. Cook for about 30 seconds or until the mushrooms absorb the vinegar. Transfer the mushrooms to a bowl and keep warm.

3. Wipe out the same pan and reheat on medium-high. Add another 2 tablespoons of the olive oil and all the butter. Heat until the butter stops bubbling, then add the onions. Season with salt and pepper and continue to cook, stirring occasionally, until the onions turn a deep brown color and start to look a bit "melted." When the onions are deeply caramelized, add them to the mushrooms. Keep warm.

4. Heat the smallest nonstick skillet you have (a 6-inch skillet is a good size) over medium heat. Brush the pan with a thin film of olive oil. Sprinkle ½ cup of the cheese in the pan, covering the entire surface. The cheese will begin to melt, then bubble, and then come together as mass. Check the underside to see when it starts to become golden. Just as the cheese begins to turn a golden color, spread half of the mushroom-onion mixture on top.

5. Cook for another minute or so, then slide the frico onto an ovenproof platter. Place in a warm oven. Repeat the process to make the second frico.

6. When ready to serve, use a spatula to carefully fold each frico in half onto a plate, much like an omelet. Sprinkle with the parsley and serve immediately

Frico Out!

If you are having difficulty finding the Montasio cheese called for in this recipe, you can substitute any semisoft cow's milk cheese, such as fontina. I recommend tracking down the Montasio, though—for the real deal.

Oysters Mexicana

All the flavors of Mexico in a broiled oyster dish.

1 ounce chorizo sausage
½ teaspoon dried oregano
¼ cup chopped fresh cilantro leaves
3 tablespoons Cotija cheese
2 tablespoons cold butter
Kosher salt, as needed
1 dozen oysters on the half shell

Preheat broiler. Place all the ingredients except the oysters in a food processor and pulse to form a paste. Spread out the kosher salt in an ovenproof dish. Place the oysters in the salt bed, and spoon an equal amount of the paste on the top of each oyster. Broil for about 3 minutes or until hot and bubbly. Serve hot.

Cotija Cheese

Cotija cheese is an aged Mexican white cheese much like a cross between Parmesan and feta. In fact, if you cannot find this cheese, mix together equal parts of grated Parmesan and feta to use in place of the Cotija.

Broiled Clams on the Half Shell

These little treats are extremely addictive. Make more to serve at parties—your guests will love them.

Kosher salt, as needed
12 cherrystone clams, washed, shucked, and loosened from their shells
2 strips bacon, minced
1 shallot, minced
2 garlic cloves, minced
Juice and grated zest of ½ lemon
2 teaspoons chopped fresh chives
Pinch cayenne
Salt and pepper, to taste
5 tablespoons panko bread crumbs (also called "Japanese bread crumbs")

1. Spread a ¼-inch layer of kosher salt on the bottom of an ovenproof dish large enough to accommodate all the clams. (The salt will act as a platform to keep the clams stable so their juices don't spill out.) Place the clams in the salt.

2. To make the topping, cook the bacon slowly over medium heat in a small skillet until crispy. Be careful not to burn the fat. Transfer the bacon to paper towels to drain, but leave the fat in the pan. Add the shallot and garlic, and sauté for about 1 minute. Remove from heat.

3. Crumble the bacon into a small bowl. Add the sautéed shallot and garlic, along with any leftover bacon fat from the pan, and all the remaining ingredients. Stir to mix.

4. Preheat your broiler and place the rack on the second level down from the heat source (about 4 inches away). Divide the topping mixture evenly between the clams in their salt bed, and broil until the tops are quite browned but not burned.

5. To serve, make small salt beds on 2 small plates and place 6 clams on each plate. These are perfect just the way they are and need no additional seasoning.

Shuck You

To shuck a clam, insert a thin-bladed knife where the shells meet, and start pushing inward and slightly rocking the blade of the knife up and down. When the clam begins to open, simply rotate the knife to act as a wedge to open the clam. With the knife, scrape all the flesh from the top shell into the bottom shell. Run the knife between the shell and the muscle of the clam to separate it from its shell.

Shrimp with Arugula "Pesto"

Classic pesto is from Genoa in Italy and consists of basil leaves, pine nuts, garlic, olive oil, and Parmesan cheese. Experiment with different herbs and greens to make your own variation.

1 cup washed and roughly chopped arugula leaves (spinach can be substituted)
1 garlic clove, smashed
¼ cup toasted walnuts
2 tablespoons grated Parmesan cheese
¼ cup extra-virgin olive oil
Salt and pepper, to taste
¾ pound 16-20 shrimp, heads and shells on
¼ cup dry white wine

1. To make the pesto, combine the arugula, garlic, walnuts, cheese, and oil in a blender or food processor. Blend until smooth, and season with salt and pepper.

2. Heat a heavy skillet, preferably cast iron, on medium-high until a drop of water skates across the surface. Season the shrimp with salt and pepper and place in the pan in a single layer. Do not stir right away. Allow the shells to blister and burn a bit, about 1 minute. Toss the shrimp around in the pan or turn over onto the uncooked side and repeat the process until the shells are a bit charred and blistered, and the shrimp are pink.

3. Add the white wine and toss with the shrimp. Cook until the wine has completely evaporated. (The entire cooking time should be around 3 minutes.)

4. To serve, toss the hot shrimp with the pesto and place in 2 bowls. To properly eat, twist the heads off the shrimp and suck the juices from them. Then eat the entire shrimp, shell and all. (The shells impart a subtle smoky flavor.) You can also peel and eat if you prefer.

Shells and All
Cooking shrimp with their shells on has its benefits. First, the shell keeps valuable moisture inside the shrimp. Second, the shell itself provides a great deal of flavor on its own, especially if slightly burned or charred.

Steamy Smoked Oyster Dip

This dish was invented at the restaurant Little Sadie in New York City. Although no longer open, it once offered some very innovative dishes.

1. Preheat oven to 500°F. Cut the bread into sticks, each about 4 inches long and 1 inch thick.

2. Toast the bread in the oven until golden.

3. Combine the remaining ingredients in a bowl and mix well. Transfer to a nonstick pan and heat on medium until the mixture is bubbling.

4. Spoon into two 4-ounce ramekins placed on 2 plates, arrange the breadsticks around the ramekins, and dip away!

Pearl of the Oyster Bar
New York City once had the richest oyster beds in the country. They were so thick in and around New York City that in the 1700s the oyster bars were marked on navigational charts. Although not as thick today, the oysters are making a strong comeback.

Crusty bread
1 (4-ounce) tin smoked oysters in oil
8 ounces cream cheese, softened
2 garlic cloves, smashed
1 small red onion, finely minced
2 teaspoons Worcestershire sauce
A few good dashes Tabasco
1 tablespoon chopped fresh parsley
Juice of 1 lemon

Crab Cakes Baltimore

*Maryland has been famous for crabs and crab cakes for more than 100 years.
The Chesapeake Bay has always been a rich fishery and has provided
the region with an abundance of culinary treasures,
none of which have equaled the popularity of the blue crab.*

¾ pound fresh lump or jumbo
    lump blue crabmeat
½ cup mayonnaise
1 teaspoon brown mustard
1 egg, lightly beaten
½ cup finely minced scallions
Dash Tabasco sauce
2 teaspoons Old Bay
    Seasoning
½ cup bread crumbs
Salt and pepper, to taste
¼ cup melted butter
½ lemon

1. Preheat oven to 425°F.

2. Carefully inspect the crabmeat for bits of shell, being careful not to break up the lumps. In a mixing bowl, gently fold together all the ingredients except the butter and lemon until just incorporated.

3. Prepare a baking sheet by lightly brushing it with half the melted butter. Form the mixture into 4 loosely packed balls and place on the baking sheet, spacing the cakes evenly apart. Press down on the balls with the palm of your hand to flatten slightly, leaving the cakes about 1 inch thick.

4. Brush the crab cakes with the remaining butter. Bake for approximately 10 min or until the cakes are very golden and piping hot. Squeeze a little lemon over the cakes before serving.

Less Oil Means More Flavor
In this recipe, we will make a fundamental change to the tradition by roasting the crab cakes in a hot oven instead of frying them in oil or butter. This allows the flavor of the crab to dominate while eliminating the excessive oiliness that dominates many crab cakes.

Mini Lobster Quesadillas in Avocado Sauce

Josephina Santacruz is the executive chef at Pampano, New York's hottest modern Mexican restaurant. Her lobster empanada inspired this creation.

1 ripe Haas avocado, peeled and roughly chopped
¼ cup store-bought salsa verde or tomatillo sauce
Juice of 1 lime
1 tablespoon sour cream
Salt and pepper, to taste
½ pound cooked lobster meat
1 cup grated Monterey jack cheese
¼ cup diced fresh tomato, seeds removed
2 tablespoons chopped fresh cilantro leaves
1 garlic clove, smashed
½ teaspoon ancho chili powder
4 (6-inch) flour tortillas
2 tablespoons vegetable oil

1. In a food processor or blender, purée the avocado with the salsa verde, lime juice, sour cream, and salt and pepper until smooth. Set aside.

2. In a bowl, mix together the lobster, cheese, tomato, cilantro, garlic, and chili powder. Equally divide the mixture between 2 of the tortillas, spreading it out evenly.

3. Heat a small sauté pan on medium and add 1 tablespoon of the oil. Place 1 of the lobster-topped tortillas in the pan and cover it with 1 of the plain tortillas, forming a "sandwich."

4. Fry until golden brown, flip over, and fry the opposite side until golden and the cheese has melted, about 4 minutes total. Transfer the quesadilla to a plate and keep warm. Repeat the process for the second quesadilla.

5. To serve, cut each quesadilla into quarters and arrange on a plate. Spoon some of the avocado sauce over the top and enjoy.

Finding Ingredients
Salsa verde and tomatillo sauce can both be found in the ethnic or Mexican section of the supermarket. Tomatillos are a papery-husked green fruit more related to a gooseberry than to a tomato. They are usually boiled or roasted before being puréed into a sauce. They have a pleasing sour taste, and they are widely used in Mexico.

Salt Cod Fritters (Baccilaoitos)

Temperature is everything when frying. If the oil is too hot, the fritter will be cooked on the outside and raw in the center. If the oil is too cool, the fritter will absorb excess fat and be greasy.

½ pound salt cod
1 cup milk
¼ cup all-purpose flour
1 egg, lightly beaten
2 garlic cloves, smashed
2 tablespoons chopped fresh parsley
2 teaspoons ground black pepper
½ cup good-quality mayonnaise
Juice and grated zest of 1 lemon
2 teaspoons chopped fresh chives
Salt and pepper, to taste
Olive oil (not virgin or extra-virgin), for frying

1. To rehydrate the salt cod, soak it in 4 quarts of cold water for 24 hours in the refrigerator. Change the cold water at least 3 times during that period.

2. Place the salt cod in a small saucepan with enough water to cover by 2 inches and bring to a boil. Reduce to a simmer and cook for about 7 minutes or until the fish begins to flake. Remove the fish from the water (discard the water) and cool in the refrigerator.

3. When the fish is cold, mix together the fish, milk, flour, egg, half of the garlic, the parsley, and black pepper. Let rest in the refrigerator for about 30 minutes.

4. Make the sauce by combining the mayonnaise, lemon zest and juice, chives, and the remaining garlic. Season with salt and pepper. Set aside.

5. Heat a small saucepan with about 5 inches of olive oil on medium-high. Check the temperature of the oil with a candy or deep-frying thermometer. The temperature should be 350°F. You can also gauge the temperature by dropping a small drop of the batter in the oil. If it sizzles to the surface immediately, it is hot enough. Do not allow the oil to reach the smoking point.

6. Drop tablespoons of the fish batter into the hot oil about 4 at a time, being careful not to overcrowd the pan. (Overcrowding the pan will cause the oil to cool off excessively, which will result in greasy fritters.) Fry the fritters for about 2 to 3 minutes, turning them occasionally with a spoon to allow all sides to brown. When deep golden and crispy, drain on paper towels. Serve with the sauce on the side to dip.

Bacon-Wrapped Figs Stuffed with Blue Cheese

*The Greeks and Romans considered the fig to be an aphrodisiac,
and consequently ate a lot of 'em! These are smoky, sweet, earthy,
and luxurious all at the same time.*

ℒℰ

8 strips bacon
About 8 teaspoons blue
cheese
8 ripe green or black figs,
trimmed
2 cups baby greens

1. Preheat oven to 475°F.

2. Bring a small pan of water (about 2 cups) to a boil and blanch the bacon for 2 minutes. (This will eliminate some fat and precook the bacon very slightly.) Remove the bacon and place on paper towels to drain.

3. Take about 1 tablespoon of blue cheese and roll it into a small cylinder. Insert it into the bottom of 1 of the figs. (Depending on the ripeness of the fig, you may have to make a small incision in the bottom, but a very ripe fig is soft enough to allow penetration.) Wrap a strip of bacon around the fig and secure it with a toothpick. Repeat with the remaining figs.

4. Place the wrapped figs in an ovenproof dish. Roast for about 8 minutes or until the bacon begins to crisp and some cheese oozes out. Let cool for 1 minute before serving. Arrange a small pile of greens in the center of each serving plate and top with the hot figs. Any juices and cheese that ooze out will act as a dressing for the greens.

Parmesan-Stuffed Mushrooms

1 (10-ounce) package white
   mushrooms
3 tablespoons extra-virgin
   olive oil
½ small red onion, minced
2 garlic cloves, smashed
½ cup plain bread crumbs
½ cup grated Parmesan
   cheese
¼ cup finely chopped fresh
   parsley leaves
Juice of ½ lemon
2 lemon wedges
Salt and pepper, to taste

Experiment with different mushrooms at your local market. They can all be treated the same way as the white mushrooms called for here.

1. Preheat oven to 400°F. Remove the whole stems from the mushrooms. Roughly chop the stems and set aside the caps.

2. In a small sauté pan, heat 2 tablespoons of the olive oil on medium until barely smoking. Add the mushroom stems, onion, and garlic, and sauté over medium heat for about 2 minutes, until slightly softened and fragrant. Season with salt and pepper. Remove from heat and let cool slightly.

3. In a small bowl, mix together the sautéed mushroom mixture, the bread crumbs, cheese, parsley, lemon juice, and remaining olive oil. Season to taste with salt and pepper. (The cheese has a high salt content, so taste before adding salt.) The mixture should now be moist enough to form into balls without it crumbling apart. If it is too dry, add a bit more olive oil.

4. Stuff each mushroom cap with the mixture, slightly packing the filling down using a small spoon.

5. Place the mushrooms in an ovenproof dish and bake for about 10 minutes, until the tops are golden brown. Squeeze the lemon wedges over the mushrooms and enjoy.

Shroomin'

In the summer, many people spend their free time in the Catskill Mountains foraging for mushrooms. The types of mushrooms they frequently liberate from the woods include chanterelles, hen of the woods, black trumpets, porcini, chicken of the woods, and numerous others. If you have an interest in wild mushroom foraging, contact the North American Mycological Association or pick up a copy of The Audubon Society Field Guide to North American Mushrooms.

Mudda's Mini Meatballs

From my pal in Brooklyn. Nothing says Brooklyn quite like real, Italian-American meatballs in Carroll Gardens, cooked in the "gravy" as they say.

1. Soak the bread crumbs in the milk for 10 minutes.

2. Mix the bread crumbs with all the remaining ingredients except the olive oil and marinara. Roll the mixture into 1-inch balls and chill in the refrigerator for 1 hour.

3. In a large skillet, heat the olive oil until barely smoking and brown the meatballs well.

4. Transfer the meatballs to a saucepan along with the marinara sauce. Cook for 30 minutes over medium heat. Enjoy on their own with toothpicks or with your favorite pasta as a meal.

Gravy or Marinara
Many Italian-Americans refer to marinara sauce as "gravy." This puzzles many non-Italians, as they turn down what seems like a disgusting invitation for "spaghetti with gravy." When they finally accept, they are surprised when the table is crowned with a steaming bowl of spaghetti with tomato sauce.

½ cup plain bread crumbs
¼ cup milk
¾ pound ground beef (or ¼ pound beef, ¼ pound veal, ¼ pound pork)
1 egg, lightly beaten
½ cup grated pecorino Romano cheese
2 garlic cloves, smashed
3 tablespoons chopped fresh parsley
Pinch dried red pepper flakes
Salt and pepper, to taste
¼ cup extra-virgin olive oil
1 recipe Quick Marinara Sauce (page 99)

Miso-Broiled Eggplant with Sesame Seeds

*Miso is a paste made from fermented soy beans. It is a staple in
Japanese cooking and is best known for being
the main component of miso soup. It has many uses.*

2 Japanese eggplants or 1
    medium Italian eggplant
2 tablespoons miso paste
1 tablespoon soy sauce
2 teaspoons sesame oil
1 teaspoon honey
1 teaspoon finely minced
    gingerroot
2 teaspoons sesame seeds

1. Preheat broiler.

2. Cut the eggplant in half lengthwise and score the flesh with a small
   knife in a crosshatched pattern about 2/3 the way through the flesh.

3. Mix together all the other ingredients except the sesame seeds to form
   a thin paste. Rub the paste into the cut side of the eggplants and let
   marinate for 10 minutes.

4. Broil the eggplant on a baking sheet, cut-side up, about 5 inches from
   the heat source for about 8 minutes, until the tops are well browned
   and bubbly and the eggplant is soft. Sprinkle with the sesame seeds
   and serve immediately.

Why "Egg"plant?

*Eggplant is so named because at one time most eggplants had a white
skin. These crops resembled fields of eggs hanging from plants. It was only
in the last 100 years that the purple-skinned variety became dominant.*

Oysters with Horseradish-Scented Whipped Cream

Using whipped cream as a broiling agent results in a magically silky texture that complements the oysters perfectly.

12 oysters on the half shell
Kosher salt, as needed
¼ cup whipping cream
1 teaspoon prepared horseradish
Salt and pepper, to taste

1. Preheat broiler. Spread out the kosher salt in an ovenproof dish. Place the oysters in the salt bed. (This keeps the oysters stable during cooking.)

2. Whip the cream until stiff peaks form, and season with salt and pepper. Fold in the horseradish.

3. Place a generous spoonful of the whipped cream on top of each oyster and broil as close to the heat source as possible until the tops are browned, about 2 to 3 minutes. Serve immediately.

Whip It Good
When whipping cream, it is important to have a very clean bowl. If the bowl has any traces of oil or fat in it, your efforts will be in vain and the cream will not inflate. It also helps if your bowl, whisk, and cream are cold.

Creamy Cabbage Spring Rolls

Peanut oil, as needed
1 tablespoon minced fresh
    gingerroot
2 garlic cloves, smashed
3 scallions, thinly sliced
1 small head napa cabbage,
    thinly sliced
2 tablespoons soy sauce
2 teaspoons sesame oil
1 teaspoon granulated sugar
4 spring roll wrappers
3 tablespoons honey
1 tablespoon Chinese chili
    paste or sambal

Napa cabbage is essential to this dish. Only this soft and supple cabbage will provide the silky, almost "creamy" texture for the filling in these crispy spring rolls.

1. In a large, heavy sauté pan or wok, heat about 3 tablespoons of the peanut oil until barely smoking. Add the ginger, garlic, and scallion, and sauté for 1 minute.

2. Add the cabbage and stir-fry for about 3 minutes or until the cabbage is well wilted. Add the soy sauce, sesame oil, and sugar. Continue cooking for 1 minute. Transfer the cabbage to a colander and let drain for 10 minutes. Cool until comfortable to handle.

3. Place about 2 tablespoons of the cabbage in the center of each spring roll wrapper. Tuck in the sides of the wrapper and roll up like a burrito. Seal the edge with a drop of water.

4. In a pot, heat about 1 inch of the peanut oil to 350°F. Fry the spring rolls for about 2 minutes or until very crispy. Drain on paper towels.

5. Mix together the honey and chili paste and serve on the side to dip.

Keep It Hot
Invest in a candy thermometer or deep-fat thermometer. Using this tool makes it easy to ensure that your frying temperatures are accurate and you will have crispy, greaseless fried foods every time.

Deep-Fried Scallops

Kewpie mayo is available in Asian markets. It has a great "eggy" flavor.

8 sea scallops
1 teaspoon finely minced lemon zest
All-purpose flour, as needed
1 egg, beaten
Panko bread crumbs (also called "Japanese bread crumbs")
Peanut oil, as needed
Fine sea salt, to taste
Kewpie mayonnaise

1. Toss the scallops with the lemon zest. Dredge the scallops in the flour, shaking off any excess. One at a time, dip the scallops in the egg, then in the bread crumbs to coat.

2. Fill a deep-fryer or deep, heavy skillet with enough oil to fry all of the scallops at the same time. Heat the oil to 375°F. Fry the scallops for about 2 minutes or until they float to the top.

3. Drain the scallops on paper towels and sprinkle with the salt. Arrange on 2 plates and top each with a dollop of the mayonnaise.

Kewpie Mayo

Kewpie mayonnaise was created in Japan after World War II when the Japanese developed a taste for mayonnaise. It has a homemade flavor and tastes very much like eggs. It is packaged in a unique plastic squeeze bottle that resembles the cartoon character "Kewpie." The top is equipped with a star tip, which makes decorative presentations easy and fun.

Sautéed Parmesan

It may sound strange, but this is a very sophisticated treat.

½ pound Parmigiano-
Reggiano cheese
All-purpose flour, as needed
Extra-virgin olive oil, as
needed
1 lemon
1 cup fresh basil leaves

1. Cut the Parmesan cheese into chunks about ¼ of an inch thick, in the longest pieces possible. Dredge each piece of cheese in flour.

2. Heat about half an inch of olive oil in a pan on medium and sauté the cheese pieces for about 30 seconds per side. They should be golden.

3. Squeeze the lemon over the cheese and use the basil leaves to pick up the morsels. Eat the leaf and the cheese together.

Individual Pâté en Croûte

A classic pâté en croûte is very involved to make. This recipe takes the flavors and makes it easy and fun. These little appetizers are also great for a cocktail party.

¼ pound ground beef
¼ pound liverwurst
1 egg yolk
¼ teaspoon ground allspice
1 teaspoon brandy
1 shallot, minced
Salt and pepper, to taste
2 sheets puff pastry, thawed

1. Preheat oven to 400°F.

2. Mix together all the ingredients except the pastry to form a smooth mixture. Roll into 12 small balls.

3. Cut the puff pastry into circles about three times as wide as the meatballs. Wrap each meatball in the puff pastry and crimp the tops shut.

4. Place on a lightly greased baking sheet and bake for 15 minutes. Serve warm.

chapter 4
salads

Endive, Walnut, and Blue Cheese Salad

3 cups washed, dried, and
    chiffonade endive (see
    "Chiffonade," page 61)
2 tablespoons hazelnut oil
2 teaspoons apple cider
2 tablespoons finely minced
    fresh chives
Salt and pepper, to taste
½ cup crumbled blue cheese
6 cherry or grape tomatoes,
    cut in half
½ cup toasted walnut halves

*The combination of blue cheese and nuts, especially walnuts, is a classic.
Served for eons in Great Britain, Stilton blue cheese and walnuts
is often served for dessert with port wine.*

1. Toss the endive with the hazelnut oil, vinegar, chives, and salt and pep-
    per. Arrange in the center of a large salad plate.

2. Top with the blue cheese and tomatoes and a scattering of the walnuts.

Spicy Caesar Salad with Chipotle Dressing

1 lime
¼ cup grated Parmesan
    cheese
2 anchovy fillets, rinsed and
    minced
2 garlic cloves, smashed
1 teaspoon Dijon mustard
2 tablespoons mayonnaise
1 teaspoon (or to taste)
    minced chipotle pepper
    in adobo sauce
¼ cup extra-virgin olive oil
Salt and pepper, to taste
4 cups washed, dried, and
    chopped romaine lettuce
½ cup chopped black olives
1 cup croutons

*Not an Italian invention at all, the Caesar salad was first made in Tijuana,
Mexico. This tidbit offers creative license to use a uniquely Mexican ingredient,
chipotle peppers, in this dressing.*

1. Juice the lime into a large mixing bowl. Add the Parmesan, anchovy,
    garlic, mustard, mayonnaise, and chipotle. Whisk together well. Slowly
    whisk in the olive oil in a slow stream. When incorporated, taste and
    adjust seasoning with salt and pepper.

2. Add the lettuce and toss well. Place in the center of a large salad plate
    and toss the olives and croutons over the salad.

Where There Is Smoke, There's Fire
*Chipotle peppers are dried and smoked jalapeño peppers. They can be
found in the Mexican section of the supermarket and are usually in
small cans labeled "chipotle in adobo." Store the unused portion of the
can in an airtight container in the fridge.*

Warm Spinach Salad with Deviled Egg Croutons

This recipe uses a sort of "deviled egg salad" on crunchy croutons to serve alongside this classic salad. This can easily be a main course for lunch.

3 large hard-boiled eggs, peeled and roughly chopped
1 tablespoon mayonnaise
1 teaspoon Dijon mustard
1 teaspoon paprika
Salt and pepper, to taste
6 small slices (about 3 inches long and ½ inch thick, cut on the bias) baguette, toasted
8 strips bacon, cut widthwise into ¼-inch pieces
1 red onion, sliced in thin half-moons
1 cup sliced button mushrooms
1 cup diced ripe tomatoes
6 cups washed and dried baby spinach
2 tablespoons red wine vinegar

1. Mix together the eggs, mayonnaise, mustard, paprika, and salt and pepper. Crush with a fork until the egg pieces are no larger than peas. Divide the egg salad among the croutons.

2. In a large sauté pan, cook the bacon over medium heat until very crispy. Be careful not to burn the fat. Transfer the bacon to paper towels to drain and leave the fat in the pan over medium heat.

3. Add the onions and mushrooms to the bacon fat in the pan. Cook over medium-high heat until the moisture from the mushrooms has evaporated, about 2 minutes.

4. When the mushrooms are dry, add the spinach and tomatoes and remove the pan from the heat. Add the vinegar and a pinch of salt and pepper, and toss very quickly to coat the greens with the dressing you have created in the pan.

5. Divide the salad between 2 large salad plates. Crumble the bacon and sprinkle it over the salads. Place 3 croutons on each plate and serve immediately.

Time Is of the Essence
The final steps of this salad demand speed. If the spinach remains in the pan too long, it will cook. The idea is to gently wilt the leaves in the warm dressing and slightly warm them. The time from the spinach hitting the pan to the plate should be about 45 seconds.

Broiled Goat Cheese Salad

Chicory is sometimes referred to as curly endive or frisée. This sturdy green stands up to heating very well.

4 cups washed and dried chicory
3 tablespoons extra-virgin olive oil
1 tablespoon red wine vinegar
1 cup crumbled goat cheese
1 egg, beaten with 1 tablespoon water
½ cup dried cranberries
Salt and pepper, to taste

1. Preheat broiler with a rack set at the lowest level.

2. Toss together the chicory, oil, vinegar, and some salt and pepper. Arrange in 2 equal piles on a baking sheet and press down to form flat, disklike shapes about 6 inches across.

3. Top each disk with enough goat cheese to cover the greens almost entirely. Brush the cheese with the beaten egg mixture.

4. Broil until the cheese is golden and begins to bubble. Carefully slide the salads onto large plates and toss the dried cranberries on and around the salad. Serve immediately.

Chock-full of Chickory
The chicory plant has been used as a coffee substitute for decades. During World War II the roots of the chicory plant were roasted and brewed like coffee because of shortages. This tradition continues in New Orleans, where much of the coffee has a bit of chicory brewed with it.

Sautéed Mushroom Salad

This dish relies entirely on the quality of the ingredients. Purchase the best prosciutto and mushrooms that you can afford and serve this salad as the first course for a special occasion.

1. Arrange the tender inner leaves of the lettuce on 2 large salad plates, covering almost the entire surface.

2. Sauté the mushrooms over medium-high heat in the olive oil until the water they release has evaporated, and season with salt and pepper. Keep warm.

3. Drizzle the lettuce leaves with the balsamic vinegar and about 1 tablespoon of the olive oil per plate.

4. Tear the prosciutto into bite-size pieces and sprinkle it over the lettuce leaves. Top with the warm mushrooms and sprinkle with the cheese. Serve immediately.

1 head butter lettuce (Boston lettuce) separated into leaves
½ pound mushrooms (such as porcini, chanterelles, or hen of the woods), cleaned and cut into ¼-inch slices
¼ cup extra-virgin olive oil, plus extra for drizzling
2 tablespoons balsamic vinegar
¼ pound thinly sliced prosciutto
¼ cup grated Parmigiano-Reggiano cheese
Salt and pepper, to taste

Tunisian Salad

North Africa rests along the southern Mediterranean Sea, and hence shares many culinary attributes with its Mediterranean neighbors such as Italy, Greece, and Spain. This salad is a prime example.

Mix together all the ingredients in a bowl and let marinate for 1 hour in the refrigerator. Serve on chilled plates. That's it!

1 (15.5-ounce) can chickpeas, rinsed and drained
1 (6-ounce) can tuna packed in olive oil
2 anchovy fillets, minced
Juice of 1 lemon
4 scallions, thinly sliced
1 small cucumber, diced the same size as the chickpeas
8 cherry or grape tomatoes, quartered
¼ cup extra-virgin olive oil
1 teaspoon ground cumin
Salt and pepper, to taste

Classic Steakhouse Salad

1 cup balsamic vinegar
½ cup honey
2 tablespoons Dijon mustard
2 garlic cloves, smashed
3 cups canola oil
1 large or 2 small beefsteak
    tomatoes, cored and
    sliced into ¼-inch-thick
    rounds
1 large Vidalia onion, sliced
    into ¼-inch-thick rounds
Salt and pepper, to taste
½ cup crumbled blue cheese

This vinaigrette was developed for Eric Rifkin, co-owner and executive chef of the Crazy Dog Restaurant in Long Island. It has become his house dressing and guests buy quarts of it to take home. Make extra.

1. Make the vinaigrette by combining the vinegar, honey, mustard, and garlic in a food processor. With the processor running, slowly add the oil in a thin stream until it is emulsified and the dressing has a light brown color.

2. Arrange the tomato and onion in alternating slices in the center of 2 salad plates. Season with salt and pepper.

3. Top with the crumbled blue cheese and a generous amount of the vinaigrette.

Vidalia Onions
Supersweet and available only in the summer, Vidalia onions are a uniquely American treat. Seek them out and enjoy this sweet onion. They are great raw, cooked, and even as an onion sandwich on buttered bread!

Stale Bread "Panzanella"

A clever use for yesterday's bread, this salad was originally made as a good way to stretch a penny. Buy fresh bread just to let it go stale for this dish.

Simply mix together all the ingredients and let stand at room temperature for 20 minutes. Adjust seasoning with salt and pepper and serve.

Chiffonade
To easily shred, or "chiffonade," basil leaves, stack washed and dried leaves on top of one another about 6 or 7 at a time. Use a sharp knife to cut through them all together. Make the slices as close to each other as possible. The results will astonish you.

About 3 cups cubed sourdough bread (about 2-inch cubes), left out overnight
1 cup diced ripe tomatoes
1 small red onion, finely minced
6 ounces fresh mozzarella cheese, diced
½ cup extra-virgin olive oil
4 tablespoons red wine vinegar
½ cup shredded basil leaves
2 tablespoons capers, rinsed
Salt and pepper, to taste

Roasted Beet Salad

If you haven't had a beet in years, it is time to try again. This is a good dish to reintroduce you to beets.

1. Preheat oven to 375°F.

2. Wrap the beets in foil and place in the oven for about 1 hour or until a knife inserted into the deepest part comes out with no resistance.

3. When the beets are cool enough to handle, peel off the skin with your hands or a paper towel and chop the beets into 1-inch pieces.

4. While still warm, toss the beets with the remaining ingredients and serve at any temperature.

2 medium beets
1 small red onion, thinly sliced
¼ cup flat-leaf parsley leaves, washed
3 tablespoons walnut oil
1 tablespoon red wine vinegar
3 tablespoons toasted walnut pieces
Salt and pepper, to taste

Wild Rice Salad

Wild rice is actually a grass and not rice at all.
Some Native American tribes "cooked" the rice by soaking it in
many changes of cold water until soft enough to eat.

½ cup wild rice
¼ cup extra-virgin olive oil
2 tablespoons apple cider
    vinegar
6 dried apricots, finely diced
¼ cup toasted pecans
1 cup baby spinach leaves,
    washed and dried
3 scallions, finely sliced
2 teaspoons chopped fresh
    tarragon
Salt and pepper, to taste

1. Cook the rice by boiling it in about 4 cups of salted water for 45 minutes.

2. Drain the rice, and while it is still hot, mix in the oil and vinegar. Let cool in the refrigerator, uncovered, for 1 hour.

3. Add the remaining ingredients and adjust seasoning with salt and pepper. Serve immediately.

Tarragon

Tarragon is not used very frequently in the United States. Its strong licorice-like flavor is so assertive that some feel it has limited uses. It is nice in some chicken dishes and in some butter-based sauces. This salad benefits greatly from the small amount added.

Crunchy Jicama Slaw

Jicama is a root vegetable that resembles a flattened brown turnip. It is eaten raw and tastes like a cross between a potato and an apple.

1 medium jicama (about ½ pound) peeled and cut into thin julienne strips
1 red bell pepper, seeds and ribs removed and cut into thin julienne strips
1 small red onion, thinly sliced
Salt and pepper, to taste
½ loosely packed cup cilantro leaves, washed and dried
1 garlic clove
Juice of 1 lime
¼ cup extra-virgin olive oil
Pinch granulated sugar

1. Place the jicama, pepper, and onion in a mixing bowl and season with salt and pepper. Let stand for 10 minutes at room temperature, uncovered.

2. In a blender, combine the cilantro, garlic, lime juice, olive oil, and sugar. Purée until very smooth. You may have to add a few tablespoons of water to get the blender to spin.

3. After the jicama mixture has stood, dab it with paper towels to absorb any water that has been pulled out by the salt. Mix with the dressing and chill well. Serve cold.

Juicing Limes
Here are a couple tricks to getting the most juice out of a lime. First, roll the lime on the counter, pressing down firmly to "loosen" the juice. Second, slice the lime in half through the stem end instead of the "middle"; this produces much more juice.

Baby Potato and String Bean Salad

Serve this German-inspired dish as a first course in the summer. It also goes great alongside boiled sausages or a crispy veal cutlet.

½ pound string beans, trimmed

½ pound new potatoes

1 tablespoon whole-grain mustard

2 tablespoons apple cider vinegar

6 tablespoons vegetable oil

Pinch granulated sugar

6 slices bacon

2 tablespoons chopped fresh dill

Salt and pepper, to taste

1. Boil the green beans in plenty of salted water until crisp-tender, about 4 minutes. Cool in ice water and drain.

2. Boil the potatoes in gently simmering salted water until tender. (A paring knife inserted in the center of the potato should come out with no resistance.) Drain and let cool. When the potatoes are cool enough to handle but still warm, peel off the skins and cut into slices about ¼ inch thick. Place the potato slices in a mixing bowl.

3. In a small bowl, mix together the mustard, vinegar, oil, and sugar. Pour over the warm potato slices and mix well. Spread out the potatoes on a plate and let cool in the refrigerator for 30 minutes.

4. Slice the bacon into ¼-inch pieces and cook in a small pan over medium heat until crisp. Drain on paper towels.

5. When the potatoes are cool, add the green beans, bacon, and dill. Adjust the seasoning with salt and pepper, and serve.

The Basics of Olive Oil
Olive oil is labeled as "pure," "virgin," and "extra-virgin." Extra-virgin is the first pressing of the olives with no added heat. Virgin is the second pressing with added heat. Pure is the final pressing with added heat and pressure. Extra-virgin has the deepest flavor and health benefits.

Mom's Cucumber Salad

*Mom always made a salad similar to this in the summer,
when the garden produced some mutant cucumbers.*

1 medium or 2 small
  cucumbers, sliced into
  thin rounds
Salt and pepper, to taste
½ cup sour cream
2 tablespoons chopped fresh
  dill
1 large garlic clove, smashed

1. Place the cucumbers in a colander and season with salt and pepper. Let drain for 20 minutes.

2. Squeeze the cucumbers gently to get a bit more water out of them. In a bowl, toss the cucumbers with the sour cream, dill, and garlic. Adjust seasoning if necessary with salt and pepper. Serve cold.

Mutant Cukes
Gardeners are always giving gifts of giant cucumbers in the summer to unsuspecting friends and neighbors. These veggies grow very large quickly. Unfortunately, the bigger the cuke, the less flavor it packs. Choose medium or small cukes for better flavor and texture.

Nectarine and Cucumber Summer Salad

Summer fruit is so versatile, yet most people only think of eating these delights out of hand. Here is another unconventional use of fruit that will have everyone asking for the recipe.

2 nectarines, cut into thin
  slices
1 small cucumber, cut into
  small dice
½ small red onion, finely
  minced
2 tablespoons finely chopped
  fresh chives
3 tablespoons extra-virgin
  olive oil
1 tablespoon white wine
  vinegar
Salt and pepper, to taste

Mix together all the ingredients and serve immediately. That simple.

Citrus and Sesame Soybean Salad

1 (8-ounce) bag frozen
    shelled soybeans
1 sheet nori seaweed
1 orange, separated into
    sections
2 tablespoons soy sauce
1 tablespoon sesame oil
1 tablespoon toasted sesame
    seeds
Salt, to taste

*Fresh soybeans can now be found in the frozen section of many supermarkets.
If you have difficulty finding them,
baby lima beans make an acceptable substitute.*

1. Boil the frozen beans in salted water for 5 minutes. Cool in ice water and drain.

2. Toast the seaweed by passing it over the burner of your stove quickly on each side. The sheet will smell toasty and shrink slightly. Crumble the sheet into small pieces.

3. Mix together all the ingredients in a bowl and let marinate in the refrigerator for 1 hour. Adjust seasoning with salt only.

Beans at the Bar

In Japan soybeans or "edamame" are served as bar snacks the way pretzels are served in the United States. The beans are boiled whole, in the pod, then tossed with sea salt. Warm bowls are placed on the bar to be enjoyed with beer. The whole pod is put in the mouth then pulled out, leaving behind the salty beans.

Sicilian-Inspired Zucchini Salad

In Sicily mint is used in the same way basil is in the more northern regions of the boot. You will find it tossed in pasta, in salads, and in other savory preparations.

3 medium-sized green
  zucchini
½ loosely packed cup mint
  leaves
2 tablespoons toasted pine
  nuts
¼ cup extra-virgin olive oil
Juice and grated zest of 1
  lemon
Salt and pepper, to taste

1. Prepare the zucchini by cutting off the ends and looking to see where the seeds meet the flesh. Lay the zucchini on a cutting board and cut down the length between the flesh and the seeds. You should have a strip of zucchini about 1 or 2 inches wide with minimal seeds. Turn the zucchini onto its cut side and repeat the process until you have 4 strips of zucchini flesh and 1 rectangular "core" of seeds. Discard the seeds and cut the flesh into small batons about 1 inch long by ¼ inch wide.

2. Bring a pot of salted water to a rapid boil. Drop the zucchini into the boiling water for 2 minutes. Cool in ice water and drain on paper towels.

3. Pat the zucchini dry and toss with the remaining ingredients. Adjust seasoning and let marinate in the refrigerator for at least 30 minutes before serving.

Pignoli (Pine Nuts)
Pignoli, or pine nuts, are just what they sound like. Taken from a species of pine that grows in Europe and Asia, the nuts are extracted from the pine cone, then packed for shipment. Toast the nuts in a 350°F oven for 5 minutes to enhance their flavor.

Brutus Salad with Roasted Garlic Dressing

1¼ cups shredded Parmesan
cheese
2 anchovy fillets
3 roasted garlic cloves
2 tablespoons lemon juice
1 tablespoon mayonnaise
1 teaspoon Dijon mustard
Salt and black pepper, to
taste
6 tablespoons extra-virgin
olive oil
1 head romaine lettuce,
shredded

A unique version of the Caesar salad that is playfully called "The Brutus"—just as Brutus put an end to the great Caesar, this salad puts the others to shame.

1. Preheat oven to 350°F. Line a small baking sheet with parchment paper.

2. Using 1 cup of the Parmesan cheese, make 4 rough disks of cheese about 4 to 5 inches in diameter each on the baking sheet. Bake for 10 minutes. Remove from oven and let cool. They will become brittle and crispy.

3. Prepare the dressing by smashing the anchovy and garlic into a paste in a small bowl. Whisk in the lemon juice, mayonnaise, mustard, black pepper, and the remaining cheese. When well combined, whisk in the olive oil in a slow stream until smooth and emulsified.

4. Toss the lettuce with the dressing. To assemble the salads, mound some of the lettuce in a small, neat ball (about the size of a medium-sized apple) on each serving plate. Top each pile of lettuce with a Parmesan crisp. Repeat the process so you have 2 mounds of lettuce stacked on top of each other with a crisp in the middle and a crisp on top. Serve immediately.

Raw Eggs in Dressings
Unless you have access to pasteurized eggs, it is best to avoid raw eggs in dressings. You can replace the eggs with mayonnaise in many recipes with great success.

Dominican Avocado Salad

This salad is inspired by the many Dominican restaurants in New York City that serve something very similar.

1. Make the dressing by whisking together the oil, lime juice, garlic, cilantro, oregano, and salt and pepper.

2. Toss the watercress with the dressing and arrange in the center of 2 plates. Arrange the tomato and onion slices on top of the greens. Season them with salt and pepper.

3. Cut the avocado in half and remove the pit. Scoop out the flesh and cut into ¼-inch slices. Place on top of the salad and season the avocado with salt and pepper. Serve immediately.

Taking the Bite Out of Onions
When onions are too strong, slice them thinly and soak them in ice water for 10 minutes. This removes the bite and crisps up the onions nicely. Another option is to marinate the onions in a mixture of equal amounts of red vinegar and granulated sugar. Completely cover the onions in this mixture like pickles in brine. They will last for 2 weeks in the refrigerator.

¼ cup extra-virgin olive oil
Juice of 1 lime
1 garlic clove, smashed
2 tablespoons finely chopped fresh cilantro leaves
1 teaspoon dried oregano
Salt and pepper, to taste
2 bunches watercress, large stems removed
1 small ripe tomato, thinly sliced
1 small red onion, thinly sliced
1 Haas avocado

Calamari and Rice Salad

*Make this salad when you have some leftover white rice.
It works fine with rice from the local takeout joint.*

½ pound cleaned calamari
    rings
1 cup cooked and cooled
    white rice
1 celery stalk, thinly sliced
12 pimiento-stuffed olives,
    cut in half
½ loosely packed cup flat-leaf
    parsley leaves
1/3 cup extra-virgin olive oil
3 tablespoons white wine
    vinegar
Salt and pepper, to taste

1. Bring a small pot of salted water to a boil and drop the calamari rings in it for exactly 2 minutes. Drain and chill the calamari in ice water. Drain, and dry on paper towels.

2. Mix together all the ingredients and let marinate in the refrigerator for 20 minutes before serving. (Leave the parsley leaves whole in this recipe—they act as a sort of green to the salad.)

Parsley 101
For years every plate on earth it seemed was adorned with a sprig of curly parsley. This turned parsley into a "garnish" rather than the true ingredient it is. Use the flat-leaf parsley (also called Italian parsley) for its superior flavor and texture.

Chopped Lobster Cobb Salad

This salad can easily serve as a light entrée, or make more and serve it on a huge platter as a buffet dish. Substitute cheaper seafood such as shrimp if throwing a bash.

1. Make the dressing by combining the liquid from the artichokes, half of the avocado, and the sour cream in a blender. Purée into a smooth sauce and season to taste with salt and pepper.

2. Chop the greens so they are about the size of parsley leaves and mound them in 2 bowls.

3. Arrange the remaining ingredients on top of the greens in neat rows. (Try to alternate colors: first the cheese, then cucumber, egg, tomato, avocado, onion, lobster, for example.) Drizzle the dressing over the salad and serve immediately.

The Legend of the Cobb

Bob Cobb, manager of the Brown Derby Restaurant in Los Angeles, invented the Cobb salad in 1926. He was simply using leftovers and made the salad for himself. Word of this salad got out to the famous Sid Grauman (Grauman's Chinese Theatre), and he asked for a sample. He loved it, and the rest is history.

1 small jar marinated artichokes, drained and liquid reserved
1 avocado, medium diced
½ cup sour cream
Salt and pepper, to taste
4 cups mixed mesclun greens
½ cup crumbled blue cheese
½ cup diced cucumber
2 hard-boiled eggs, thinly sliced
½ cup diced ripe tomato
½ cup finely diced red onion
½ pound cooked lobster meat, roughly chopped

Wedge Salad with Chunky Russian Dressing

½ large head iceberg lettuce
½ cup ketchup
½ cup mayonnaise
1 hard-boiled egg, chopped finely
¼ cup finely minced red onion
¼ cup sweet relish
¼ cup capers, rinsed
1 tablespoon lemon juice
Dash Worcestershire sauce
Dash Tabasco sauce

Iceberg lettuce gets a bad rap these days because of all the fancy greens now available. It is a shame this crunchy delight doesn't show up more often.

1. Cut the iceberg into thick wedges and arrange on 2 plates.

2. Mix together all the remaining ingredients.

3. Pour the dressing over the iceberg wedges and serve immediately with fork and knife.

The Perfect Boiled Egg
Place large eggs in enough cold water to cover by 1 inch and bring to a boil. As soon as the water boils, turn off the heat. Let stand for 11 minutes. Drain, moving the eggs around a bit to crack the shells, and cool in ice water. Perfect every time. No green yolks or rubbery whites.

Butternut Squash Salad

The flavors of butternut squash and sage are perfect together.

3 cups 1-inch-diced butternut
  squash
3 tablespoons extra-virgin
  olive oil
6 sage leaves, chopped
Salt and pepper, to taste
2 tablespoons aged sherry
  vinegar
2 tablespoons minced red
  onion

1. Preheat oven to 400°F.

2. Toss the squash with the oil, sage, and salt and pepper. Place on a baking sheet and bake for 20 minutes. Remove from the oven and let cool.

3. Transfer the squash to a bowl and mix with the vinegar and onion. Adjust seasoning to taste. Serve at any temperature.

The Powers of Sage
Sage is a very powerful and potent herb. Many ancient civilizations attributed mystical and healing powers to this herb. Some people will burn sage leaves to "purify" a dwelling or as a sign of luck and hope. It also tastes great!

Wheat Berry Salad

1 cup wheat berries
½ cup minced scallions
¼ cup dried cranberries
¼ cup minced dried apricots
¼ cup toasted pistachios
2 tablespoons toasted pine
    nuts
¼ cup extra-virgin olive oil
3 tablespoons red wine
    vinegar
Salt and pepper, to taste

Wheat berries are the whole wheat before the bran and husk are removed.
They are a great complex carbohydrate.

1. Boil the wheat berries in plenty of salted water for 30 minutes. Drain and let cool.

2. Toss the wheat berries with the remaining ingredients and let marinate in the refrigerator for about 1 hour before serving.

Complex Carbs

In this day of popular low-carb diets, many people do not understand the difference between simple and complex carbohydrates. In a nutshell, simple carbs are usually refined and ground grains like white flour, white rice, and pasta. These carbs burn quickly in the body and are not a very efficient fuel. Complex carbs such as whole grains and brown rice are much more efficient fuels for the body and are therefore much healthier.

chapter 5
soups

"Souper" Fast Black Bean Soup

*Make this soup when you are short on time
but want something warm and comforting.*

3 tablespoons olive oil
1 ounce dried chorizo
    sausage
1 small white onion, small
    diced
1 garlic clove, minced
1 teaspoon dried oregano
½ cup frozen corn kernels
1 (15.5-ounce) can black
    beans
4 cups low-sodium chicken
    broth
Salt and pepper, to taste
2 tablespoons sour cream

1. Heat the oil in a small saucepot until barely smoking. Add the chorizo, onion, garlic, and oregano. Sauté over medium heat until the onions have softened, about 3 minutes.

2. Add all the remaining ingredients except the sour cream and bring to a boil.

3. As soon as the soup boils, reduce to a low simmer and cook for 15 minutes, uncovered. Season to taste with salt and pepper.

4. Divide into 2 warmed bowls and top each with a dollop of the sour cream.

Carrot and Ginger Bisque

Creamy and luscious, this soup is very comforting.

3 tablespoons butter
3 cups peeled and chopped
    carrots
1 medium white onion,
    roughly chopped
2 celery stalks, roughly
    chopped
1 garlic clove, smashed
1 tablespoon grated
    gingerroot
½ cup uncooked long-grain
    white rice
5 cups chicken or vegetable
    broth
Salt and pepper, to taste

1. Heat the butter in a pot on medium until it stops bubbling. Add the carrots, onion, celery, garlic, and ginger. Sauté for about 5 minutes, until the vegetables begin to soften.

2. Add the rice, broth, and salt and pepper. Bring to a boil. Reduce to a gentle simmer and cook for 30 minutes, covered.

3. Purée the soup in a blender until smooth, working in batches if necessary. Adjust seasoning and serve.

Portobello Bisque with Parmesan

You can substitute any mushrooms you wish for this soup. Portobellos are nice because of their very deep flavor, which holds up well in this rich soup.

1. Heat the butter in a small saucepot over medium heat. When the butter stops bubbling, add the onion and garlic and sauté for 3 minutes.

2. Add the mushrooms, rice, and broth. Bring to a boil. Reduce to a gentle simmer and cook for 30 minutes, uncovered.

3. Remove from heat and add the half-and-half.

4. Working in batches, purée the soup in a blender until smooth. After puréeing, return the soup to the pot and heat to serving temperature. Season to taste with salt and pepper.

5. Divide the soup between 2 bowls and garnish each with the tarragon, the Parmesan and a splash of the sherry.

Rice Is Nice

Rice makes an excellent thickening agent for puréed soups. The starch thickens the broth and lends a silky texture to the soup. Other such thickening agents are potatoes, bread, and even pasta.

2 tablespoons butter
1 small onion, roughly chopped
2 garlic cloves, sliced
10 ounces portobello mushroom caps, roughly chopped
¼ cup uncooked white long grain rice
5 cups chicken or vegetable broth
½ cup half-and-half
Salt and pepper, to taste
2 teaspoons chopped fresh tarragon
1 tablespoon dry sherry
4 tablespoons grated Parmesan cheese

Fall Pumpkin Soup with Dumplings

It is nice to serve this soup in small, hollowed-out sugar pumpkins. Do not try to make this with a large jack-o'-lantern pumpkin; it will be lousy.

2 tablespoons butter or olive oil

1 red onion, roughly chopped

1 celery stalk, roughly chopped

1 tablespoon chopped fresh gingerroot

¼ teaspoon freshly grated nutmeg

2 cups large-diced sugar pumpkin or butternut squash, peeled

5 cups chicken or vegetable broth

8 ounces cream cheese

1 egg yolk

2 tablespoons all-purpose flour

2 teaspoons chopped fresh chives

1 teaspoon ground cinnamon

Salt and pepper, to taste

1. Heat the butter or oil on medium in a saucepot until it has stopped bubbling. Add the onion, celery, ginger, and nutmeg. Sauté for about 5 minutes.

2. Add the pumpkin and the stock, and bring to a boil. Reduce to a simmer and cook gently for 30 minutes, uncovered.

3. Remove from heat and stir in half of the cream cheese.

4. Working in batches, purée the soup in a blender until smooth. Return the soup to the pot and bring to a very low simmer over medium heat.

5. Mix together the remaining cream cheese, the egg yolk, flour, chives, cinnamon, and a bit of salt and pepper until smooth. Spoon teaspoons of the dumplings into the soup and cook uncovered for 10 minutes. Serve in warmed bowls.

Pumpkin Patch

Another option to prepare sugar pumpkin for soup is to cut off the top, scoop out the seeds, and roast the pumpkin in a 350°F oven until the meat is tender. Scoop out the meat, being careful not to pierce the skin, and proceed with the soup recipe as is. Use the pumpkin as a soup terrine.

Curried Cauliflower and Green Grape Soup

Curry and cauliflower are a natural combination and widely paired in India. Even people who do not like Indian food will love this soup.

1. Heat the butter on medium in a saucepot until it has stopped bubbling. Add the onion, garlic, ginger, and curry powder. Sauté for about 5 minutes.

2. Add the tomato paste and sauté for 2 minutes.

3. Add the cauliflower, broth, and all but 6 of the grapes. Bring to a boil. Reduce to a simmer and cook gently for 30 minutes, uncovered.

4. Remove from heat and stir in the cream.

5. Working in batches, purée the soup in a blender until very smooth. Season to taste with salt and pepper. After puréeing, return the soup to the pot and reheat to serving temperature. Serve in warmed bowls. Slice the remaining grapes into disks and float in the soup for garnish.

Peeling Ginger
Fresh gingerroot is an awkward thing to peel. An easy way to navigate the many contours is to use a small spoon as a peeler. Simply scrape the skin off while following the curves and ridges. This is a simple and effective trick.

2 tablespoons butter or vegetable oil
1 white onion, roughly chopped
3 garlic cloves, sliced
1 tablespoon chopped fresh gingerroot
3 tablespoons mild curry powder
2 tablespoons tomato paste
3 cups chopped cauliflower
5 cups chicken or vegetable broth
1 cup green grapes
½ cup half-and-half or heavy cream
Salt and pepper, to taste

Mexican Chicken Soup

1 bunch washed cilantro
2 skinless chicken thighs
5 cups chicken broth
1 small white onion, medium
   diced
1 celery stalk, thinly sliced
1 small carrot, peeled and
   sliced into thin rounds
½ cup frozen corn kernels
3 garlic cloves, thinly sliced
2 teaspoons ground cumin
Salt and pepper, to taste
1 lime, cut in half

The inspiration for this soup comes from Chef John Santiago, who could not eat chicken soup without a load of fresh cilantro floating in it.

1. Separate the stems and leaves of the cilantro. Tie the stems in a bunch with twine and roughly chop the leaves. Set aside the leaves. In a pot, combine the cilantro stems, chicken, broth, onion, celery, carrot, corn, garlic, and cumin. Bring to a boil and simmer gently for 45 minutes, covered.

2. Remove the cilantro stems and chicken. Discard the stems. Pull the chicken meat off the bones and cut into small pieces. Return the chicken to the pot.

3. Season to taste with salt and pepper, and add the cilantro leaves.

4. Serve in warmed bowls with a lime half beside each bowl. Squeeze the lime over the soup at the table.

Dark Vs. White Meat
Contrary to other people around the world, Americans put much more value on the breast of the chicken than the legs and thighs. Dark meat has more fat, more flavor, and is much better suited to long-cooked dishes such as soups and stews.

Barbecued Beef and Barley Soup

A twist on a classic, serve this soup in the dead of winter when you are missing the grill the most.

1. Heat the oil in a saucepot on medium-high. Brown the beef well.

2. Add the onion, celery, carrot, mushrooms, paprika, garlic powder, sugar, and dry mustard. Sauté for about 5 minutes or until the vegetables soften.

3. Add the barley, tomatoes, consommé, broth, and Worcestershire sauce. Bring to a boil, then reduce to a simmer. Cook gently for 40 minutes, uncovered.

4. Season to taste with salt and pepper, and serve in warmed bowls.

Consommé 101

A consommé is a stock that has been enriched with flavor and then clarified. A mixture of ground vegetables, meat, and egg whites—called a "raft"—is poached in the stock like a giant omelet, which flavors and clarifies the soup.

---

2 tablespoons vegetable oil
½ pound lean beef chuck, cut into ½-inch dice
1 small white onion, small diced
1 celery stalk, thinly sliced
1 small carrot, peeled and thinly sliced into rounds
6 white mushrooms, thinly sliced
2 teaspoons paprika
1 teaspoon garlic powder
1 teaspoon brown sugar
1 teaspoon dry mustard
1/3 cup dry pearl barley
½ cup canned diced tomatoes
1 (16-ounce) can beef consommé
3 cups chicken broth
1 tablespoon Worcestershire sauce
Salt and pepper, to taste

Quick and Easy Midtown Clam Chowder

This is a simple and tasty soup.
Using canned clams make life easy when preparing this dish.

2 tablespoons vegetable oil
2 strips bacon, finely minced
1 small white onion, small diced
1 celery stalk, thinly sliced
1 small carrot, peeled and sliced into thin rounds
1 garlic clove, smashed
1 tablespoon fresh thyme leaves
3 tablespoons all-purpose flour
1 (10-ounce) can baby clams, juice and clams separated
1 cup clam juice
3 cups chicken broth
1 tablespoon Worcestershire sauce
1 cup diced canned tomatoes
¾ cup small-diced Idaho potato
Dash Tabasco sauce
Salt and pepper, to taste

1. In a saucepot, heat the oil on medium-high and add the bacon, onion, celery, carrot, garlic, and thyme. Sauté until the vegetables soften, about 10 minutes.

2. Add the flour to the pot and stir well to avoid any lumps.

3. Add the juice from the canned clams plus the additional 1 cup clam juice, the broth, Worcestershire sauce, and tomatoes. Bring to a boil. Reduce heat and gently simmer for 20 minutes, uncovered.

4. Add the potato and cook for another 15 minutes, uncovered, or until the potato is tender.

5. Add the clams and a dash of Tabasco sauce. Heat the soup through, then season with salt and pepper. Serve in warmed bowls.

What Makes a Chowder?
Classic chowder is not chowder unless it contains 3 essential ingredients: salt pork or bacon, potatoes, and milk or cream. This technically qualifies Manhattan clam chowder as a generic soup rather than a chowder. In Rhode Island they use both tomatoes and milk in the chowder to combine the best of both soups.

Baked Potato Soup

Keep some baked potatoes in the freezer in case you need some quick soup or home fries in a hurry. They last about 6 months tightly wrapped in the freezer.

2 tablespoons butter
1 medium-sized white onion, small diced
1 garlic clove, sliced
2 medium-sized baked potatoes, peeled and roughly chopped
3 cups chicken or vegetable broth
1 cup milk
1 bay leaf
Salt and pepper, to taste
4 tablespoons sour cream
2 tablespoons chopped fresh chives

1. In a saucepot, heat the butter on medium-high until it stops bubbling. Add the onion and garlic, and sauté about 3 minutes.

2. Add the potatoes, broth, milk, and bay leaf. Bring to a boil, then reduce to a gentle simmer. Cook, uncovered, for 20 minutes.

3. Remove the bay leaf. Working in batches, purée the soup in a blender until very smooth. Season to taste with salt and pepper.

4. Pour into warmed bowls. Garnish with a dollop of the sour cream and sprinkle the chives on top.

Dress Up Your Potato
Treat this soup as you would a regular baked potato. Use your creativity to incorporate other garnishes such as crumbled bacon, broccoli florets, Cheddar cheese, or even salsa. This soup is like a blank canvas just waiting to be filled. Experiment!

Cantonese Crabmeat and Egg Drop Soup

4 cups chicken broth
1-inch piece gingerroot,
    smashed with the back of
    a knife
2 garlic cloves, thinly sliced
4 tablespoons soy sauce
½ pound fresh crabmeat,
    picked over for shells
2 cups baby spinach
3 tablespoons cornstarch
    dissolved in 3
    tablespoons cold water
3 egg whites, lightly beaten
2 scallions, thinly sliced
2 teaspoons sesame oil

*Serve this soup as a first course to an Asian-inspired meal.
The trick here is to get comfortable using the cornstarch
slurry technique to give the soup that velvety feel.*

1. In a saucepot, combine the broth, ginger, garlic, and soy sauce. Bring to a boil. Reduce to a gentle simmer and cook for 10 minutes, uncovered. Remove and discard the ginger.

2. Add the crabmeat and spinach, and return to a boil. Very slowly drizzle in the cornstarch mixture while constantly stirring the soup. (It will slightly thicken the soup on contact.) Turn off the heat.

3. Stir the soup in 1 direction with a large spoon to make a whirlpool in the pot. While the hot soup is spinning, slowly drizzle in the egg whites; they will coagulate immediately. Let the soup stand for 1 minute. Adjust seasoning with soy sauce if desired.

4. Divide into 2 warmed bowls and sprinkle with the scallions. Drizzle the sesame oil over the soup.

Yellow Velvet Corn Soup

*Make this soup during the height of corn season.
The natural sweetness of great corn cannot be reproduced with
frozen corn or with inferior corn and added sugar.*

5 ears corn on the cob
6 cups chicken or vegetable
    broth
2 small white onions, medium
    diced
1 bay leaf
3 tablespoons butter
1 celery stalk, thinly sliced
2 garlic cloves, sliced
3 tablespoons all-purpose
    flour
Salt and pepper, to taste

1. Cut the kernels off the cob by sliding the knife between the kernels and the cob down the ear in a smooth motion. Cut the cobs into 2-inch pieces and add them to a saucepot along with the broth, half the onion, and the bay leaf. Cover and simmer gently for about 45 minutes to infuse the corn flavor into the broth. Strain the broth into a bowl and set aside.

2. In the same saucepot, melt the butter over medium-high heat until it stops bubbling. Add the remaining onion, the celery, and garlic. Sauté for about 5 minutes.

3. Sprinkle the flour over the sautéed vegetables and mix well.

4. Add the corn and the reserved corn broth to the pot and bring to a boil. Reduce to a gentle simmer and cook, uncovered, for about 30 minutes or until the corn is very soft.

5. Working in batches, purée the soup in a blender until smooth. Return to the pot and reheat. Season to taste with salt and pepper. Serve in warmed bowls.

Amount of Broth
Most soup recipes in this book call for 5 cups of broth for 2 people. Usually about 1 cup will evaporate during cooking. In the recipe for Yellow Velvet Corn Soup, we have started with 6 cups to allow for the infusion broth to evaporate a bit. If the soup is too thick, add more broth. If it is too thin, reduce the broth slightly.

Tuscan Tomato and Bread Soup

This soup, known as Pappa al Pomodoro, is a Tuscan classic. Chef Patrick Nuti, formerly of the restaurant Tuscan Square in New York City, inspired this dish.

½ cup extra-virgin olive oil

1 small red onion, medium diced

1 celery stalk, thinly sliced

1 small carrot, peeled and cut into thin half-moons

3 garlic cloves, minced

2 cups canned diced tomatoes and their juice

3 cups chicken or vegetable broth

1½ cups cubed stale crusty bread

Salt and pepper, to taste

½ cup grated Parmigiano-Reggiano cheese

8 basil leaves, torn into rough pieces

1. Heat half of the olive oil in a pot on medium-high. Add the onion, celery, carrot, and garlic. Sauté for about 5 minutes, until the vegetables are tender.

2. Add the tomatoes and broth, and simmer for 15 minutes.

3. Add the bread, and simmer for another 15 minutes.

4. Whisk the soup until the bread dissolves and the soup thickens. Season to taste with salt and pepper.

5. Pour into 2 warmed bowls and top each bowl with the cheese. Drizzle with the remaining olive oil and top with the basil leaves.

Olive Oil as a Seasoning

In Italy olive oil is as essential for seasoning as it is for cooking. Soups, grilled meats and fish, and all manner of vegetables are drizzled with extra-virgin olive oil as a final step to finish the dish with the great fragrance and silky texture that this liquid gold provides.

(Almost) Mom's Chicken Soup

If Mom hails from Eastern Europe, where many dishes are perfumed with dill, she probably uses this seasoning copiously.

2 large skinless, boneless chicken thighs
1 small white onion, medium diced
1 celery stalk, thinly sliced
1 small carrot, peeled and cut into thin rounds
1 cup shredded green cabbage
5 cups chicken broth
Salt and pepper, to taste
3 tablespoons chopped fresh dill
1 cup very small cooked pasta, such as stars or pastina

1. In a pot, combine all the ingredients except the dill and pasta. Bring to a boil, then reduce to a gentle simmer. Simmer for 1 hour, covered.

2. Remove the chicken thighs and break into small pieces. Return the meat to the pot. Adjust seasoning with salt and pepper.

3. Add the pasta and dill to the pot. Heat through and divide between 2 bowls to serve.

Miso Soup with Shrimp

It is easy to improvise with this soup—try adding almost any leftover fish, shellfish, or veggies to miso soup to bulk it up and change its character.

4 cups water
3 tablespoons miso paste with dashi added
½ pound raw medium shrimp, shelled and deveined
1 box silken tofu, cut into ½-inch cubes
4 scallions, thinly sliced

1. Bring the water to a boil, add the miso, and whisk well.

2. Add the shrimp and simmer for 3 minutes.

3. Divide the tofu and scallions between 2 bowls and pour the soup over them. Divide the shrimp equally between the bowls.

Miso 101
Miso is a fermented paste made mostly from soybeans. It is a staple in Japanese cuisine. Dashi is a stock made from seaweed and bonito, which is a fish that is dried and often shaved into flakes. You can purchase miso with dashi added to simplify the soup. Otherwise, dashi powder can be purchased separately.

Creamy Onion Soup

3 tablespoons butter

5 cups thinly sliced white onion

3 tablespoons all-purpose flour

4 cups chicken or vegetable broth

1 whole clove

1 bay leaf

4 ounces Stilton cheese, crumbled

¼ cup port wine

The sweet flavor of this soup is wonderfully accentuated by the sharp Stilton cheese and the port wine. If you cannot find Stilton, use any good blue cheese.

1. Heat the butter in a pot on medium-high until it stops bubbling. Add the onions. Sauté for about 20 minutes or until the onions are deeply caramelized and soft, stirring occasionally. (If the onions appear too dry during this process, add small amounts of water as necessary.)

2. Add the flour and stir well to incorporate. Add the broth, clove, and bay leaf. Simmer gently for 25 minutes, uncovered.

3. Remove the bay leaf and clove. Purée the soup in a blender, working in batches if necessary.

4. Pour into warmed bowls and garnish with the cheese. Serve the port in a small glass on the side, to be poured over the soup at the table.

Port and Stilton

A wonderful combination, port and Stilton are usually served together at the end of a meal as a dessert. The combination is considered a classic, and deservedly so. Walnuts, pears, and apples are also great counterparts to this cheese.

Half-Purée of Chickpeas

This soup is a typical dish in Moroccan households,
where chickpeas are a staple.

1. Heat half of the olive oil in a pot until barely smoking. Add the onion, garlic, celery, carrot, and coriander. Sauté for about 3 minutes, until the vegetables begin to soften.

2. Add the chickpeas, along with their liquid, and the broth. Simmer for 15 minutes, uncovered. Season to taste with salt and pepper.

3. Purée half of the soup in a blender, and return it to the unpuréed portion in the pot.

4. Divide the soup between 2 warmed bowls and top with the parsley, the remaining olive oil, and harissa. Serve a lemon half on the side of each bowl to squeeze over the soup.

Harissa
As widely used in Morocco and Tunisia as ketchup is in the United States, harissa is a spicy paste made from hot chilies, garlic, caraway, lemon, salt, and olive oil. It is put on just about everything, and it adds a perfect spicy kick to this soup. It is available in any Middle Eastern or Arabic market.

4 tablespoons extra-virgin olive oil, divided
1 small white onion, small diced
2 garlic cloves, minced
1 celery stalk, small diced
1 small carrot, peeled and small diced
2 teaspoons ground coriander
1 (15.5-ounce) can chickpeas and their liquid
3 cups chicken or vegetable broth
Salt and pepper, to taste
2 tablespoons chopped fresh parsley
1 teaspoon, or to taste, harissa sauce
1 lemon, cut in half

Roasted Sweet Potato Soup

*Roasting sweet potatoes in their skins is an incredible way
to maximize their already sweet flavor.*

2 medium-sized sweet
potatoes

2 tablespoons butter or extra-
virgin olive oil

1 small white onion, medium
diced

1 celery stalk, thinly sliced

2 garlic cloves, sliced

2 teaspoons chopped fresh
rosemary

4 cups chicken or vegetable
stock

½ cup half-and-half

4 tablespoons sour cream

1. Preheat oven to 350°F. Roast the sweet potatoes, directly on an oven rack, until a knife inserted into the deepest part comes out with no resistance. Let cool, peel, and cut into cubes.

2. Heat the butter on medium-high in a pot until it stops bubbling. Add the onion, celery, garlic, and rosemary. Sauté for about 3 minutes, until the vegetables begin to soften.

3. Add the potatoes and broth. Simmer gently for 25 minutes, uncovered.

4. Remove from heat and stir in the half-and-half.

5. Purée the soup in a blender until very smooth, working in batches if necessary. Transfer to 2 warmed bowls and garnish each with a dollop of the sour cream.

Rosemary

Rosemary is a member of the pine family and has that resinous flavor and scent reminiscent of its tree relatives. It is native to the Mediterranean region and makes a great counterpart to lamb, potatoes, and even strawberries.

Smoked Turkey and Wild Rice Soup

This soup is hearty and deeply flavorful with a subtle hint of smokiness. Serve this soup in the autumn, when these flavors seem apropos.

2 tablespoons butter or extra-virgin olive oil
1 small white onion, small diced
1 celery stalk, thinly sliced
1 small carrot, peeled and cut into rounds
2 garlic cloves, minced
1 bay leaf
1 teaspoon fresh thyme leaves
¾ cup uncooked wild rice
½ pound smoked turkey meat, medium diced
5 cups chicken stock
Salt and pepper, to taste

1. Heat the butter (or oil) in a pot on medium and add the onion, celery, carrot, garlic, bay leaf, and thyme. Sauté for about 3 minutes, until the vegetables begin to soften.

2. Add the rice and toss well with the vegetables to coat the grains with the fat.

3. Add the turkey meat and broth. Bring to a boil, then reduce to a simmer. Cover, and cook very gently for 45 minutes or until the rice kernels start breaking open. Season to taste with salt and pepper. Serve in warmed bowls.

Toasting Herbs and Spices
When sturdy herbs and spices are tossed with hot fat in a pan, they release their essential oils and become even more fragrant and flavorful. This is a great way to maximize flavors.

Hearty Lentil and Sausage Soup

*Any good sausage will do, but I prefer the French garlic sausage.
If you cannot find this, substitute a good-quality kielbasa.*

6 ounces garlic sausage,
   small diced
1 cup balsamic vinegar
2 tablespoons butter or extra-
   virgin olive oil
1 small white onion, small
   diced
1 celery stalk, small diced
1 small carrot, small diced
2 garlic cloves, minced
1 bay leaf
2 cups brown lentils
5 cups chicken broth
Salt and pepper, to taste
2 tablespoons chopped fresh
   parsley

1. In a small saucepan, reduce the balsamic vinegar over medium heat until about 2 tablespoons remain and it is very thick. Remove from heat and set aside.

2. In the soup pot, cook the sausage over medium heat until well browned. Leave the fat in the pan.

3. Add the butter or oil and heat on medium-high. Add the onion, celery, carrot, garlic, and bay leaf. Sauté for about 3 minutes, until the vegetables begin to soften.

4. Add the lentils and stir well. Add the broth. Cover, and simmer for 25 minutes.

5. Season to taste with salt and pepper. Ladle into warmed bowls. Sprinkle with the parsley and drizzle with the balsamic syrup.

Soaking Lentils
Lentils, unlike other beans, do not benefit from a soak in cold water. They are so small that they will cook evenly right from their dry state. Some people like to soak them for about 1 hour to help pull out some of the gas-causing enzymes.

White Bean and Rosemary Purée

The flavors of Northern Italy really come through with this simple soup.

3 tablespoons extra-virgin olive oil plus extra for garnish
1 garlic clove, minced
1 small red onion, small diced
1 medium carrot, peeled and small diced
1 celery, small diced
1 teaspoon chopped fresh rosemary
1 (15.5-ounce) can white beans and their liquid
4 cups chicken broth
1 lemon, cut in half
½ cup grated Parmesan cheese
Salt and pepper, to taste

1. Heat the olive oil in a pot on medium. Sauté the garlic, onion, carrot, celery, and rosemary for about 5 minutes, until the vegetables begin to soften.

2. Add the beans and broth. Bring to a boil, then reduce to a simmer for 25 minutes, uncovered.

3. Purée the soup in a blender, working in batches if necessary. Return to the pot and reheat.

4. Ladle the soup into 2 warmed bowls. Squeeze a lemon half over each, sprinkle with the Parmesan cheese, and drizzle with extra-virgin olive oil.

Lemon Instead of Salt?
Many times a cook will reach for salt when finishing a dish to give it a boost. Try to use acids such as lemon or vinegar first to see if what is really needed is a "brightening" of a dish rather than more salt.

Tortellini en Brodo

This is so simple, yet so satisfying. Buy frozen cooked tortellini to make life easy.

5 cups rich chicken or beef broth
3 cups cooked cheese tortellini
Salt and pepper, to taste
1 cup freshly grated Parmesan cheese
¼ cup chopped fresh parsley

Heat the broth in a saucepot. Add the tortellini and cook for just a minute or so, until warmed through. Season to taste with salt and pepper. Pour into bowls and garnish with the cheese and parsley.

The Importance of Broth
Store-bought broth is pretty respectable these days, but nothing beats a real homemade broth. Use plenty of bones and meat scraps, and avoid boiling your broth too vigorously. (This will cause it to be cloudy and greasy.) Cook the broth for at least 3 hours and freeze in portions for later use.

Quick Chinese Broth

This broth is delightful and really seems to help with a cold or flu.

4 cups chicken stock
1 (3-inch) piece fresh gingerroot, smashed lightly
¼ cup soy sauce
1 teaspoon dashi powder or 1 tablespoon dried bonito flakes
6 scallions
½ cup washed and roughly chopped cilantro leaves

Place everything in a pot except the cilantro and simmer gently for 40 minutes, uncovered. Strain the soup and add the cilantro. Drink hot.

Using Fish Flavors in Unusual Places
The use of dried fish or dashi powder in this dish is a prime example of how fish and fish flavors are used in dishes that are not considered "fishy." Much like anchovy in a Caesar dressing, the dried fish adds a salty complexity without making the dish taste like fish. Most people who say they hate anchovy have never even tried one!

chapter 6
pastas

Lora's Linguini with White Clam Sauce

½ pound linguini
2 tablespoons extra-virgin olive oil
½ small red onion, minced
3 garlic cloves, minced
1 tablespoon fresh thyme leaves
Pinch dried red pepper flakes
½ cup dry white wine
1½ cups chicken broth
1 can baby clams separated from the juice, juice reserved
2 tablespoons cornstarch dissolved in 2 tablespoons cold water
1 tablespoon butter
Salt and pepper, to taste
1 cup grated Romano cheese

Inspired by the great fashion stylist Lora Jackson, this dish is so delicious and easy to prepare that you may virtually stop ordering it in restaurants.

1. Bring a pot of water to a boil for the pasta. Boil the pasta according to package directions.

2. Meanwhile, heat the olive oil in a saucepot on medium-high until barely smoking. Add the onion, garlic, thyme, and pepper flakes. Sauté for about 3 minutes, until the onion begins to soften.

3. Add the wine and reduce the volume by half.

4. Add the broth and the juice from the clams. Simmer gently for about 7 minutes, uncovered.

5. Slowly drizzle the cornstarch slurry into to the simmering sauce, constantly stirring the sauce. Remove from heat and add the clams and butter. Keep warm.

6. When the pasta is cooked, drain well and toss with the sauce. Season to taste with salt and pepper. Divide the pasta between 2 serving plates, and serve the cheese at the table to be sprinkled on top.

Proper Pasta Etiquette

In Italy the pasta is almost always tossed with the sauce, not put in a bowl with the sauce ladled on top. Also, Italians do not use a spoon to load up a fork with pasta; they take smaller bites. It is not common to add cheese to fish-based sauces, but many do like cheese on this dish.

Orecchiette with Chicken Sausage and Broccoli

*You can substitute sweet or hot Italian pork sausage
for the chicken sausage if you wish.*

1. Heat a pot of water for the pasta.

2. In a large sauté pan, heat half of the oil on medium until barely smoking and brown the sausage very well. Add the garlic and red pepper flakes. Cook until the garlic is golden and fragrant, about 1 minute. Add the roasted red pepper, and remove the pan from the heat.

3. Drop the pasta in the water and begin cooking it according to package directions. Exactly halfway through the cooking process, add the broccoli to the pot. (This eliminates the step of cooking the broccoli separately.) When the pasta is cooked, the broccoli will be perfect.

4. Return the pan with the sausage to medium heat and bring up to temperature. Drain the pasta/broccoli and add to the pan. Add the remaining olive oil and season with salt and pepper. Divide into 2 bowls and serve the cheese at the table to be sprinkled on top.

Save Yourself the Mess

Adding the broccoli to the pasta water during the cooking process is a good technique. You can save a step, keep another pot clean, and simplify your cooking life. Experiment a bit with cooking times of different veggies and add them to your pasta repertoire.

¼ cup extra-virgin olive oil
½ pound chicken sausage,
    cut into 1-inch pieces
3 garlic cloves, minced
Pinch dried red pepper flakes
1 roasted red pepper, cut into
    1-inch strips
½ pound orecchiette pasta
2 cups broccoli florets
Salt and pepper, to taste
1 cup grated Romano cheese

Spaghetti with Mussels and Pancetta

½ pound spaghetti
2 tablespoons extra-virgin
    olive oil
2 ounces pancetta or bacon,
    small diced
3 garlic cloves, minced
Pinch dried red pepper flakes
1 cup dry white wine
1 recipe Quick Marinara
    Sauce (page 99)
1½ pounds fresh mussels,
    washed and debearded
Salt and pepper, to taste
4 tablespoons chopped fresh
    parsley

*When buying fresh mussels, always make sure they are either
closed or close when tapped. If not, discard them,
as this means they are dead and dangerous to eat.*

1. Bring a pot of water to a boil for the pasta. Cook the pasta according to package directions.

2. In a large sauté pan, heat the oil on medium. Add the pancetta, and cook slowly until crispy. Transfer the pancetta to paper towels to drain, and leave the fat in the pan.

3. Place the pan with the fat over medium-high heat and add the garlic and red pepper flakes. Sauté for about 1 minute, then add the wine. Increase heat to high and cook until the wine is reduced by half.

4. Add the marinara and mussels. Keep the heat on high, and cover the pot. Check the pot after about 3 minutes. The mussels are done when 95 percent of them have opened. Turn off the heat at this point and remove any unopened mussels. Keep warm.

5. When the pasta is cooked, drain well and toss with the mussel sauce. Season to taste with salt and pepper. Divide into 2 bowls. Top with parsley and serve.

Mussel 101
Fresh mussels are available year-round. Many are farmed near Prince Edward Island and have the designation "PEI" mussels. Green-lipped mussels are from New Zealand, are much larger, and are always frozen. They are inferior in both flavor and texture. Always ask your fishmonger to tell you the date the mussels were harvested. By law, he or she must have this information.

Quick Marinara Sauce

This sauce freezes well. Just make sure the sauce is well cooled in the refrigerator before placing it in the freezer.

4 tablespoons extra-virgin olive oil
1 white onion, medium diced
3 garlic cloves, smashed
½ cup chopped fresh parsley leaves
Pinch dried red pepper flakes
1 (28-ounce) can whole Italian plum tomatoes
Salt and pepper, to taste

1. In a sauté pan, heat the olive oil until barely smoking. Add the onion, garlic, parsley, and red pepper flakes. Sauté for about 5 minutes, and season with salt and pepper.

2. Add the tomatoes and simmer gently for 30 minutes, uncovered.

3. Purée the sauce in a blender and adjust seasoning with salt and pepper.

Perciatelli with Artichokes

Using frozen artichokes as opposed to canned makes a big difference in this dish. Seek them out.

2 tablespoons extra-virgin olive oil
1 garlic clove, sliced
1 small red onion, minced
½ pound frozen artichokes, thawed
½ cup heavy cream
Salt and pepper, to taste
½ pound perciatelli pasta
¼ cup grated Parmesan cheese
2 tablespoons chopped fresh dill

1. Heat the oil in a skillet over medium-high heat. Sauté the garlic and onion for 3 minutes. Add the artichokes and cream, and reduce the cream by half. Season with salt and pepper, and keep warm.

2. Cook the pasta according to package directions. Drain the pasta, and toss with the warm sauce. Top with the Parmesan and dill, and serve.

Easy Low-Fat Meat Sauce

½ pound ground beef or pork
1 recipe Quick Marinara
   Sauce (page 99)
1 cup canned beef consommé
   or chicken broth

*Boiling the ground meat is the key to reducing the fat content of this dish.
If you are not concerned with the extra calories,
brown the meat in olive oil instead.*

1. Place the ground beef in a saucepan with 1 quart of water and whisk well to break up the meat. Bring to a boil and cook for 5 minutes. Drain through a fine-meshed strainer.

2. Combine the beef, marinara, and broth in a saucepan. Cook for 30 minutes at a low simmer, uncovered.

Cold Pasta with Butter Beans and Tuna

3 cups any cooked pasta,
   cooled
1 can butter beans, rinsed
   and drained
1 can good-quality tuna,
   drained and flaked
3 scallions, finely sliced
1 large ripe tomato, diced
2 tablespoons capers, rinsed
½ cup kalamata olives
Juice of ½ lemon
¼ cup extra-virgin olive oil
½ cup grated Parmesan
   cheese
Salt and pepper, to taste

A great summer treat, this combination is a snap to prepare and truly satisfies.

Mix together all the ingredients in a bowl and serve. That's it!

Tuna 101
There are many kinds of canned tuna in the market these days. Look for albacore tuna that is "dolphin safe." Solid tuna packed in water or olive oil works well for this dish. Tuna from Italy packed in extra-virgin olive oil is also a great choice for this dish. If using this type, do not drain the tuna, and cut back on the oil in the recipe.

Israeli Couscous "Risotto" Primavera

*Not Moroccan couscous, but a small, round pasta from Israel,
Israeli couscous is available in most well-stocked supermarkets.
Look for it near the pasta or rice.*

1 quart chicken or vegetable broth
4 tablespoons extra-virgin olive oil
½ pound Israeli couscous
1 small white onion, finely diced
1 small red bell pepper, finely diced
1 small zucchini, finely diced
½ cup asparagus tips
2 garlic cloves, minced
½ cup grated Parmesan cheese
2 tablespoons finely minced fresh chives
Salt and pepper, to taste

1. In a saucepan, heat the broth on medium until almost boiling.

2. Meanwhile, in a small sauté pan, heat half of the olive oil over medium heat. Add the couscous and toss well in the oil. Cook until golden, about 5 minutes, stirring often. Remove the couscous from the pan and set aside.

3. In the same pan, heat the remaining olive oil until barely smoking. Add the onion, bell pepper, zucchini, asparagus, and garlic. Sauté for about 3 minutes.

4. Return the couscous to the pan with the vegetables and add about one-third of the hot broth. Cook uncovered over low heat until the broth has been absorbed, stirring occasionally. Repeat the process, adding more broth in portions until the couscous is al dente and almost all of the broth has been absorbed.

5. Turn off heat and add the Parmesan cheese and chives. Season with salt and pepper, and serve.

The Risotto Method
Usually associated with the classic Italian rice dish, adding hot broth gradually to short-grained starchy rice results in a creamy texture that is prized in a good risotto. This pasta is unique and acts much in the same way.

Fragrant Basil Pasta

½ pound long pasta
½ cup extra-virgin olive oil
6 garlic cloves, thinly sliced
2 cups cleaned and
    chiffonade basil leaves
1 cup grated pecorino
    Romano cheese
Salt and pepper, to taste

Serve this dish using long, spaghetti-type pasta. Any good pasta will do. Do not attempt this pasta with dry basil; it will not come out right.

1. Cook the pasta according to package directions.

2. In a sauté pan, heat the olive oil with the garlic until the garlic begins to turn golden. Immediately dump the garlic into a bowl large enough to handle all the ingredients.

3. Drain the pasta and add it to the bowl along with all the remaining ingredients. Toss well and serve immediately.

Cold Sesame Noodles with Cucumber and Cilantro

½ pound lo mein noodles or
    spaghetti
1 tablespoon minced fresh
    gingerroot
2 garlic cloves, minced
3 tablespoons peanut butter
¼ cup water or chicken broth
2 tablespoons soy sauce
1 tablespoon sesame oil
1 teaspoon Asian hot chili
    sauce
1 tablespoon rice vinegar
1 cup finely julienned
    cucumber
½ loosely packed cup washed
    cilantro leaves

A fantastic summer dish, these cold noodles are rich enough to satisfy a large hunger, yet surprisingly light.

1. Boil the pasta according to package directions. Drain and set aside to cool.

2. Make the sesame sauce by combining all the other ingredients except the cucumbers and cilantro in a blender. Purée until very smooth.

3. Toss the sauce with the pasta, cucumbers, and cilantro. Serve cold.

Baked Penne with Roasted Mushrooms and Ricotta

A very hearty and satisfying meatless pasta, this can be assembled up to a day in advance. Bake 1 hour before serving.

1 (10-ounce) package white mushrooms, cut into quarters
2 tablespoons extra-virgin olive oil
Salt and pepper, to taste
½ pound penne pasta
1 egg
1 cup ricotta cheese
½ cup grated Parmesan cheese
2 garlic cloves, minced
1 teaspoon dry oregano
½ cup shredded mozzarella cheese

1. Preheat oven to 400°F. Lightly oil a baking dish large enough to hold the pasta. Bring a pot of water to a boil for the pasta.

2. Toss the mushrooms with the oil and salt and pepper. Place the mushrooms on a baking sheet and roast for 10 minutes. Remove from oven and let cool. (Leave the oven at 400°F.)

3. While the mushrooms are roasting, boil the pasta al dente according to package directions.

4. Mix together the egg, ricotta, Parmesan, garlic, and oregano. Season with salt and pepper.

5. Mix together the mushrooms, the ricotta mixture, and the drained pasta. Spoon the mixture evenly into the prepared baking dish. Bake for about 25 minutes, until the center is very hot (above 165°F).

6. Top the pasta with the mozzarella and bake for an additional 10 minutes or until the top is well browned and bubbly. Remove from the oven and let rest for 5 minutes before serving.

Variations on a Theme
You can substitute an endless variety of vegetables in this dish. Try butternut squash and sage in the fall, sun-dried tomatoes in the winter, asparagus in the spring, and zucchini in the summer.

Japanese-Italian Angel Hair Pasta

Inspired by a similar dish in New York City, where the restaurant Basta Pasta specializes in "Japanese-Italian" cuisine.
Prepare to be blown away by this combination.

½ pound angel hair pasta
3 tablespoons extra-virgin olive oil
1 tablespoon butter
½ cup grated Parmesan cheese
½ cup "tobiko" (also called "flying fish") caviar
10 shiso leaves, chiffonade
Salt and pepper, to taste

1. Cook the pasta al dente according to package directions.

2. Drain the pasta and toss with the oil, butter, and cheese.

3. When the butter is melted, add the caviar and shiso. Season to taste with salt and pepper, and toss to mix. Serve immediately.

The Similarities of Japan and Italy

The common theme in Italian and Japanese cuisines is the respect for superior ingredients that are simply prepared. As an example, when sardines are in season, the Italians will prepare them by grilling them over wood and serving them with sea salt and lemon. In Japan they will also grill them, then sprinkle them with citrus-flavored soy sauce. Practically the same!

Farfalle with Calamari Fra Diavlo Sauce

*The trick with calamari is to cook it for either 2 minutes or 2 hours;
anything in between will be tough and chewy.*

3 tablespoons extra-virgin
  olive oil
1 small red onion, finely diced
4 garlic cloves, minced
1 teaspoon dried red pepper
  flakes
¾ pound cleaned calamari,
  cut into rings and legs cut
  in half
1 cup dry red wine
1 recipe Quick Marinara
  Sauce (page 99)
1 cup clam juice
Salt and pepper, to taste
½ pound farfalle pasta

1. In a heavy saucepot, heat the oil until barley smoking. Add the onion, garlic, and red pepper flakes. Sauté for about 3 minutes, until the onion begins to soften.

2. Add the calamari and red wine. Reduce the wine over high heat until almost dry.

3. Add the marinara and clam juice. Reduce heat and simmer very gently for 2 hours, covered.

4. When the sauce is nearly finished, cook the pasta according to package directions. Season the sauce with salt and pepper, toss with the drained pasta, and serve.

Calamari 101

Calamari is the Italian word for "squid." There are many species and sizes of squid in the sea, but what we commonly see in the fish market are small squid about 6 to 10 inches long. Most cleaned squid have previously been frozen. Fresh squid are superior in flavor but are difficult and messy to clean.

Spinach Noodles with Smoked Ham

This creamy pasta dish is extremely satisfying.
Experiment with different hams as well as salamis for this dish.

2 tablespoons extra-virgin olive oil
1 cup sliced mushrooms
1 cup frozen peas, thawed
½ cup julienned smoked ham
½ cup heavy cream
Salt and pepper, to taste
½ pound spinach fettuccini
¼ cup grated Parmesan cheese

1. Heat the olive oil in a skillet over medium-high heat. Add the mushrooms. Sauté for about 3 minutes, until they just begin to soften. Add the ham and peas, and sauté for 3 more minutes.

2. Add the cream and reduce by half. Season with salt and pepper.

3. Meanwhile, cook the pasta according to package directions. Drain, and toss with the warm sauce. Top each bowl with the Parmesan, and serve.

Cavatelli with White Beans and Arugula

Try to find baby arugula for this dish.
It usually comes washed and dried and ready to go.

4 tablespoons extra-virgin olive oil
2 garlic cloves, sliced
½ pound cavatelli pasta
1 (15.5-ounce) can small white beans, rinsed and drained
2 cups washed arugula leaves
½ cup grated Parmesan cheese
Salt and pepper, to taste

1. In a skillet, heat the olive oil on medium-high with the garlic until it turns golden. Immediately remove from heat.

2. Cook the pasta according to package directions. Drain the pasta, and mix together all the ingredients in a large pasta bowl. The arugula will wilt and collapse. Serve immediately.

The Simplest Sauce

The combination of Parmesan cheese and olive oil transforms plain pasta into a real treat. This combination, with the addition of any number of pantry ingredients, can create countless pasta masterpieces.

Rigatoni with Simple Shrimp Scampi Sauce

Scampi is the Italian word for "shrimp."
So, ordering "shrimp scampi" is really ordering "shrimp shrimp."

½ pound rigatoni pasta
2 tablespoons extra-virgin
 olive oil
½ pound medium shrimp,
 shelled and deveined
4 garlic cloves, minced
1 teaspoon fresh thyme
 leaves
½ cup dry white wine
1 cup clam juice
1 tablespoon butter

1. Bring a pot of water to boil, and cook the pasta according to package directions.

2. While the pasta is cooking, prepare the sauce: Over medium–high heat, heat the olive oil in a large skillet until barely smoking. Add the shrimp and brown quickly. Remove from the pan. The shrimp should be undercooked in the center at this point.

3. Add the garlic and thyme to the pan and sauté for about 1 minute. Add the wine and reduce until almost dry.

4. Add the clam juice and reduce by half. Add the shrimp and cook gently for 2 minutes.

5. Turn off the heat and add the butter. Stir to melt, then toss the hot pasta with the sauce.

Clam Juice

This is a great convenience item available in the supermarket. Substitute this for fish stock, which is tough to make. The only consideration is that clam juice is sometimes too salty. Taste the juice before adding it to a dish and reduce your salt content if necessary.

Garganelli with Porcini and Tomato Sauce

Dried porcini mushrooms are essential for this dish. Do not substitute other mushrooms. Look for them near the spices or produce in the supermarket.

1 cup dried porcini mushrooms

3 tablespoons extra-virgin olive oil

1 small white onion, small diced

Pinch dried red pepper flakes

½ cup dry red wine

1 recipe Quick Marinara Sauce (page 99)

Salt and pepper, to taste

½ pound garganelli pasta

½ cup grated Parmesan cheese

¼ cup chopped fresh parsley

1. Soak the porcini mushrooms in 2 cups of warm water for 1 hour. Remove the mushrooms from the water and roughly chop them. Strain the soaking liquid to remove any sand. Reserve 1 cup of the liquid.

2. Heat the olive oil on medium-high in a heavy saucepot. Sauté the onion with the red pepper flakes for about 3 minutes, until the onion begins to soften. Add the wine and reduce by half.

3. Add the mushrooms, the mushroom soaking water, and the marinara. Simmer gently for 1 hour, uncovered. Season with salt and pepper, and keep warm.

4. Cook the pasta according to the package directions, drain, and toss with the warm sauce. Serve with the cheese and parsley sprinkled over the top.

The King

Porcini literally translates to "little pig" in Italian. These mushrooms are the most sought after wild mushroom on earth. The Latin Boletus edulis is the scientific name for these earthy delights. Some mushroom foragers in the Pacific Northwest of the United States have been killed for encroaching on other mushroom foragers, "turf."

Classic Gnocchi

Gnocchi are a potato dumpling from the north of Italy.
They are often listed as a pasta, and although not a classic pasta,
they are quite worthy of placement in this book.

2 large russet potatoes (about 1 pound)
1 cup all-purpose flour
1 teaspoon salt

1. Bake the potatoes in a 350°F oven for about 1 hour, until tender.

2. While the potatoes are still warm, peel them and put them through a food mill or a ricer. (Do not process in a food processor; they will get gummy.) Place the potatoes in a large bowl and gradually stir in the flour until a sticky dough forms. Add the salt.

3. Knead the dough for about 3 minutes. It may require a bit more flour if it is too wet. The finished dough will be a bit sticky.

4. Flour your hands and divide the dough into 2 equal balls. Roll out the balls into long snake-shaped lengths about as thick as your finger. Cut the "snakes" into 1-inch pieces.

5. Press each gnocchi with the tines of a fork to put ridges into the dumplings. (These will help capture any sauce you pair them with.)

6. Bring a pot of salted water to a boil. Add the gnocchi and cook until they rise to the surface. Toss the gnocchi with your favorite sauce, and enjoy your hard work!

You Say Potato
Potatoes are originally from South America. They were imported into Europe in the 1600s and were used as an ornamental plant until someone figured out how good they were to eat.

Spaghetti with Sand

A funny-sounding dish. Kids love this dish for that reason, and it tastes great!

½ pound thin spaghetti
¼ cup extra-virgin olive oil
1 tablespoon butter
½ cup plain bread crumbs
1 garlic clove, minced
¼ cup grated Parmesan
    cheese
¼ cup chopped fresh parsley
Salt and pepper, to taste

1. Bring a pot of water to boil, and cook the pasta according to package directions.

2. While the pasta is cooking, heat the olive oil and butter together in a skillet until the butter stops bubbling.

3. Add the bread crumbs and the garlic. Toast the bread crumbs over medium heat for about 4 minutes, stirring frequently. (Be careful not to burn the bread crumbs.)

4. Drain the pasta, toss with the bread crumb mixture, and then toss with the cheese and parsley. Season with salt and pepper, and serve.

Crummy Business
Bread crumbs are a simple and effective way to add texture to a variety of dishes. Toasted bread crumbs are great on top of boiled veggies. They can also be used as a simple thickener for sauces and soups.

Simple Filling for Stuffed Pastas

This simple mixture is a great filling for stuffed pastas such as ravioli, cannel-loni, or manicotti. It can also be used as the cheese layer in lasagna.

Mix together all the ingredients and fill any pasta you wish. Make sure it cooks to 165°F because of the raw eggs in the filling.

2 cups ricotta cheese
1 egg, lightly beaten
½ cup grated Parmesan cheese
2 tablespoons chopped fresh parsley
1 garlic clove, minced
Salt and pepper, to taste

Linguini with Ricotta Salata and Olive Sauce

This is a very earthy and savory pasta dish.
Seek out whole-wheat linguini for this dish.

1. Cook the pasta according to package directions.

2. In a blender or food processor, purée the olives and olive oil together to form a smooth paste.

3. Drain the pasta, and toss with the olive sauce. Place in warm bowls and top with the cheese, basil, and pepper.

½ pound whole-wheat linguini
½ cup pitted oil-cured black olives
½ cup extra-virgin olive oil
¾ cup ricotta salata cheese crumbles
¼ cup chopped fresh basil
Freshly ground black pepper, to taste

Whole-Wheat Pasta
Whole-wheat pasta more closely resembles the classic Italian rustic pastas of old. The larger milled wheat and the addition of bran make for a rich and nutty flavor. This pasta is also a more complex carbohydrate than plain white pasta, and therefore is more healthful.

Slammin' Macaroni and Cheese

This is the real deal.

½ pound elbow macaroni
1 cup heavy cream
½ cup scallion cream cheese
½ pound sliced American cheese
1 garlic clove, minced
Salt and pepper, to taste
¾ cup plain bread crumbs
4 tablespoons melted butter

1. Preheat oven to 375°F. Grease a 9" × 13" ovenproof casserole dish.

2. Cook the pasta according to package directions, drain, and rinse under cold water.

3. Combine the cream, cream cheese, American cheese, and garlic in a saucepot over medium heat. Heat until just melted together.

4. Toss the pasta with the cheese sauce, and season with salt and pepper.

5. Transfer the pasta to the prepared casserole dish, spreading it out in an even layer. Sprinkle the top with the bread crumbs and then the melted butter. Bake for 35 minutes or until it is browned and bubbly.

The Magic of Cream Cheese
Cream cheese has a unique ability to melt into almost anything and create a great texture. Whether you are making a cheesecake, scrambled eggs, mac and cheese, or a myriad of other dishes, adding cream cheese is an easy, fast, and effective way to enhance creamy textures.

chapter 7

fish demystified

Moroccan-Spiced Salmon

*A very hearty fish entrée, serve this in wintertime
when you desire a more warming dish.*

1 cup dry lentils
Juice of 1 lemon
3 tablespoons extra-virgin
    olive oil, divided
2 tablespoons roughly
    chopped fresh cilantro
    leaves
Salt and pepper, to taste
1 teaspoon ground cumin
1 teaspoon ground coriander
½ teaspoon ground
    cinnamon
Pinch cayenne
2 (6-ounce) skinless salmon
    fillets
3 scallions, thinly sliced
6 black oil-cured Moroccan
    olives, pitted and
    chopped

1. Make a lentil salad by boiling the lentils in salted water for about 20 minutes or until they are firm but tender. Drain the lentils, and while they are still warm, add half of the lemon juice, 2 tablespoons of the olive oil, the cilantro, and salt and pepper. Keep warm.

2. Mix together the cumin, coriander, cinnamon, and cayenne. Dust one side of the salmon fillets with the spice mixture. Season the salmon with salt and pepper.

3. Preheat oven to 400°F. Heat a large, heavy, ovenproof skillet on high.

4. Add the remaining olive oil to the pan, and place the salmon in the hot pan, spice side down. Cook over high heat for about 3 minutes or until the spice side is well browned and beginning to crisp.

5. Turn the salmon over in the pan and place the entire pan in the oven. Cook for about 7 minutes, or until the salmon is cooked through but not flaking apart. Remove from the pan and blot the fillets on a paper towel. Serve on top of a pile of the lentil salad in the center of a large plate. Sprinkle the remaining lemon juice, the scallions, and olives over the fish.

Pan Roasting
Browning one side of the fish (or meat) and then placing the pan in a hot oven to finish cooking is a restaurant technique rarely used by the home cook. Just make sure the pan you are using has a metal handle!

Soy and Honey Roasted Black Cod

Black cod is a great substitute for Chilean sea bass, which is being fished to extinction. Don't order Chilean sea bass at restaurants, and let them know you disapprove of its presence on their menu.

2 cups trimmed string beans
1 tablespoon toasted sesame seeds
1 tablespoon sesame oil
Salt and pepper, to taste
3 tablespoons soy sauce
1 tablespoon vegetable oil
3 tablespoons honey
2 (6-ounce) black cod fillets

1. Boil the string beans in salted water until they are tender but still crisp, about 5 minutes. Cool them in ice water and drain well. Toss the beans with the sesame seeds, sesame oil, and a bit of salt and pepper. Set aside.

2. Mix together the soy, oil, and honey. Coat the cod in the mixture and let marinate for about 2 hours (an hour on each side) in the refrigerator.

3. Preheat oven to 425°F.

4. Place the fish in a small, ovenproof sauté pan. Roast in the oven for about 12 minutes or until the fish has browned well on top and is piping hot in the middle. Serve with the sesame string beans on a large plate.

Temperature Trick
To judge the internal temperature of a piece of meat or fish without a thermometer is easy. Simply insert a small knife or metal skewer into the deepest part of the meat, then touch it carefully to your lower lip or wrist. If it feels lukewarm, you know it is about body temperature (98.6°F) If it is piping hot, you can be sure it is fully cooked (above 140°F).

Monkfish Medallions with Provençal Salsa

1 cup ripe diced tomato

¼ cup finely minced red onion

2 tablespoons chopped pitted niçoise olives

1 tablespoon capers, rinsed

1 garlic clove, minced

2 tablespoons chopped fresh basil leaves

4 tablespoons extra-virgin olive oil, divided

Salt and pepper, to taste

1 teaspoon fresh thyme leaves

1 (12- to 16-ounce) monkfish fillet, cut into 6 medallions

Monkfish is also known as poor man's lobster.
It has a similar texture and is a fine eating fish.

1. To make the salsa, combine the tomatoes, onion, olives, capers, garlic, basil, 2 tablespoons of the olive oil, and salt and pepper. Set aside.

2. Toss the monkfish medallions with the remaining olive oil, the thyme, and salt and pepper. Heat a nonstick pan on medium, and sauté the fish for about 2 minutes per side or until piping hot in the center.

3. Mound the salsa in the center of the serving plates and arrange 3 medallions around the salsa on each plate.

The Flavors of Provence

Provence is a region in France famous for its tomatoes, garlic, olive oil, and olives. The climate and agriculture provide France with superior produce and a cuisine unique to the area. Visit if you can.

Sautéed Mako Shark Steaks

Mako shark has a truly sweet flavor, reminiscent of scallops.
The secret is not to overcook this (or any other) fish.

2 (6–8-ounce) mako shark
    fillets, about 1 inch thick
Salt and pepper, to taste
½ cup all-purpose flour
2 tablespoons butter, divided
2 tablespoons extra-virgin
    olive oil, divided
1 (10-ounce) package white
    mushrooms, thinly sliced
Juice of 1 lemon
2 tablespoons chopped fresh
    chives

1. Season each piece of fish with salt and pepper and dust with flour. Be sure to shake off any excess flour.

2. Preheat a heavy skillet over medium heat and add 1 tablespoon of the butter and 1 tablespoon of the oil. Heat until the butter stops bubbling, and sauté the fish for about 5 minutes per side. The outside should be golden brown and the center piping hot. Remove the fish from the pan and keep warm.

3. Wipe out the same pan and add the remaining butter and oil. Heat over medium-high heat until the butter stops bubbling. Sauté the mushrooms until all of the water they release has evaporated. Add the lemon juice and cook for 1 minute. Add the chives and adjust seasoning with salt and pepper. Serve the mushrooms on top of the mako steaks.

Practice Makes Perfect

The secret to not overcooking fish is to trust in yourself. This means lots of trial and error. Even professional cooks have a tendency to overcook fish. Do not be afraid to cut into the fish to gauge temperature and doneness. The fish should be a bit translucent in the center. If the fish flakes apart, it is probably overdone.

Crispy and Rare Tuna Slabs

2 medium cucumbers, thinly sliced
2 tablespoons rice vinegar
2 tablespoons granulated sugar
1 (12- to 16-ounce) slab tuna
2 tablespoons soy sauce
2 tablespoons peanut oil or vegetable oil

Choose the reddest tuna you can find. If the tuna appears gray or brown, pass on it and save this dish for another day.

1. Toss the cucumbers with the vinegar and sugar, and let marinate for 30 minutes. Drain off the liquid released by the cucumbers.

2. Marinate the tuna in the soy sauce for 15 minutes, then blot dry.

3. Heat the oil in a heavy pan until barely smoking. Sear the tuna quickly on all sides, no more than 20 or 30 seconds per side. Remove from the pan.

4. To serve, place a pile of the cucumbers in the center of each plate. Slice the tuna into slabs about ½ inch thick and arrange around the cucumbers. You can also serve this dish with wasabi and ginger as a sashimi course.

Peanut Oil
Peanut oil is used in high-heat cooking because of its ability to withstand higher temperatures than most other oils. The Chinese usually use peanut oil in their wok cookery, and many people fry in peanut oil. Be aware that people with nut allergies will be allergic to peanut oil.

Tilapia with "Marmalade"

The "marmalade" for this dish is also a great topping for steaks, sandwiches, or just about anything else.

1 large white onion, thinly sliced
1 large sweet red bell pepper, julienned
½ cup balsamic vinegar
½ cup granulated sugar
2 (6- to 8-ounce) tilapia fillets
2 tablespoons butter, softened
2 teaspoons dried oregano
Salt and pepper, to taste
½ cup dry white wine

1. Make the marmalade by combining the onion, pepper, balsamic vinegar, and sugar in a small pot. Simmer gently until the liquid has been absorbed, about 10 minutes. Let cool at room temperature.

2. Preheat broiler with an oven rack set in the top position. Rub each fillet with the softened butter and season with the oregano and salt and pepper. Place in a greased ovenproof pan and pour the wine over the fish.

3. Broil for about 4 minutes or until the fish is very hot. Save any liquid that remains to pour over the fish. Serve with the marmalade on the side.

Tilapia 101

Tilapia is a freshwater fish originally native to the Amazon River. The fish is now regularly farmed in many parts of the world including Asia, South America, and even in the Bronx! The fish has a very mild flavor and reminds me of flounder or sole in both flavor and texture.

Flounder Stuffed with Scallops and Dill Mousse

½ pound scallops, very cold
¼ cup heavy cream or half-and-half
1 egg white
1 teaspoon lemon juice
3 tablespoons chopped fresh dill, divided
Salt and pepper, to taste
2 (6-ounce) flounder fillets (sole can be substituted)
½ cup dry white wine
2 tablespoons softened butter

You can substitute almost any lean meat or fish to make this mousse.
To get the scallops cold enough, put them in the freezer
for 20 minutes before preparing.

1. Make the mousse by combining the scallops, cream, egg white, lemon juice, 1 tablespoon of the dill, and salt and pepper in a food processor. Process for about 1 minute, until smooth. Chill in the refrigerator until it is firm enough to spread on fillets.

2. Preheat oven to 425°F. Lightly grease a baking dish.

3. Cut each fish fillet in half lengthwise to form a total of 4 long strips. Season the fillets with salt and pepper, and spread one-quarter of the mousse on each. Roll up each fillet jelly–roll style and secure with a toothpick.

4. Place the fish in the prepared baking dish. Top each roll with an equal amount of the butter, and pour the wine over the fish. Bake for 15 minutes.

5. Transfer the fish to serving plates and add the remaining dill to the liquid in the baking dish. Pour this sauce over the fish, and serve.

Scallops
Scallops are a bivalve much like a clam. The part eaten is the adductor muscle, which is responsible for opening and closing the shell. The reason the mussel is so large in scallops is that scallops actually swim by opening and closing their shells rapidly to propel themselves!

Crispy and Mustardy Roasted Rainbow Trout

*If you cannot find the Japanese bread crumbs for this dish,
substitute fresh bread crumbs.*

1. Preheat oven to 425°F. Lightly grease a baking sheet.

2. Place the trout on a cutting board and cut off the head, fins, and tail (or have your fishmonger do this for you).

3. Mix together all the remaining ingredients in a small bowl.

4. Place the trout on the prepared baking sheet. Distribute the bread crumb mixture equally over both fish, covering as much of the flesh as possible with the topping. Bake for about 6 minutes, until the topping is golden brown. Serve immediately.

Wild or Fresh?
Many fish today are being raised in aquaculture farms. Trout are among them. Trout have been successfully raised in pens for almost 100 years. Today, most farmed trout comes from Idaho.

2 (8 to 10-ounce) boneless whole rainbow trout, skin on
½ cup panko bread crumbs (also called "Japanese bread crumbs")
2 garlic cloves, minced
1 tablespoon whole-grain mustard
1 teaspoon chopped fresh tarragon
2 teaspoons fresh thyme leaves
1 egg white
3 tablespoons extra-virgin olive oil
Salt and pepper, to taste

Caribbean-Style Cod Cakes

Salted cod is traditionally used for this dish.
Here, fresh cod is substituted for a lighter flavor.

¾ pound cod fillet
1¼ cups plain bread crumbs
¼ cup mayonnaise
1 egg, lightly beaten
Juice of 2 limes
6 scallions, thinly sliced
1 teaspoon grated fresh
    gingerroot
1 tablespoon fresh thyme
    leaves
½ teaspoon cayenne pepper
¼ teaspoon ground allspice
Salt and pepper, to taste
1 cup peeled and small-diced
    papaya
2 tablespoons chopped fresh
    cilantro

1. Simmer the cod in salted water until it begins to flake apart. Drain in a colander and break apart well. Let cool.

2. Preheat oven to 400°F. Lightly grease a baking sheet.

3. When the fish is cool, mix together the fish, bread crumbs, mayonnaise, egg, half of the lime juice, half of the scallions, the ginger, thyme, allspice, cayenne, and salt and pepper. Form into 4 equal patties and place on the prepared baking sheet. Bake for 20 minutes.

4. Meanwhile, make the salsa by mixing together the papaya, the remaining lime juice and scallions, the cilantro, and salt and pepper. Serve the salsa on top of the fish.

To Fry or Bake?
These cakes would most often be fried. Baking them at a high temperature has great results. The cakes will be less greasy, lighter, and lower in calories. If you crave something fried, you can fry these cakes in 1 inch of peanut oil at 370°F for 5 minutes per side.

Pineapple-Glazed Mahi-Mahi

Mahi-mahi is also known as Dorado and dolphinfish. This is a very tasty and firm fish. Seek it out.

1 tablespoon butter
1 tablespoon peanut oil
2 (8-ounce) mahi-mahi fillets
Salt and pepper, to taste
2 tablespoons pineapple jam
½ cup coconut milk
1 teaspoon grated fresh
    gingerroot
1 tablespoon Madras curry
    powder
2 tablespoons cornstarch
    dissolved in 2
    tablespoons cold water

1. Preheat oven to 400°F. Heat the butter and oil in an ovenproof skillet over medium-high heat until the butter stops bubbling. Season the mahi-mahi with salt and pepper, and brown well on one side. Turn the fish over and top each fillet with 1 tablespoon of the pineapple jam.

2. Place the pan in the oven and bake for 10 minutes.

3. While the mahi cooks, begin preparing the sauce by combining the coconut milk, ginger, and curry in a saucepan over medium heat.

4. When the fish is done, transfer the fillets to a plate and keep warm. Add the pan juices from the cooked fish to the sauce and bring to a boil. Slowly drizzle the cornstarch mixture into the boiling sauce, stirring the sauce throughout until it thickens. Serve the sauce over the mahi-mahi.

Storing Fresh Ginger
Keep fresh gingerroot at room temperature where you keep onions and garlic. It will dry out slightly, but it will retain its natural sweetness. When refrigerated too long, the ginger looses some sweetness and becomes tougher and stringy.

Old Bay Catfish with Roasted Corn Salsa

Roasting the corn for this dish is a snap.
Use this roasted corn as a side dish for other meats and fish.

1 cup frozen corn kernels (do not defrost)
Salt and pepper, to taste
2 tablespoons extra-virgin olive oil
¼ cup finely sliced scallions
¼ cup finely minced pimiento
2 (8-ounce) catfish fillets
Juice of ½ lemon
2 tablespoons Old Bay Seasoning
1 tablespoon softened butter

1. Preheat oven to 400°F. Lightly grease a baking sheet. Heat a heavy skillet on high until very hot.

2. Season the frozen corn with salt and pepper, and mix with the olive oil. Place the corn in the hot pan in a single layer and do not move around in the pan. After about 2 minutes, check to see that the corn is beginning to char. If there is visible blackening of the corn, move the corn around a bit. Cook for about 4 minutes total. Remove from pan and let cool at room temperature.

3. When the corn is cool, add the scallions and pimiento. Adjust seasoning to taste with salt and pepper.

4. Rub the fish fillets with the lemon juice and the Old Bay. Place on the prepared baking sheet and rub the tops with the softened butter. Season with salt and pepper. Bake for about 12 minutes. Serve the salsa over the fish.

Catfish 101
Catfish is a freshwater fish native to every continent except Antarctica. Most of the catfish consumed in the United States is farm raised either in the southern United States or in Southeast Asia. Ask your fishmonger where the fish comes from and buy American if you can.

Steam-Grilled Striped Bass

A lovely firm-fleshed and meaty fish, striped bass is worth seeking out.
You can also substitute halibut for this dish.

2 (8-ounce) striped bass fillets, scaled, skin on
1 medium-sized red onion, thickly sliced
4 tablespoons extra-virgin olive oil
Salt and pepper, to taste
3 garlic cloves, sliced
1 large, meaty beefsteak tomato, thickly sliced
2 sprigs fresh thyme

1. Preheat grill to medium heat.

2. Make a sturdy pouch of tinfoil for each fillet. Place the onions on the bottom, and place the fish on top. Drizzle with the oil and season with salt and pepper. Top with the garlic, tomato, and thyme. Seal up the tinfoil pouches.

3. Place on the grill and let steam for 15 minutes.

4. Place the tinfoil pouches on paper plates and slice open. Serve.

Stripers
Each spring and fall, the northeast coast of the United States is blessed with some of the greatest striped bass fishing on earth. Anglers up and down the coast revel in this magnificent game fish and its succulent flesh.

Swordfish with Anchovy and Caper Sauce

*A very meaty fish, swordfish is well suited for all
cooking styles and is incredibly versatile.*

2 tablespoons extra-virgin
    olive oil
2 (8-ounce) swordfish fillets
Salt and pepper, to taste
2 tablespoons butter
2 anchovy fillets, chopped
Juice of 1 lemon
2 tablespoons capers, rinsed
2 tablespoons chopped fresh
    parsley

1. Heat a heavy skillet on medium-high. Add the olive oil and heat until barely smoking.

2. Season the swordfish on both sides with salt and pepper and brown well on both sides. Cook until the center of the fish is hot. Transfer the fish to a plate and keep warm.

3. Wipe out the same pan and return to medium-high heat. Add the butter and anchovy to the pan, and heat until the butter begins to turn slightly brown. Immediately add the lemon juice, capers, and parsley. Turn off the heat, and stir the sauce to mix.

4. Pour the sauce over the fish, and serve.

The Ecology of Eating
It is important to remember that large pelagic fish such as swordfish and tuna are a natural resource that can easily be depleted. Limit your consumption of these giants to a few times a year to help ensure the species' survival.

Drunken Floribbean Snapper

Floribbean is a term describing the wonderful pairing of Florida's cuisine with that of its neighbor, the Caribbean.

2 medium-ripe plantains, peeled
6 tablespoons peanut oil, divided
Salt and pepper, to taste
Juice of 1 lime
¼ cup minced red onion
2 tablespoons chopped fresh cilantro
2 (8-ounce) snapper fillets, scaled, skin on
1 ounce dark rum
2 teaspoons fresh thyme leaves

1. Preheat oven to 400°F. Lightly grease a baking sheet. Cut the plantains into diagonal slices about ¼ inch thick. Toss with 2 tablespoons of the oil, and season with salt and pepper. Place on the prepared baking sheet, and bake for 15 minutes.

2. Toss the cooked, hot plantains with half of the lime juice, the onion, and the cilantro. Keep at room temperature.

3. Mix together the remaining lime juice, the rum, thyme, and salt and pepper. Coat the fish in the mixture and let marinate for 10 minutes in the refrigerator.

4. Heat the remaining oil in a heavy skillet and blot the fish lightly to remove excess liquid. Sauté the fish on both sides until the skin is crisp and the flesh is cooked through. Serve alongside the plantain salad.

Go Bananas

Plantains are sometimes called "cooking bananas." They are a close relative of the banana but need to be cooked. Many Caribbean cultures use the plantain much like potatoes. If they are green, they are under-ripe; if they are black, they are ripe (both ripe and unripe are used).

Broiled Pickled Mackerel with Citrus Soy Sauce

2 fillets from a small mackerel (about 1½ pounds total), top skin removed
1 cup granulated sugar
2 cups rice vinegar
2 tablespoons peanut oil
Salt, to taste
4 tablespoons citrus soy sauce

In Japan, oily fish such as mackerel and sardines are often pickled to complement their strong flavor. This is an easy home method.

1. Score the skin side of the mackerel every 2 inches or so, just slicing through the skin.

2. Mix together the sugar and vinegar well, and soak the fish in this mixture for 3 hours. Drain and use paper towels to blot the fish completely dry.

3. Preheat broiler. Place the fish on a lightly oiled baking sheet, skin side up. Rub the skin with the oil and season with salt.

4. Broil until well browned and bubbling. Don't turn the fish. (The fish will cook through even though only one side is being broiled.) Slide the fillets onto plates and sprinkle with citrus soy.

Mackerel Skin
The mackerel has 2 layers of skin. The outermost layer contains the very small scales of the mackerel. Peeling this layer eliminates the scales but keeps the underlayer of skin, which is nice when crispy.

Sesame-Roasted Salmon with Snow Pea "Slaw"

Almost too easy to put in print, this dish always gets requests for recipes.

2 (8-ounce) skinless salmon
 fillets
4 tablespoons soy sauce
1 cup sesame seeds
Cooking spray
2 cups finely shredded snow
 peas
¼ cup shredded raw carrot
2 teaspoons rice vinegar
½ teaspoon sesame oil
Salt and pepper, to taste

1. Marinate the salmon in the soy sauce for 1 hour in the refrigerator.

2. Preheat oven to 400°F. Press the top of each fish in the sesame seeds to coat the top completely. Spray a baking dish with cooking spray, and place the salmon seed-side up in the dish. Spray the sesame seeds well with the cooking spray. Bake for about 10 minutes or until the center of the salmon is piping hot and the sesame seeds are golden.

3. Mix together the snow peas, carrots, rice vinegar, and sesame oil. Season with salt and pepper, and serve under the salmon.

Easy Shred

To shred the snow peas, place them on your cutting board in a long row, slightly overlapping, and perpendicular to the board. This way, you can shred them with your knife in a single motion rather than doing them one at a time. This trick also works for anything relatively flat, such as shiitake mushrooms.

Crispy Whitebait "Fries"

Peanut oil, as needed
All-purpose flour, as needed
Salt and pepper, to taste
1 pound whitebait, rinsed in
     cold water and patted dry
½ cup mayonnaise
3 garlic cloves, smashed into
     a paste
Juice of 1 lemon

Whitebait are very small fish also called spearing. They are about 2 to 3 inches long and require no cleaning of any kind. Look for them in the spring.

1. Heat about 4 inches of the oil in a pot to 375°F.

2. Season the flour with salt and pepper, and dredge the fish very thoroughly in the flour. Place the fish in a strainer and shake off all of the excess flour.

3. Fry the fish in 3 batches. (This keeps the oil from cooling down too much.) When the fish are golden and float to the surface, they are done (about 1 minute). Drain on paper towels and sprinkle with salt while still hot.

4. Mix together the mayonnaise, garlic, and lemon juice. Serve as a dip for the whitebait. Eat the fish while hot and crispy.

Eat It All

Eating a whole uncleaned fish may seem very unappetizing to most Americans. In actuality, these little fish are delightfully flavorful and not "fishy." The scales, bones, and the rest of it are unnoticeable while eating and virtually melt away during the frying process. Do not fear!

Buttery Sea Trout with Oranges

Sea trout is also known as speckled trout in the South and weakfish and sque-teague in New England. Whichever name you use, this fish is fantastic.

2 (8-ounce) sea trout fillets, scaled, skin on
Salt and pepper, to taste
¼ cup dry white wine
2 oranges
2 tablespoons butter
1 garlic clove, thinly sliced
1 tablespoon chopped fresh chives

1. Preheat oven to 450°F. Season the fish with salt and pepper. Pour the wine into a sauté pan large enough to hold both pieces of fish. Squeeze all the juice from 1 of the oranges into the pan. Place the fish in the pan, and add the butter and garlic.

2. Place the pan in the oven. Bake for about 13 minutes or until the fish is fully cooked.

3. While the fish is cooking, segment the other orange by cutting away all of the skin and pith and running a small knife between the segments. Avoid any membrane and seeds.

4. When the fish is done, place the pan on the stovetop and transfer the fish to a platter. Add the orange segments to the pan and heat through. Add the chives and adjust seasoning with salt and pepper. Serve the sauce over the fish.

What You Need to Know about Sea Trout

This fish has very delicate flesh when cooked and has a tendency to want to fall apart. Keep this in mind when transferring from pan to plate and use caution and a good spatula. The meat is also excellent raw as sushi and sashimi, and in the spring finds its way into the finest sushi bars in the Northeast.

Stir-Fried Blackfish with Black Bean Sauce

Blackfish is available in the fall and has a very sweet and succulent flesh that is similar in flavor to scallops.

3 tablespoons peanut oil
1 cup sliced shiitake
    mushrooms
½ cup julienned red bell
    pepper
3 scallions, thinly sliced
2 garlic cloves, minced
2 teaspoons grated fresh
    gingerroot
¾ pound skinless blackfish
    fillet, cut into 2-inch
    chunks
½ cup chicken stock or water
2 tablespoons soy sauce
1 tablespoon prepared
    Chinese black bean sauce
Pinch granulated sugar
2 tablespoons cornstarch
    dissolved in 2
    tablespoons cold water

1. In a large, heavy pan or wok, heat the peanut oil on high until smoking.

2. Add the mushrooms, bell pepper, scallions, garlic, and ginger. Stir-fry for about 2 minutes. Add the fish, and cook for another 2 minutes.

3. Add the stock, soy sauce, black bean sauce, and sugar. Bring to a boil, and let boil for 2 minutes.

4. With the sauce still boiling, slowly drizzle in the cornstarch slurry, stirring the sauce constantly. Turn off the heat immediately, and serve.

Black Bean Sauce
This interesting ingredient can be found in almost any supermarket these days. It is a mixture of small fermented black beans, soy, and seasonings. A little goes a long way, so experiment with how much you like.

Swordfish Slabs with Roasted Olives

Meaty and firm, swordfish has become an American favorite. Look for fish with a bright red "blood line" running through the meat.

क्ष

1 cup Sicilian green olives
3 tablespoons extra-virgin
   olive oil
2 (8-ounce) swordfish steaks
Salt and pepper, to taste
½ lemon

1. Preheat oven to 350°F. Place the olives in a towel and "crack" them with a heavy pan or mallet.

2. Heat the olive oil in a large ovenproof pan until barely smoking. Season the fish with salt and pepper, and brown well on one side. Remove from heat.

3. Turn over the fish in the pan, and add the olives. Place the pan in the oven, and bake for about 8 minutes or until the fish is piping hot in the center. Transfer the fish to serving plates and scatter the olives around the fish. Squeeze lemon over the top, and serve.

The Plight of the Swordfish

The popularity of swordfish has unfortunately led to its being overfished. Try to limit your consumption of this great fish to only a few times a year to ensure that our children and grandchildren will be able to share our planet with this magnificent creature, which can easily reach 500 pounds or more.

Poached Grouper Fillets

Poaching is a great way to reduce fat and keep flavor. As usual, not over-cooking the fish is the key to a moist piece of flesh.

2 (8-ounce) skinless grouper fillets
½ cup vermouth
¼ cup chicken stock
2 tablespoons minced shallots
1 tablespoon butter
Salt and pepper, to taste
2 teaspoons chopped fresh dill

1. Place the fish, vermouth, chicken broth, shallots, butter, and salt and pepper in a shallow pan.

2. Bring the liquid to a boil, then reduce heat to the lowest setting. Cover the pan, and cook for about 6 minutes or until the centers of the fillets are hot.

3. Transfer the fish to shallow bowls. Add the dill to the sauce in the pan, then pour the sauce over the fish. Serve with a lot of sauce, with a spoon to eat it like soup.

Shallot Substitution
Shallots are a member of the onion family. They resemble small red onions and are prized for their mild flavor. If you cannot find shallots in your market, use red onion that has been minced, then rinsed in cold water. Do not use dried shallots; they are practically tasteless.

Dill and Mustard Roasted Salmon

Salmon has a strong flavor, so other strong flavors like mustard work well with it.

2 tablespoons Dijon mustard
1 egg yolk
1 tablespoon chopped fresh dill
Salt and pepper, to taste
2 (7-ounce) skinless salmon fillets

1. Preheat oven to 400°F. Lightly grease a baking dish. Mix together the mustard, egg yolk, dill, and salt and pepper.

2. Place the salmon in the prepared pan, and brush the mustard mixture over the tops of the fillets. Bake for 12 to 14 minutes or until the tops are well browned and the meat is piping hot in the center. Serve hot.

Pairing Fish and Flavors
Delicate and white-fleshed fish tend to marry better with lighter and more delicate flavors. Their fragile flesh will be overwhelmed by strong flavors. Conversely, strong-flavored fish such as salmon, mackerel, and bluefish can stand up to very aggressive and strong flavors. Just experiment and be creative.

Steamed Cod with Chinese Flavors

2 tablespoons soy sauce
1 teaspoon sesame oil
1 teaspoon dry sherry
Pinch granulated sugar
2 (7-ounce) cod steaks, scaled, skin on
2 large napa cabbage leaves
6 scallions, white part only, julienned
1-inch piece gingerroot, thinly julienned
2 garlic cloves, sliced paper-thin

Pick up a bamboo steamer at the nearest Chinese marketplace. They are cheap and very versatile.

1. Mix together the soy, sesame oil, sherry, and sugar. Coat the fish in the mixture and let marinate for 2 hours in the refrigerator.

2. Fill a pot with 1 or 2 inches of water, and bring to a boil. Line a bamboo steamer with the cabbage leaves and lay the fish on top of the leaves. Pile the scallions, ginger, and garlic on top of the fillets.

3. Place the steamer over the pot of boiling water. Steam for approximately 10 minutes or until the fish is piping hot. Serve hot, as is.

Chinese Seasoning 101

The mixture of soy sauce, dry sherry, and sesame oil is a trinity used in much Chinese cookery. It is a simple, versatile, and flavorful Chinese marinade. These flavors are easy for the American palette to "understand," and all the ingredients are easy to find. Try this marinade on anything!

chapter 8
not the same old chicken

Shredded Chicken Enchilada Pie

Buy enchilada sauce in the can; it makes life a lot easier.
Making it from scratch is quite involved.

1 pound skinless, boneless chicken thighs
½ cup chicken broth
Juice of 2 limes
1 tablespoon ground cumin
Salt and pepper, to taste
2 tablespoons vegetable oil
9 (6-inch) soft corn tortillas
1 (20-ounce) can enchilada sauce
1 cup Cotija cheese or ricotta salata
1 ripe Haas avocado, peeled and roughly chopped
2 tablespoons finely minced red onion
2 tablespoons chopped fresh cilantro

1. Place the chicken, broth, half of the lime juice, cumin, and salt and pepper in a small pot. Cover, and gently simmer for 40 minutes or until the chicken shreds apart easily. Shred and let cool slightly.

2. Preheat oven to 400°F. Lightly grease a 9-inch square baking dish with the vegetable oil.

3. Place a layer of 3 tortillas on the bottom of the baking dish. Pour a thin layer of enchilada sauce on top of the tortillas. Place one-third of the meat on top of the sauce, spreading it out in an even layer. Repeat with another layer of tortillas, sauce, and meat. Finish with a final layer of tortillas, and pour the remaining sauce over the top. Sprinkle with the cheese. Bake for about 30 minutes, until the top is brown and the dish is bubbling.

4. Mix together the avocado, onion, cilantro, the remaining lime juice, and salt and pepper.

5. Allow the enchilada pie to rest for about 5 minutes before serving. Serve with the salsa on the side.

Looks like Lasagna!
A good way to view this dish is like a "Mexican lasagna." The tortillas replace the pasta, and the enchilada sauce replaces the tomato sauce. Get creative and experiment with different meat and vegetable fillings. This is a great way to use leftovers.

Greek-Style Taverna Oregano and Lemon Chicken

*The only secret here is allowing enough time for
the marinade to flavor the chicken. Overnight is best.*

½ cup dry white wine
½ cup extra-virgin olive oil
Juice of 2 lemons
6 garlic cloves, minced
2 tablespoons dried oregano
Salt and pepper, to taste
1 (2½-pound) roaster chicken,
   cut into 6 pieces

1. Mix together the wine, oil, lemon juice, garlic, oregano, and salt and pepper. Coat the chicken with the mixture, and let marinate overnight in the refrigerator.

2. Preheat oven to 425°F. Drain the chicken, and reseason slightly with salt and pepper. Place the chicken in a baking pan, and bake for 40 minutes. Serve hot.

Tavernas

A taverna is a Greek tavern. These taverns are known for having great, cheap food, belly dancers, and a rowdy and fun crowd. Often, whole lambs will be roasting in the windows for customers to see from the street.

Quick Chicken Cacciatore with Mushrooms

Here is a great way to use the cheaper parts—legs and thighs—of the chicken. Breasts will just dry out in this preparation.

2 whole chicken legs, thighs attached
Salt and pepper, to taste
All-purpose flour, as needed
8 tablespoons extra-virgin olive oil, divided
3 garlic cloves, sliced
1 small white onion, sliced
1 medium carrot, peeled and cut into thin half-moons
1 (10-ounce) package white mushrooms, sliced
1 cup dry red wine
1 (16-ounce) can crushed tomatoes
1 cup chicken broth
1 bay leaf
1 sprig fresh oregano or rosemary

1. Separate the chicken legs and thighs, and season well with salt and pepper. Dust with flour and shake off the excess.

2. Heat half of the oil in a large skillet on medium-high. Brown the chicken well on all sides. Remove the chicken from the pan and set aside.

3. Add the remaining oil to the same pan and add the garlic, onion, carrot, and mushrooms. Sauté for about 5 minutes, or until the vegetables begin to soften.

4. Add the wine, broth, tomatoes, bay leaf, and oregano. Season with salt and pepper. Return the chicken to the pan, and bring to a gentle simmer. Cook, partially covered, for 45 minutes or until the chicken is very tender and the broth has slightly thickened. Serve hot over pasta or polenta, or alone.

Hunters' Stew

Cacciatore means "hunter" in Italian. Since hunters prowl the forest for their prey, and mushrooms inhabit these same woods, the term cacciatore will almost always signify the addition of mushrooms in a dish.

Baked Chicken Cordon Bleu

Baking takes much of the fat from this dish.
The secret is generous use of cooking spray.

2 (6-ounce) skinless, boneless
    chicken breasts, pounded
    thin
Salt and pepper, to taste
2 slices smoked ham
2 slices Swiss cheese
Flour, for dredging
2 eggs, beaten
Bread crumbs, for coating
Cooking spray

1. Season the chicken on both sides with salt and pepper. Place a slice of ham and cheese on each chicken breast, and roll up the breast so the cheese and ham are inside. Place the chicken in the freezer for 2 hours to allow them to freeze partially. (This makes it easier to bread the chicken.)

2. Preheat oven to 400°F. Dredge the chicken rolls in the flour. Shake off excess flour. Dip in the egg, then coat in the bread crumbs.

3. Spray a baking sheet with the cooking spray, and place the chicken on the sheet. Spray the tops and the sides of the breaded chicken very heavily with cooking spray. Bake for 30 minutes or until the chicken is 165°F. Serve hot.

Skin or No Skin?
The delightful texture and taste of crispy, salty chicken skin is hard to beat. If you have real health concerns with fat intake, feel free to discard the skin before or after cooking. If not, enjoy this treat occasionally.

Curried Yogurt Chicken

Once again, the marinating time is key here.
Allow this chicken a full day to tenderize and pick up flavors.

1 (2-pound) roaster chicken, cut into 6 serving pieces (breasts, thighs, wings)
2 cups plain yogurt
2 tablespoons grated fresh gingerroot
2 garlic cloves, minced
4 tablespoons Madras curry powder
Salt and pepper, to taste
1 cup store-bought mango chutney (such as Major Grey's)

1. Mix together the yogurt, ginger, garlic, and curry powder. Coat all the chicken pieces completely in the mixture, and let marinate overnight in the refrigerator.

2. Preheat oven to 425°F. Place the chicken on a lightly greased baking sheet, and season the top with salt and pepper. Cook for about 40 minutes, or until the chicken is deeply colored and the internal temperature reaches 165°F.

3. Serve the mango chutney alongside the chicken for dipping.

Caesar-Style Chicken Breasts

With the "Chicken Caesar" craze in full swing,
everyone will appreciate this easy and tasty treat.

2 (8-ounce) boneless chicken breasts, skin optional
1 cup store-bought Caesar dressing
Cooking spray
½ cup grated Parmesan cheese

1. Marinate the chicken in the Caesar dressing for at least 3 hours or up to 12 hours.

2. Preheat oven to 400°F. Spray a baking sheet with the cooking spray. Place the chicken breasts skin-side up on the sheet. Top with the Parmesan cheese and spray the cheese layer lightly with cooking spray. Bake for about 15 minutes, until the top is browned and the center reaches 165°F. Serve hot or cold.

Rotisserie-Style Whole Chicken

You'll be surprised how close this comes to a real rotisserie chicken—the key is the rub smeared on the bird.

1 (2-pound) roaster chicken, giblets removed
2 tablespoons paprika
2 teaspoons brown sugar
1 tablespoon garlic powder
1 tablespoon onion powder
1 tablespoon dried thyme
2 tablespoons mayonnaise
Salt and pepper, to taste

1. Preheat oven to 375°F. Rinse the chicken and pat dry with paper towels.

2. Mix together all the remaining ingredients. Rub the mixture over the entire chicken.

3. Place the chicken on a lightly greased rack set inside a roasting pan. Roast for about 50 minutes or until the deepest part of the thigh reaches 165°F.

4. Remove from the oven and let rest for 10 minutes before carving.

Resting Meat

Whether you are cooking a 6-ounce steak or a 30-pound turkey, all meat should have a period of resting time after it is removed from the heat source. This allows the hot juices inside the meat to settle back into the fibers of the meat, which results in a much juicier and more tender piece of meat. The bigger the piece of meat, the longer the resting time should be.

Chicken Breasts Stuffed with Asparagus and Parmesan

8 medium-sized asparagus spears
2 (6-ounce) boneless chicken breasts, butterflied
Salt and pepper, to taste
1 cup shredded Parmesan cheese, divided
Cooking spray

Easy, healthy, and delicious, this is sure to please.
Make it in the spring when asparagus is at its best.

1. Preheat oven to 400°F. Trim the bottoms of the asparagus and boil the spears in salted water for 4 minutes. Shock in cold water and drain.

2. Season the inside of each chicken breast with salt and pepper. Sprinkle ¼ cup of the cheese evenly inside each breast. Top each with 4 asparagus spears, so the asparagus tips peek out when the chicken breast is folded back together. Fold the chicken breasts closed, so they are as close to their original shape as possible.

3. Spray a baking sheet with the cooking spray. Place the chicken on the sheet, and top the skin side with the remaining cheese. Spray the tops lightly with cooking spray. Bake for about 12 minutes or until the center registers 165°F. Serve hot.

Butterflying
Butterflying a piece of meat is essentially cutting it in half widthwise to make the piece thinner and larger without cutting it completely into 2 pieces. Use a sharp, thin-bladed knife and place your hand on top of the meat horizontally with your palm on the meat and fingers up. Practice makes perfect.

Unfried Chicken Parmesan

This "oven-frying" technique works well with almost any breaded item. Just be sure not to skimp on the cooking spray.

1. Preheat oven to 400°F. Put some flour in a shallow bowl, and season with salt and pepper. In another shallow bowl, mix together the bread crumbs, Parmesan, and parsley, and season with salt and pepper. Lightly beat the eggs with the water in another bowl.

2. Dredge the chicken in the flour, and shake off any excess. Dip the chicken in the egg, then coat in the bread crumb mixture. Press the bread crumbs firmly into the meat. Shake off excess.

3. Spray a baking sheet with the cooking spray. Place the chicken on the sheet. Spray the chicken with the cooking spray so that all the bread crumbs are well moistened. Bake for 10 minutes.

4. Remove from the oven and top each chicken breast with half of the marinara, and then the mozzarella . Bake for 3 to 4 more minutes, or until the cheese is melted and the chicken is 165°F.

Spray and Bake

Try this technique on any breaded item that you wish to fry but don't want the extra fat. This works well with chicken fried steak, fish fillets, calamari, crab cakes, and all manner of cutlets.

All-purpose flour, as needed
Salt and pepper, to taste
2 cups plain bread crumbs
¼ cup grated Parmesan cheese
2 tablespoons finely chopped fresh parsley
2 eggs
1 tablespoon water
2 (6-ounce) skinless, boneless chicken breasts, slightly pounded
Cooking spray
1 cup Quick Marinara Sauce (page 99)
½ pound smoked fresh mozzarella, sliced

Garlic-Brined Chicken Thighs

1 quart water
½ cup salt
6 garlic cloves, smashed
*4 chicken thighs, bone in and
    skin on*
¼ cup real maple syrup
¼ cup Dijon mustard

Extremely juicy and flavorful, this chicken is a smash hit.

1. Boil the water with the salt and the garlic for 5 minutes. Cool in the refrigerator for 2 hours.

2. After the brine has cooled, soak the chicken in the brine for 4 hours. Drain, and pat the chicken dry with paper towels.

3. Preheat oven to 400°F. Mix together the maple syrup and mustard. Coat the chicken with the mixture.

4. Place the chicken in a baking dish. Bake for about 20 minutes or until the center reaches 165°F. Serve hot.

Brine Is Fine
Brining is an excellent way to impart flavor and moistness to white meats such as chicken and pork. It is the technique that gives smoked hams their characteristic texture, and it is the secret to the great flavor of kosher chicken.

Almost from Scratch Chicken Potpies

Buying the pie shells and the puff pastry at the supermarket makes this homey treat easy to make, and the homemade filling is the cat's meow.

4 tablespoons butter
½ cup medium-diced white onion
½ cup peeled and medium-diced carrot
½ cup medium-diced celery
6 white mushrooms, sliced
4 tablespoons all-purpose flour
3 cups chicken broth
Dash Worcestershire sauce
½ cup defrosted baby peas
1 tablespoon fresh thyme leaves
½ pound leftover cooked chicken meat, cut into ½-inch cubes
Salt and pepper, to taste
2 (6-inch) frozen pie shells
2 (8-inch) rounds prepared puff pastry, defrosted
Cooking spray

1. Heat the butter in a medium-sized saucepan until it stops bubbling. Add the onion, carrot, celery, and mushrooms. Sauté for 3 minutes.

2. Add the flour, and stir well to coat the vegetables. Slowly add the chicken stock, stirring to avoid lumps. Add the Worcestershire sauce and thyme. Simmer gently for 20 minutes, uncovered.

3. Add the peas and chicken, and remove from heat. Season with salt and pepper.

4. Preheat oven to 400°F.

5. Divide the chicken mixture between the 2 pie shells and top with the puff pastry, pressing it into the pie shell slightly to seal. Make a small incision in the top of the puff pastry and spray the tops with the cooking spray. Bake for about 25 minutes or until the tops are well browned and the mixture is bubbling.

Roux It

A roux (pronounced roo) is a mixture of an equal amount of flour and fat. This combination gives many sauces and soups their creamy and velvety texture while also acting as a thickening agent. The key is cooking the roux in the liquid for at least 20 minutes to eliminate the "raw" flour taste.

Chicken Medallions with Sweet Sherry and Mushroom Sauce

¾ pound skinless, boneless chicken breast, cut into thin 3-inch medallions
Salt and pepper, to taste
All-purpose flour, as needed
3 tablespoons butter
1 (10-ounce) package white mushrooms, sliced
¼ cup finely minced red onion
1 garlic clove, minced
½ cup sweet sherry
1 cup prepared brown gravy
2 tablespoons minced fresh chives

*Very similar to the classic chicken Marsala,
this dish gets a nice kick from the sweet sherry.*

1. Season the chicken with salt and pepper, and dust with flour. Shake off any excess.

2. Heat half the butter in a skillet on medium-high until it stops bubbling. Add the chicken and cook for about 1 minute on each side until light golden. Transfer the chicken to a plate and keep warm.

3. Wipe out the same pan, add the remaining butter, and heat on medium-high until it stops bubbling. Add the mushrooms, onion, and garlic. Sauté until the water released from the mushrooms evaporates.

4. Add half of the sherry, and boil for 1 minute. Add the gravy, and bring to a simmer.

5. Return the chicken to the pan along with the remaining sherry and the chives. Cook for about 3 minutes to heat through, and serve.

Fortified Wine
Sherry is a fortified wine, which is wine that has had brandy added to it and that is then aged to achieve a complex flavor. Other examples of fortified wines are port, Madeira, and Marsala. All can be used interchangeably.

Stir-Fried Chicken

This is a good introductory dish to learn the basics of a stir-fry.

1 ounce dry sherry
5 tablespoons soy sauce, divided
4 teaspoons sesame oil, divided
½ pound skinless, boneless chicken thighs, cut into thin strips
6 tablespoons peanut oil, divided
1 small white onion, thinly sliced
3 scallions, thinly sliced
3 garlic cloves, minced
1 tablespoon grated fresh gingerroot
2 cups snow peas, julienned
½ cup chicken stock
2 tablespoons cornstarch dissolved in 2 tablespoons water

1. Mix together the sherry, 3 tablespoons of the soy sauce, and 2 teaspoons of the sesame oil. Coat the chicken thoroughly in the mixture. Let marinate in the refrigerator for at least 1 hour, or up to overnight.

2. Place about 3 tablespoons of the peanut oil in a wok or cast-iron pan and heat until very hot. Add the chicken, and stir-fry on high heat for about 2 minutes. Transfer the chicken to a plate and set aside.

3. Wipe out the pan and add another 3 tablespoons of peanut oil. Add the onion, scallions, garlic, ginger, and snow peas. Stir-fry for about 1 minute.

4. Return the chicken to the pan. Add the remaining soy sauce and the chicken stock, and bring to a boil. Let boil for about 1 minute, then slowly stir in the cornstarch slurry until the sauce thickens. Turn off the heat, add the remaining sesame oil, and serve immediately.

Make It Snappy
There are three keys to a successful stir fry. First, you must have a very hot pan or wok. Secondly, you must have all the ingredients ready to go and organized. Thirdly, you must be able to move quickly, because once it starts, it is a very quick process.

Buffalo-Style Crispy Chicken

For all those buffalo wing fans,
here is a way to enjoy all the flavors during dinnertime.

Peanut oil, as needed
2 (6-ounce) skinless, boneless
   chicken breasts, slightly
   pounded
Salt and pepper, to taste
All-purpose flour, as needed
Milk, as needed
4 tablespoons butter
½ cup Frank's RedHot
   Cayenne Pepper Sauce
¾ cup crumbled blue cheese
2 celery stalks, finely diced

1. Heat 1 inch of peanut oil in a heavy skillet to 375°F. Preheat oven to 350°F.

2. Season the chicken with salt and pepper, and dredge in the flour. Shake off any excess. Dip in the milk, then back in the flour.

3. Fry the chicken in the peanut oil for about 3 minutes per side or until the chicken is at least 150°F. Blot on paper towels and transfer to a baking sheet.

4. In a saucepan, melt the butter with the hot sauce, and keep warm.

5. Divide the blue cheese between the chicken breasts, mounding it on top. Bake until the cheese is melted and the chicken reaches 165°F. Transfer to a plate and sprinkle with the celery.

The Buffalo Legend
Legend has it that in a small bar in Buffalo, New York, the cook slapped together the ingredients for buffalo wings because there was nothing else left to eat. Little did he know how the trend would take off.

Buttermilk and Mustard Fried Chicken

This dish requires some commitment to fry the chicken in a cast-iron pan. This can get a bit messy, but be prepared for some incredible chicken.

1 (2-pound) roaster chicken, cut into 8 serving pieces (breasts, thighs, wings, and legs)
4 cups buttermilk
½ cup Dijon mustard
2 tablespoons kosher salt
4 cups all-purpose flour
2 teaspoons baking powder
1 tablespoon garlic powder
1 tablespoon ground paprika
1 teaspoon ground cayenne
Salt and pepper, to taste
Shortening, as needed

1. Marinate the chicken overnight in a mixture of the buttermilk, mustard, and salt.

2. Remove the chicken from the marinade, but do not discard the liquid.

3. Mix together the flour, baking powder, all the dry spices, and some salt and pepper.

4. Dredge the chicken in the flour mixture, and shake off any excess. Dip the chicken into the buttermilk marinade, then return it to the flour for a final dredging. Shake off any excess flour.

5. In a cast-iron skillet, melt enough shortening to come halfway up the pan. Heat to 300°F, and add the chicken to the skillet. Fry the chicken for 12 to 15 minutes per side, covered. Turn the chicken only once. The chicken should reach 165°F.

6. Transfer the chicken to paper towels to drain, and blot off any excess grease. Enjoy hot or cold.

True Fried Chicken
True fried chicken is not deep-fried, but uses the technique detailed in this recipe, which is called shallow-frying. The most authentic fried chicken is cooked in lard, not shortening, and yields incredible results. Try it if you wish; nothing else changes in this recipe.

Chicken Cutlet "Katzu" Style

A crispy cutlet breaded with Japanese bread crumbs. Seek out these bread crumbs, as they are integral to the dish.

2 (6-ounce) chicken breasts, slightly pounded
Salt and pepper, to taste
1 cup all-purpose flour
3 eggs, beaten with 3 tablespoons water
2 cups panko bread crumbs (also called "Japanese bread crumbs")
Peanut oil, for frying
½ cup store-bought barbecue sauce
¼ cup A1 Steak Sauce
2 tablespoons soy sauce
2 teaspoons grated fresh gingerroot
¼ cup finely minced scallions

1. Season the chicken with salt and pepper, and dust in flour. Shake off excess flour. Dip the chicken in the egg, then coat in the bread crumbs.

2. Heat the peanut oil to 350°F in a heavy skillet. Fry the chicken for about 5 minutes per side, until it reaches 165°F. Transfer the chicken to paper towels to drain, and blot off excess grease.

3. Mix together the barbecue sauce, A1, soy sauce, and ginger. Serve the sauce over the chicken, and sprinkle with the scallions to garnish.

Japanese Tradition
In Japan, many restaurants serve this "Katzu Don" using pork cutlets instead of chicken. The sauce used is called tongatsu and very much resembles the sauce made for this dish. It is traditionally served with sautéed napa cabbage and rice.

Stuffed Cornish Game Hens

The game hens make a very elegant option instead of "just chicken." The stuffing is easy to prepare and delicious.

2 (12- to 16-ounce) Cornish game hens, giblets removed

2 tablespoons extra-virgin olive oil

¼ cup small-diced white onion

¼ cup small-diced celery

¼ cup peeled and small-diced carrot

2 garlic cloves, minced

2 cups cooked and cooled wild rice

2 eggs, beaten

½ cup dried cranberries

2 tablespoons fresh thyme leaves

Salt and pepper, to taste

2 tablespoons softened butter

1. Preheat oven to 375°F. Rinse the hens with cold water and dry well with paper towels.

2. Heat a small skillet on medium and add the olive oil. Sauté the onion, celery, carrot, and garlic for about 5 minutes, until the vegetables begin to soften. Remove from heat.

3. Transfer the sautéed vegetables to a bowl. Add the rice, and mix well. Add the eggs, cranberries, thyme, and salt and pepper. Stuff the mixture inside the cavities of the birds.

4. Place the birds on a rack set inside a roasting pan. Rub the birds with the butter, and season with salt and pepper. Roast, uncovered, in the oven for about 50 minutes or until the center of the stuffing reaches 165°F. Let rest for 7 minutes, and serve.

Check the Temperature!
It is important when cooking any stuffed poultry to make sure that the stuffing reaches a safe temperature. Many times, when the meat is cooked, the juices have gone into the stuffing and it is still not up to a safe temperature. Be sure to measure the temperature of the stuffing, not just the bird.

Chicken Breasts in Lemon Sauce with Dill

Adding cold stock to hot roux is a good way to prevent lumps in the sauce. Also, use fresh lemon juice, not that stuff in the bottle.

2 (8-ounce) skinless, boneless chicken breasts, slightly pounded
Salt and pepper, to taste
¼ cup all-purpose flour, plus extra for dusting
4 tablespoons extra-virgin olive oil
2 tablespoons butter
2 cups chicken stock
¼ cup fresh-squeezed lemon juice
2 tablespoons chopped fresh dill

1. Season the chicken with salt and pepper, and dust with flour. Heat the olive oil in a skillet on medium-high. Brown the chicken on both sides. Remove from pan and set aside.

2. In the same pan, melt the butter and stir in the flour. When smooth, slowly add the stock, whisking well. Bring to a simmer, and cook gently for 20 minutes, uncovered.

3. Add the lemon juice to the sauce and return the chicken to the pan. Simmer gently, turning the meat occasionally, for about 5 minutes or until the chicken reaches 165°F. Add the dill to the sauce, and serve.

Velute

This sauce is based on a classic French sauce known as a velute. It is simply a stock thickened with a roux and cooked until the flour can no longer be tasted. This simple and versatile sauce is easy to make, and its variations are only limited by your imagination.

Grilled Chicken Cooked under a Brick

The results of this cooking method are moist, smoky, and very flavorful. Try this in the summer when the grill is getting a lot of use.

1. Since the backbone has been removed from the chicken, you can press the 2 sides apart to flatten the chicken. (You can have your butcher remove the backbone.)

2. Mix together all the ingredients, and smear all over the chicken. Let marinate for about 1 hour in the refrigerator.

3. Heat a charcoal or gas grill to medium–high. Place the chicken skin-side up on the grill, and put an ovenproof plate or pan on top of the chicken to press the bird down slightly. You can add a brick to help. Grill, uncovered, for about 12 minutes or until the chicken is nicely charred.

4. Flip the bird over, skin-side down, and repeat the weighting process. Grill for another 12 minutes or so. The bird is done when it is well charred and reaches an internal temperature of 165°F at its thickest point. Let rest for 7 minutes, and serve.

Check Your Grill
All grills are different. They all have varying amounts of BTUs (British thermal units), and all have "hot spots" and "cool spots." Only experience will tell you how your particular grill behaves.

1 (2½-pound) fryer chicken,
 backbone removed
¼ cup extra-virgin olive oil
2 tablespoons whole-grain
 mustard
Juice of 2 lemons
3 garlic cloves, minced
2 tablespoons finely chopped
 fresh rosemary
2 tablespoons fresh thyme
 leaves
Pinch dried red pepper flakes
Salt and pepper, to taste

"Polpette" Chicken and Ricotta Meatballs

A wonderful treat from Tuscany, these light chicken meatballs can be served on their own or with pasta. They also make a nice sandwich.

¾ cup plain bread crumbs
½ cup milk
½ pound ground chicken
4 ounces whole-milk ricotta cheese
1 egg, beaten
¼ cup grated Parmesan cheese
2 garlic cloves, minced
4 tablespoons chopped fresh parsley
Salt and pepper, to taste
Olive oil, as needed
1 recipe Quick Marinara Sauce (page 99)

1. Soak the bread crumbs in the milk for 10 minutes. Mix together all of the ingredients except the olive oil and marinara sauce. Mix well, using your hands. Divide the mixture into eighths, and roll into meatballs.

2. Heat the olive oil in a skillet on medium-high. Brown the meatballs well, and blot dry with paper towels.

3. Pour the marinara into a saucepan, and add the meatballs. Simmer for 25 minutes. Serve hot.

Selecting Meat for Meatballs
Most packages of ground meats today advertise the amount of fat in the meat. When making meatballs or meatloaf, it is advisable to use meat with a fat content higher than 10 percent. The finished product will be superior in flavor and texture.

The Simplest Roast Chicken

Try to make sure the chicken is cooked to exactly 160°F when you remove it from the oven. Roasting the chicken upside down also adds to this recipe.

1 (2½-pound) roaster chicken, giblets removed
1 lemon
4 tablespoons (½ stick) softened butter
Salt and pepper, to taste

1. Preheat oven to 375°F. Rinse the chicken and pat dry with paper towels.

2. Squeeze the lemon over the bird, and rub the juice all over it. Place the squeezed lemon in the cavity of the bird. Rub the chicken all over with the butter, and season well with salt and pepper.

3. Place the chicken upside down on a rack set in a roasting pan. Roast for 45 minutes. Turn the chicken over, baste, and continue cooking for another 15 minutes.

4. When the thickest part of the thigh registers 160°F, remove the chicken from the oven and let it rest for 10 minutes. The internal temperature of the bird will increase to 165°F as it sits.

Carryover Cooking
All foods continue to cook after they have been removed from the heat source. The larger the item, the more heat will be stored in it. To prove this to yourself, remove a bird from the oven and place a meat thermometer in it. Come back 10 minutes later and you will find the temperature has risen by about 10 degrees. A good thing to remember.

Steamed Chicken with Shredded Cabbage and Ginger

4 tablespoons soy sauce, divided

2 teaspoons sesame oil

2 teaspoons dry sherry

Pinch sugar

2 (6-ounce) skinless, boneless chicken breasts, slightly pounded

2 cups shredded napa cabbage

2 teaspoons minced fresh gingerroot

2 garlic cloves, minced

2 large napa cabbage leaves

Simple, low calorie, and delicious. Break out that bamboo steamer again.

1. Mix together 2 tablespoons of the soy sauce, the sesame oil, sherry, and sugar. Coat the chicken in the mixture, and let marinate for 1 hour in the refrigerator.

2. Mix together the shredded cabbage, ginger, garlic, and the remaining soy sauce. Let stand for 20 minutes to allow the cabbage to "collapse."

3. Bring a pot of water to a boil. Line a bamboo steamer basket with the cabbage leaves. Place the marinated chicken on the cabbage leaves. Top with the marinated shredded cabbage and all the juices that have leached out. Place the steamer basket over the pot of boiling water. Steam for approximately 12 minutes or until the chicken has reached 165°F. Serve hot.

Balance in Chinese Cuisine

Chinese cuisine is very ancient and sophisticated. Most Americans are only familiar with "Chinese-style" cuisine, which has unfortunately been tailored for unadventurous palettes. The Chinese have a philosophy of balance that includes salty, sweet, sour, and bitter, and they try to incorporate all of these components in a single dish.

chapter 9
steaks, chops, and meats

Simple Pan-Roasted Rib Steaks

A great technique to cook steaks at home.
Open a window though; it gets a bit smoky.

1 (10-ounce) package white
  mushrooms, chopped
  into pea-size pieces
1 cup rice vinegar
1 cup granulated sugar
2 tablespoons chopped fresh
  parsley
2 (8- to 10-ounce) rib or
  Delmonico steaks, about
  1 inch thick
Salt and pepper, to taste

1. Combine the mushrooms, vinegar, and sugar in a pot, and bring to a boil. Boil for 5 minutes, then cool in the refrigerator. Drain, and toss with parsley.

2. Season the steaks well with salt and pepper. Heat a cast-iron skillet or a heavy pan on high for at least 5 minutes. Add the steaks to the dry skillet. Don't turn the steaks until a few drops of juices appear on the tops of the meat.

3. Turn the steaks and cook for about 2 minutes for medium-rare (130 to 135°F). Let the steaks rest for about 3 minutes before serving. Serve with the mushroom relish.

Beef Cooking Temperatures
Here are some guidelines for cooking beef: Rare is 120 to 125°F. Medium-rare is 130 to 135°F. Medium is 140 to 145°F. Medium-well is 150 to 155°F. Anything over 160°F is well done.

Red Wine–Marinated Hanger Steak with Onions

Hanger steak is sometimes called butchers tender or onglet. Ask your butcher for some. It is fantastic and inexpensive.

1 (1½-pound) hanger steak
2 large white onions, thinly sliced
2 cups dry red wine
¼ cup Worcestershire sauce
3 tablespoons extra-virgin olive oil, divided
Salt and pepper, to taste
2 tablespoons butter

1. Mix together the onions, wine, Worcestershire sauce, and 2 tablespoons of the oil. Coat the beef in the mixture, and let marinate overnight in the refrigerator.

2. Drain the marinade off the steak. Discard the liquid, but save the onions. Blot the meat dry with paper towels, and season all over with salt and pepper.

3. Heat a heavy pan on medium-high for about 5 minutes. Rub the remaining oil over the seasoned steaks and place them in the hot pan. Evenly brown all sides, and cook to desired temperature (see "Beef Cooking Temperatures," page 160). Remove from pan and let rest.

4. While the meat rests, melt the butter over medium heat in a sauté pan. Sauté the marinated onions about 5 minutes. Season with salt and pepper.

5. Cut the meat into slices about ½ inch thick. Serve the sautéed onions atop the steak.

Go Against the Grain
All meat has a "grain," which is the direction that the fibers in the flesh run. In order to have the most tender bite, it is important to identify the grain and cut against it. This shortens the muscle fibers and results in a good chew, not a leathery chew.

Mustard-Crusted Filet Mignon

*A tender but less flavorful cut of meat, filet mignon,
or tenderloin, benefits greatly from aggressive flavors such as
mustard and bacon. This is sure to impress.*

*3 tablespoons extra-virgin
olive oil*
*2 (8-ounce) filets mignons,
preferably cut from the
center*
Salt and pepper, to taste
*½ cup fresh, not dry, bread
crumbs*
2 strips bacon, finely minced
1 tablespoon Dijon mustard
1 garlic clove, minced
*1 tablespoon finely minced
fresh chives*

1. Heat the oil in a heavy pan on medium-high until barely smoking. Season the filets with salt and pepper, and brown well on all sides. Remove from the pan, and blot the meat dry with paper towels.

2. Preheat oven to 400°F. Mix together the remaining ingredients, and divide over the tops of the filets.

3. Place the filets in a baking pan. Bake for about 7 minutes for medium-rare, or to desired doneness. (See "Beef Cooking Temperatures," page 160.) Let rest for 5 minutes, and serve.

Cooking Muscles?
The tenderloin is so named because it is the most tender muscle in the cow and comes from the loin of the animal. This muscle does almost no work and therefore is underdeveloped and tender. A general rule of thumb is muscles that work hard (legs, shoulders, etc.) are tougher and require slow, moist cooking, while other muscles are more tender and can be cooked quickly over high heat.

Seared Skirt Steak with Cilantro and Lime

Jicama is available in many markets today. It tastes like a cross between a potato and an apple, and it makes a great, crispy salsa.

1. In a blender, combine the oil, half of the lime juice, the garlic, 2 tablespoons of the cilantro, and some salt and pepper. Purée until smooth. Pour the mixture over the steaks and let marinate for 1 hour in the refrigerator.

2. Mix together the jicama, tomato, onion, jalapeño, and the remaining lime juice and cilantro. Season with salt and pepper, and set aside.

3. Heat a heavy pan on medium-high and spray with the cooking spray. Drain the steaks, and wipe off most of the marinade. Sear well on both sides, about 2 minutes per side or to desired doneness (see "Beef Cooking Temperatures, page 160). Remove from the pan and let rest for 3 minutes. Serve with the salsa.

Skirt Steak 101
Skirt steak is a thin muscle that acts as a diaphragm inside the cow. It is a great and underutilized cut of beef, although it is now commonly used for fajitas, a popular Southwestern dish. It is very thin and has a conspicuous grain to the meat.

¼ cup extra-virgin olive oil
Juice of 2 limes
3 garlic cloves, minced
4 tablespoons chopped fresh cilantro leaves, divided
Salt and pepper, to taste
2 (8-ounce) skirt steaks
1½ cups small-diced jicama
¼ cup diced ripe tomato
¼ cup finely minced red onion
½ jalapeño pepper, seeded and minced
Cooking spray

Slow-Cooked Beef Brisket with Teriyaki Glaze

1 (1½-pound) beef brisket,
    trimmed
¼ cup peanut oil
½ cup soy sauce
2 cups chicken broth
½ cup sake
6 garlic cloves
1 (2-inch) piece fresh
    gingerroot, smashed flat
½ cup store-bought teriyaki
    glaze

*This is a great weekend dish when you have
the time to let a dish cook for 3 hours or so.*

1. In a heavy pot large enough to accommodate all the ingredients, heat the oil on medium-high until barely smoking. Brown the brisket well on both sides. Wipe out the excess oil in the pot and add all the remaining ingredients except the teriyaki glaze.

2. Bring the liquid to a boil, then reduce to a very gentle simmer. Cover the pot and simmer as gently as possible for about 3 hours, or until a knife inserted into the deepest part of the meat comes free with no resistance.

3. Preheat broiler. Carefully transfer the meat to a foil-lined baking sheet and pour the teriyaki glaze over the top. Broil for about 4 minutes or until the glaze is well browned and bubbling. Serve hot.

Braising Methods
This dish uses stovetop braising. Another way to braise is in the oven. Follow all the steps exactly as they appear in this recipe, except use an ovenproof pot and place it in a 350°F oven after the liquid has come to a boil. If using this method, the pot should be checked about halfway through to determine if any more liquid needs to be added.

Honey Mustard Pork Chops

Pork pairs well with sweet flavors and fruit. They don't put the apple in the roast pig's mouth for nothing!

2 tablespoons olive oil
2 (8-ounce) center-cut, bone-in pork chops
Salt and pepper, to taste
2 tablespoons butter
2 Granny Smith apples, peeled, cored, and cut into 8 wedges each
4 tablespoons Dijon mustard
3 tablespoons honey

1. Preheat oven to 450°F. Heat the olive oil in a heavy skillet on medium-high. Season the pork chops with salt and pepper, and brown well, about 2 minutes per side.

2. Wipe out the pan and add the butter. Heat on medium until it stops bubbling, and add the apples. Season with salt and pepper, and sauté for about 5 minutes or until the apples soften slightly and brown. Remove the apples from the pan and keep warm.

3. Mix together the honey and mustard, and rub on top of the pork chops. Place the chops on a baking sheet, and roast for 6 minutes or until the tops are glazed and the center reaches 155°F. Let rest for a few minutes, and serve with the apples on top of the chops.

Picking Good Apples
Apples are in peak season from September until November in the United States. Choose apples that are firm, heavy for their size, and display a smooth, tight skin. Many apples available in off-peak season are actually last year's apples that have been stored in nitrogen-filled warehouses. These apples tend to loose flavor and become mealy.

Incredibly Easy Pork Spare Ribs

Cooking these ribs in the oven takes the stress out of long procedures such as preboiling or smoking. The results are fantastic.

2 tablespoons brown sugar
1 tablespoon sweet paprika
1 tablespoon garlic powder
1 tablespoon dry mustard
   powder
1 tablespoon onion powder
1 tablespoon salt
1 teaspoon cayenne pepper
1 rack pork spare ribs
2 cups store-bought barbecue
   sauce
¼ cup red vinegar
2 tablespoons chopped
   rosemary

1. Mix together all of the dry spices and distribute evenly over the ribs. Allow the ribs to marinate in this "rub" for about 1 hour in the refrigerator.

2. Preheat oven to 300°F.

3. Place the ribs on a rack over a roasting pan with 3 inches of water in the roasting pan. Place in the oven for about 3½ hours or until you can easily pull a bone from the meat. Let rest for 5 minutes, then cut into individual ribs.

4. In a small saucepan, mix together the barbecue sauce, vinegar, and rosemary, and simmer for 5 minutes. Serve this sauce alongside the ribs.

Rib Lingo
Spare ribs are the most popular ribs because of their price as well as their meatiness. Baby back ribs have less meat but are easier to work with and are consequently more expensive. "Country-style" ribs are sort of like a small pork chop and are the meatiest ribs. They have a large section of meat not attached to a bone and do not have that great gelatinous texture that rib lovers crave. They are better suited for grilling.

Grilled Pork Tenderloin with Grilled Pears

*Pork tenderloins are readily available in most supermarkets.
They are lean, tender, and have great flavor.*

1 (1½-pound) pork tenderloin
1 teaspoon caraway seeds
Salt and pepper, to taste
3 tablespoons extra-virgin
    olive oil, divided
2 firm Anjou pears

1. Preheat grill. Season the pork with the caraway seeds and salt and pepper. Rub the pork with half of the oil. Grill until the thickest part reaches 155°F. Transfer the tenderloin to a plate. Tent loosely with foil, and let rest.

2. Slice the pears off of the core in 4 pieces. Season with salt and pepper, and rub with the remaining oil. There is no need to peel the pears. Grill until well charred and softened, about 5 minutes.

3. Arrange the pears on a plate. Cut the pork into ¼-inch slices, and arrange over the pears.

Beware Overcooking Lean Meats
The reason pork roasts and chicken breasts are often dry is because they do not have enough fat in them to stay moist if overcooked. It is critical to use a meat thermometer when cooking these lean cuts to truly enjoy them at their juiciest. Invest in an instant-read thermometer, and remember, do not leave it in the meat in the oven!

Slow-Cooked Pork Shoulder

*Meltingly tender, this rich and sumptuous dish is enhanced by
a good dose of garlic and a hearty measure of dark beer.*

2-pound pork shoulder,
    cut into 4 pieces, skin
    removed
8 garlic cloves, minced
1 (12-ounce) bottle dark beer
1 cup chicken broth
3 bay leaves
Salt and pepper, to taste

1. Preheat oven to 375°F.

2. Combine all the ingredients in an ovenproof pot with a tight lid. Cover, and bake for 3½ hours or until the pork falls apart when touched. Serve with good mustard.

Long and Slow
The trick in this dish is to cook the meat long enough that it begins to fall apart. This is technically a braised dish even though there is no need to sear the meat. This pork can also be shredded with a fork to make sandwiches or meat sauces. Keep the broth for later uses.

Lamb Rib Chops Glazed in Port Wine

*Port wine, which comes from Portugal, is a rich, complex fortified wine that
has a similar character to sherry, Madeira, and Marsala wines.*

2 cups port wine
1 tablespoon butter
1 rack of lamb, cut into 4 thick
    chops
Salt and pepper, to taste
3 tablespoons extra-virgin
    olive oil

1. Bring the port wine to a hard boil in a saucepan until only about ¼ cup remains. Add the butter to the wine and remove from heat.

2. Preheat oven to 425°F.

3. Season both sides of each chop with salt and pepper. Heat the olive oil in an ovenproof skillet on medium-high, and sear the chops on both sides. Brush the glaze over the chops, and place the skillet in the oven. Bake for 5 minutes for medium-rare. Serve hot.

Grill-Smoked Rack of Lamb with Raspberry Glaze

If your grill will not permit heating only one side, place the meat in a small pan inside a pan of water to take advantage of indirect heat.

2 cups hardwood chips, soaked in water for 1 hour

1 rack of lamb, trimmed and frenched, bones covered with foil

Salt and pepper, to taste

2 tablespoons raspberry jam

1 teaspoon chopped fresh rosemary

1 tablespoon red wine vinegar

1. Heat one side of the grill on medium. Place one-third of the wood chips over the grill stones. Heat until the chips begin to smoke.

2. Season the lamb with salt and pepper, and place on the grill as far away from the heat as possible. Close the grill, but use a ball of foil to prop open the lid about 1 inch so smoke can escape.

3. Cook the lamb, turning occasionally and replenishing the wood chips as needed until the lamb reaches an internal temperature of 135°F (medium-rare).

4. Mix together the jam, rosemary, and vinegar. Brush the mixture over the lamb. Cook for another 5 minutes or so, glazing occasionally until the lamb reaches 140°F (medium). Remove the foil from the bones, and let the lamb rest for 5 minutes.

Frenching a Rack

When a rack of lamb, veal, or pork is trimmed to have all the bones exposed and bare, it is called a frenched rack. Your butcher can do this for you, or you can try it yourself. The trick is to "score" the bones so you can peel off all of the tissue from them to reveal a bare bone.

Roasted Top Round of Lamb

The top round is a muscle within the leg.
It is very lean, has almost no sinew, and is easy to cook.

1½-pound top round of lamb, trimmed of all fat
Salt and pepper, to taste
4 tablespoons extra-virgin olive oil, divided
¼ cup diced ripe tomato
¼ cup finely minced red onion
¼ cup chopped black olives
1 garlic clove, minced
1 tablespoon capers, rinsed
1 tablespoon chopped fresh parsley

1. Preheat oven to 375°F.

2. Season the lamb with salt and pepper, and rub with 2 tablespoons of the oil. Place the lamb in a roasting pan. Roast for about 25 minutes, until the lamb reaches an internal temperature of 140°F (for medium). Remove from the oven, tent loosely with foil, and let rest for 10 minutes.

3. Mix together the remaining ingredients. Slice the lamb thinly, and serve with the relish on top.

Variations on Roasted Top Round of Lamb

This lamb is also great served cold as a sandwich filling or just sliced thin and drizzled with olive oil and salt. Seek out this cut of lamb. You will be surprised how affordable and delicious it is. Keep your find quiet though, or everyone will catch on and this hidden gem will become more expensive.

Lamb T-Bone Steaks with Lemon-Garlic Crust

*Also known as loin chops, these little T-bones are a real treat.
Break out the red wine to serve with these babies.*

1. Preheat broiler. Mix together the bread crumbs, oil, lemon juice and zest, garlic, thyme, and salt and pepper.

2. Season the chops with salt and pepper, and place on a baking sheet. Broil for about 3 minutes on one side. Flip the chops over, and broil for 1 minute.

3. Divide the bread crumb mixture over the chops. Return to the broiler for about 1 more minute or until the tops are well browned. Let rest for 3 minutes, and serve.

T-Bone for Two
The virtue of a T-bone is that one side of the bone contains the loin, and the other side contains the tenderloin, or filet mignon. The tenderloin of a lamb is quite small and is rarely seen by itself in markets. These little chops are a good way to taste the elusive lamb tenderloin.

1 cup plain bread crumbs
3 tablespoons extra-virgin olive oil
Juice and grated zest of 1 lemon
2 garlic cloves, minced
1 teaspoon fresh thyme leaves
Salt and pepper, to taste
6 lamb loin chops, about ¾ inch thick

Slow-Roasted Lamb Shoulder Chops

Shoulder chops are more affordable than loin or rib chops.
They contain more bone and sinew, but are very tasty.

2 (8- to 10-ounce) shoulder
lamb chops
2 teaspoons dried oregano
Salt and pepper, to taste
½ cup dry white wine
¼ cup black kalamata olives,
pitted and chopped

1. Preheat oven to 325°F.

2. Rub the chops with the oregano and salt and pepper. Place in a shallow pan and pour the wine over the meat. Sprinkle the olives over the top.

3. Roast, uncovered, for 40 minutes. Let rest for 3 minutes, and serve hot.

Smooth Out the Toughness

Shoulder chops tend to be a bit tougher than other lamb chops. Slow roasting this way allows the meat to become tender even though the meat is fully cooked. This is a nice alternative to a stew that is quick and easy.

Sautéed Venison with Currants and Rosemary

Do not be afraid of venison.
The meat tastes similar to lamb and is very lean and low in saturated fat.

2 (8-ounce) venison
   medallions cut from the
   loin, about ½ inch thick
1 teaspoon chopped fresh
   rosemary
Salt and pepper, to taste
All-purpose flour, as needed
2 tablespoons butter
¼ cup chicken broth
2 tablespoons currant jam

1. Season the meat with the rosemary and salt and pepper. Dredge in the flour and shake off excess.

2. Heat the butter in a pan on medium until it stops bubbling. Add the meat and sauté gently on each side for about 4 minutes, or less if the meat is thinner than ½ inch.

3. Transfer the meat to a warm plate and add the chicken broth to the pan. Bring to a hard boil for 1 minute. Use a wooden spoon to scrape the browned bits from the bottom of the pan into the broth. Add the jam, and stir to mix. Pour the sauce over the meat, and serve.

Today's Venison
Since almost all venison available today is farm raised, the meat has a much less "gamey" flavor than people think. Because of the diet of these animals, the meat more closely resembles mild lamb than wild game. Seek out this wonderful meat.

Classic Roast Prime Rib with Horseradish Sauce

1 prime rib (2 or 3 ribs long),
   chine bone removed
Salt and pepper, to taste
¼ cup sour cream
¼ cup mayonnaise
2 tablespoons prepared
   horseradish
2 tablespoons snipped fresh
   chives

*Normally cooked in a huge slab, prime rib is available in smaller pieces.
Ask your butcher to cut you a 2- or 3-rib roast.*

1. Preheat oven to 375°F.

2. Season the roast with salt and pepper. Place on a rack set in a roasting pan, and bake for about 35 minutes or until the center reaches 140°F (for medium-rare). Remove from the oven and let rest for 15 minutes, loosely covered with foil.

3. Combine the remaining ingredients in a bowl and mix well.

4. Carve the roast by slicing straight down along a rib all the way through the meat. Serve with the sauce on the side.

Approaching Your Butcher
Most butchers are good cooks. If you have questions, do not be afraid to go into detail about what you have in mind. Your butcher may be able to offer you alternative suggestions for expensive cuts of meat as well as cooking tips and recipes. Use this resource that is available to you.

Pan-Roasted Lemon and Oregano Veal Chops

The trick with veal is not to overcook the meat.
Veal should be barely pink inside to remain juicy and tender.

2 rib veal chops, about 1½ inches thick, trimmed of most fat
Juice and grated zest of 1 lemon
2 teaspoons fresh oregano
Salt and pepper, to taste
4 tablespoons extra-virgin olive oil

1. Preheat the oven to 400°F.

2. Rub the chops with the lemon juice and zest, oregano, and salt and pepper.

3. Heat the oil in an ovenproof pan until barely smoking. Add the chops and brown well on one side. Flip the chops over and place in the oven for about 10 minutes or until the meat is 150°F in the center. Let rest for 5 minutes before serving.

Lemon Zest
The zest of the lemon contains the essential oils, which have a characteristically "lemony" flavor without the acidity of the juice. Just be sure to wash your lemons thoroughly and use a grater or peeler to remove the yellow part only. The white "pith" is quite bitter.

1 (2-pound) rolled roast of
    veal breast
Salt and pepper, to taste
3 tablespoons extra-virgin
    olive oil
1 recipe Quick Marinara
    Sauce (page 99)
1 cup dry red wine
1 (10-ounce) package white
    mushrooms, thinly sliced

Breast of Veal with Mushroom and Tomato Sauce

*The breast of veal is another inexpensive and highly
flavorful cut of meat ignored by many home cooks. Ask your butcher
to roll and tie you a roast of about 2 pounds.*

1. Preheat the oven to 375°F.

2. Season the roast with salt and pepper. Heat the oil in a heavy skillet on medium-high. Brown the roast well on all sides, and transfer to a roasting pan.

3. Pour the marinara into the pan and add the wine and the mushrooms. Place in the oven and roast for about 50 minutes or until the center registers 165°F.

4. Remove the meat from the sauce and let rest for 10 minutes, loosely covered with foil. Slice the meat as thinly as possible and serve with the sauce on top.

Judging Veal
When choosing veal in the market, look for meat that has a very light pink appearance. The fat should be very white with no traces of yellowing. Darker-colored veal is usually from an older animal, and the meat will be less tender.

Veal Scaloppini with Prosciutto and Fontina

*A scaloppini is simply a very thin cutlet. The French use
the term escalope. You can substitute chicken breasts for this dish;
just make sure they are pounded out very thin.*

2 cups plain bread crumbs, as
  needed
2 tablespoons grated
  Parmesan cheese
1 tablespoon finely minced
  fresh parsley
4–6 veal scaloppini (about 1
  pound total)
Salt and pepper, to taste
All-purpose flour, as needed
3 eggs, beaten
Extra-virgin olive oil, as
  needed
¼ pound fontina cheese
4–6 thin slices prosciutto

1. Preheat broiler. Mix together the bread crumbs, Parmesan, and parsley.

2. Season the meat with salt and pepper. Dredge in the flour and shake off excess. Dip the veal in the egg, then coat with the bread crumbs. Shake off excess.

3. Heat the oil in a skillet on medium. Sauté the cutlets for about 2 minutes per side. Transfer the veal to a baking pan.

4. Top each piece of veal with a slice of prosciutto and some of the fontina cheese. Place under the broiler for about 1 minute or until the cheese melts. Serve immediately.

Crispy Baked Orange Pork Chops

2 (8-ounce) pork chops
Juice and grated zest of 1
  orange
Salt and pepper, to taste
Bread crumbs, as needed
All-purpose flour, as needed
2 eggs, beaten
Cooking spray

Be sure to wash the orange before removing the zest for this dish.

1. Marinate the pork chops in the orange juice and salt and pepper for 6 hours or overnight in the refrigerator.

2. Preheat oven to 400°F. Mix together the orange zest and the bread crumbs.

3. Dust the chops with flour and shake off excess. Dip in the egg, then coat in the bread crumbs. Spray all sides of the chops heavily with the cooking spray and place on a baking sheet. Bake for 14 minutes or until the chops are crispy and reach an internal temperature of 155°F.

The Magic of Cooking Spray
Cooking sprays are simply oil in aerosol form. The advantage is you get great coverage of the product without using an excessive amount of fat. The "oven-frying" technique described in this recipe is a professional secret and has many uses in the home.

Filet Mignon Pinwheels

Ask your butcher to "butterfly" the filets for you.
This will open them up like a book for easy stuffing.

2 (7-ounce) filets mignons,
    butterflied
Salt and pepper, to taste
½ cup grated Parmesan
    cheese
8 basil leaves, washed
3 tablespoons melted butter

1. Preheat oven to 425°F.

2. Season both sides of the filets with salt and pepper. Sprinkle one side with the Parmesan cheese, and place the basil leaves on top of the cheese. Roll up the filets like a jelly roll and secure the seam with toothpicks.

3. Place the filets in a baking dish, and pour the melted butter over them. Bake for about 20 minutes for medium, or to desired doneness. (See "Beef Cooking Temperatures", page 160.) Serve warm.

Filet of Beef

The filet, or tenderloin, of beef is a very lean, tender, and expensive cut of meat. It lacks a pronounced "beefy flavor" that many steak lovers crave, but makes up for it with a very soft and buttery texture. It is a good option for those trying to cut out fat while still enjoying beef. Just don't overcook it or it will be very dry.

Braised Beef Short Ribs with Mushrooms

These ribs will fall right off the bone.

4 (6-ounce) short ribs, trimmed
Salt and pepper, to taste
All-purpose flour, as needed
¼ cup oil
3 cups beef broth
2 cups dry red wine
1 (10-ounce) package white mushrooms, sliced
1 cup canned diced tomatoes
2 garlic cloves, minced

1. Season the ribs with salt and pepper. Dust with flour and shake off excess. Heat the oil in a skillet on medium-high and brown the ribs well on all sides.

2. Place the ribs in a pot along with all the remaining ingredients, and bring to a boil. Immediately turn down to a simmer and cover. Cook over low heat for 1½ hours or until the meat begins to fall off the bone.

3. When the meat is done, remove it from the pot. Skim off any fat and boil the liquid until about 2 cups remain. Return the meat to the sauce to warm through, and serve.

The Basics of Braising

Braising simply means to cook slowly in liquid. Most braised items are first browned well, then placed in a flavorful liquid and cooked gently until the meat is very tender. Braising is usually reserved for tough cuts of meat that do not roast well.

chapter 10
shellfish

Two-Hour Calamari Stew with Spinach

The flavor of calamari changes drastically when it cooks for a long time. It becomes very deep and rich. Make this!

1 red onion, roughly chopped

1 medium carrot, peeled and roughly chopped

1 celery stalk, roughly chopped

4 garlic cloves, peeled

¼ cup chopped fresh parsley leaves

½ cup extra-virgin olive oil

1 pound cleaned calamari, cut into rings, legs cut in half

½ cup dry red wine

1 recipe Quick Marinara Sauce (page 99)

Pinch dried red pepper flakes

1 (10-ounce) package curly spinach, stems removed and roughly chopped

Salt and pepper, to taste

1. Place the onion, carrot, celery, garlic, parsley, and olive oil in a food processor. Pulse until the mixture is the texture of pickle relish.

2. Transfer the vegetable mixture to a saucepot and cook over medium heat, stirring frequently until it becomes golden in color, about 10 minutes.

3. Add the calamari and wine, and boil for about 2 minutes. Add the marinara and red pepper flakes. Reduce heat and simmer gently for 1½ hours, partially covered.

4. Add the spinach and simmer, partially covered, for 30 minutes. Season with salt and pepper, and serve over pasta or in a bowl with a slice of good crusty bread.

Sofrito
This mixture of ground veggies cooked in olive oil is known as a sofrito. Many Latin cultures have sofritos of some kind. Sometimes the vegetables and spices are cooked, and sometimes they're puréed raw. But they always play the same role of adding a lot of flavor.

Pan-Roasted Sea Scallops

*Ask for "dry" scallops (also called diver scallops) at the fish market,
as opposed to "wet" scallops, which have been chemically treated
to extend their shelf life. If your fishmonger doesn't know what
you are talking about, find another fish shop.*

2 tablespoons butter
1 tablespoon extra-virgin
   olive oil
¾ pound sea scallops
Salt and pepper, to taste
½ pound oyster mushrooms,
   trimmed of hard stems
   and torn into ½-inch
   strips
2 teaspoons fresh or ½
   teaspoon dried thyme
   leaves
3 tablespoons dry white wine

1. Heat the butter and oil in a large skillet on medium-high until the butter stops bubbling. Season the scallops with salt and pepper. Lay them in the pan in a single layer with some room between each scallop. Increase heat to high, and don't move the scallops for about 2 minutes. Allow them to brown well on one side.

2. Turn the scallops over, and add the mushrooms and thyme to the pan. Stir to coat the mushrooms with the butter. Cook over high heat until the water that releases from the mushrooms evaporates.

3. Add the wine and cook for about 1 minute, until evaporated. Season with salt and pepper, and serve immediately.

Bubbling Butter
The reason that the butter should be heated until it stops bubbling is simple. The bubbling is the water that is in the butter boiling away. In order for the butter to achieve maximum temperature, the water must evaporate.

Pan-Roasted Lobster in Brandy and Butter

2 (1½-pound) lobsters
Salt and pepper, to taste
½ cup (1 stick) butter
¼ cup brandy
½ cup chicken stock
3 garlic cloves, peeled and
   sliced thinly
1 sprig fresh thyme

*The only trick here is to make sure your sauté pan has a
metal handle and can go in the oven.*

1. Preheat oven to 400°F. Split the lobsters down the middle lengthwise. Remove the sack in the head, and pull out the vein in the tail. Lightly crack the claws. Season the lobster flesh with salt and pepper.

2. Heat a large ovenproof skillet on medium-high. Add half the butter, and heat until it stops bubbling. Place the lobsters flesh-side down in the pan and cook for about 3 minutes.

3. Turn the lobsters over, and add the brandy, chicken stock, garlic, thyme, and the remaining butter to the pan. Transfer the pan to the oven, and bake, uncovered, for 8 minutes. Place the lobsters on a platter, and pour the sauce over them.

Splitting Lobsters
The lobster has a slight line that runs down its body. Insert the knife point into the head to kill the lobster, then follow the line straight down. Not pretty, but a useful method.

Ultimate Soft-Shelled Crab Sandwich

A true delicacy, the soft-shelled crab is a springtime treat. Ask your fishmonger to clean them for you, as it is messy and a bit complicated.

Vegetable oil, for deep-frying
1 cup flour
1 cold egg
1 cup cold water
2 teaspoons Old Bay
  Seasoning
Salt and pepper, to taste
2 large soft-shelled crabs
2 soft buns (such as
  hamburger buns or club
  rolls)
2 cups shredded iceberg
  lettuce
1 large ripe tomato, thinly
  sliced
½ cup (or to taste) tartar
  sauce
2 lemon wedges

1. Heat the oil in a pot or deep-fryer to 375°F.

2. Mix together the flour, egg, water, Old Bay, and salt and pepper. Do not overmix. Keep cold.

3. Dip the crabs in the batter and carefully place them in the oil. Fry for about 5 minutes or until the oil stops bubbling and the crabs float, turning once. Transfer to paper towels to drain, and blot dry.

4. Split the buns and lightly toast them. Place the lettuce and tomato on the buns and place the fried crabs on top. Squeeze the lemon over the crabs, and top with tartar sauce.

Worth the Deep-Fry

The effort of deep-frying is well worth it with these crabs. It is such a treat to have a crab sandwich that many travel to Maryland just for the pleasure. These crabs are in season during spring and early summer, and they should be alive at the market.

Jumbo Sweet and Spicy Shrimp Skewers

12 jumbo shrimp, peeled and deveined
3 tablespoons peanut oil
Salt and pepper, to taste
2 tablespoons honey
1 tablespoon hot sauce
1 teaspoon fresh thyme leaves

Remember to soak your wooden skewers for 20 minutes before you grill with them to prevent them from catching fire.

1. Preheat grill or broiler on high. Thread each shrimp onto a wooden skewer so that the shrimp is positioned along the skewer straight up and down. Rub with the oil, and season with salt and pepper.

2. Grill or broil for about 2 minutes per side.

3. Mix together the honey, hot sauce, and thyme, and brush the glaze over the shrimp. Cook for 1 minute on each side. Serve hot.

Boiled Blue Crabs with Newspaper

1 white onion, cut in half
3 tablespoons Old Bay Seasoning
2 lemons, cut in half
6 garlic cloves
4 bay leaves
1 gallon water
6 tablespoons salt
2 (12-ounce) bottles of beer
8 live blue crabs
1 newspaper, day unimportant

This meal is messy, silly, and fun, and requires a sense of adventure. Have plenty of napkins, beer, and toothpicks around for this treat.

1. Place everything except the crabs and the newspaper in a large pot, and boil for 10 minutes.

2. Add the crabs to the pot and turn off heat. Cover, and let poach for 5 minutes.

3. Spread out the newspaper on a table. Place the crabs directly on the newspaper. Crack the crabs with mallets and eat. Drink much beer while doing this.

Curry and Coconut Steamed Mussels

Curry and mussels are a natural combination. The sweet briny nature of the mussel juice combines effortlessly with the pungent complexity of curry.

2 tablespoons vegetable oil
1 small white onion, minced
2 tablespoons curry powder
3 pounds mussels, washed and picked over
1 cup coconut milk
1 cup dry white wine
½ cup shredded fresh basil leaves

1. Heat the oil on medium-high in a pot large enough to accommodate all of the mussels when they open. Add the onion and curry, and sauté for about 2 minutes.

2. Add the mussels, coconut milk, and wine. Cover, and cook over high heat until the mussels open, about 4 minutes.

3. Turn off the heat and add the basil. Toss to mix. Serve in large bowls with bread to soak up the broth.

Choosing Mussels
Mussels, like all shellfish, should be closed or close when they are tapped. They should be heavy for their size and smell like the sea. They also should have a federal shellfish tag attached to them that tells the consumer when the shellfish was harvested. Ask your fishmonger to show you this tag, and do not choose shellfish that have been out of the water for more than 4 days.

Curry in a Hurry
Curry is not a singular spice, but a mixture of many different spices. Each region of India has its own unique curries and use them all differently. There is a curry plant where curry leaves come from, but that is a totally different flavor and is not used in curry powder.

Garlicky Shrimp Sauté

Chorizo is a spicy Spanish sausage.
You can substitute pepperoni if you cannot find chorizo.

2 tablespoons extra-virgin
  olive oil
2 ounces chorizo, finely
  chopped
2 garlic cloves, minced
1 small white onion, finely
  chopped
¾ pound shrimp, peeled and
  deveined
1 (15-ounce) can butter
  beans, drained and rinsed
1 plum tomato, chopped
¼ cup dry white wine
1 tablespoon butter
1 teaspoon fresh thyme
  leaves
Salt and pepper, to taste

1. Heat the olive oil in a large skillet until barely smoking. Add the chorizo, onion, and garlic. Sauté for about 3 minutes or until the onions are golden.

2. Add the shrimp, and sauté for 1 minute.

3. Add the butter beans, tomato, and wine, and cook for 2 minutes.

4. Add the butter, thyme, and salt and pepper. Turn off heat, and stir until the butter is melted. Serve immediately.

Mmmmmm Pork

A little bit of smoked pork product goes a long way. In Italy, Spain, and many other countries, a small amount of bacon or smoked sausage is often added to fish and vegetable dishes to enhance flavors. Americans carried this over mostly in the South, but it's also done in the true chowders of the Northeast.

Scallop and Corn Sauté

Only use fresh corn for this dish. Canned and frozen corn lack the flavor that these scallops demand.

2 tablespoons peanut oil
¾ pound dry sea scallops
10 white mushrooms, sliced
2 ears fresh corn, kernels cut from the cob
1 tablespoon butter
2 tablespoons chopped fresh chives
1 tablespoon truffle oil
Salt and pepper, to taste

1. In a large skillet, heat the peanut oil on medium-high until barely smoking. Season the scallops with salt and pepper, and add them to the pan in a single layer. Do not crowd the pan. Cook on one side until browned.

2. Add the mushrooms and the corn kernels, and stir well. Cook for about 3 minutes, until the mushrooms begin to release their juices and the corn starts to become tender.

3. Add the butter, chives, and truffle oil. Turn off heat, and stir to mix. Season with salt and pepper, and serve.

Aren't Truffles Chocolate?
Truffles are a member of the mushroom family and grow primarily in France and Italy. The Italian white truffle is far more fragrant than the French black truffle. Look for white truffle oil in specialty markets. Refrigerate unused oil for up to 1 year.

3 tablespoons butter
1 pound small bay scallops
Freshly ground black pepper, to taste
1 ounce sturgeon or paddlefish caviar
Juice of ½ lemon

Bay Scallop Fricassee with Brown Butter and Caviar

A luxurious dish combining scallops, caviar, and butter, this is truly for a special occasion. Buy caviar from a reputable dealer; do not buy supermarket lumpfish roe.

1. Heat the butter in a large pan on medium-high until it stops bubbling. Add the scallops, and season with pepper. Do not stir. Allow the scallops to brown well on one side.

2. Stir the scallops, and cook for about 1 more minute. Add the caviar and lemon. Turn off heat, and stir to mix. Serve immediately.

Salt Is Optional

When using salty ingredients such as caviar, Parmesan cheese, capers, or anchovy, it is wise not to salt the dish until it is complete and tasted. The salt that is present in these ingredients is often enough to provide all the saltiness a dish needs.

Classic Steamed Mussels

*This is a great way to serve mussels simply yet packed with flavor.
Make extra garlic bread for this dish!*

1 baguette, cut in diagonal slices about 1 inch thick
Extra-virgin olive oil, as needed
3 garlic cloves, peeled and left whole
3 pounds mussels, cleaned and picked over
2 cups dry white wine
4 garlic cloves, minced
½ cup minced shallots
½ cup chopped fresh parsley
2 tablespoons butter

1. Preheat broiler. Brush the tops of the bread with olive oil and place under the broiler until well toasted. Rub the tops of the bread with the whole garlic cloves. Keep warm.

2. Heat a large pot on high for about 3 minutes. Add the mussels to the dry pan. Immediately pour in the wine and add the garlic, shallots, parsley, and butter. Cover, and cook over high heat for about 4 minutes or until the mussels open.

3. Pour into a large serving bowl and discard any unopened mussels. Serve the bread on the side to dip in the broth, and enjoy!

Unopened Mussels
Any shellfish that does not open when cooked is unsafe to eat. Because shellfish are filter feeders, they can pick up harmful bacteria in the water and transfer it to whoever eats them. Always buy shellfish from a reputable store, and do not be a afraid to ask about the pedigree of the items you are buying.

Oyster "Pan Roast"

Not made in a pan, and not roasted either, this classic American oyster "stew" is famously served at New York's Oyster Bar in Grand Central Station.

2 cups half-and-half
2 cups clam juice
2 tablespoons Worcestershire sauce
Dash Tabasco sauce
Salt and pepper, to taste
12 shucked oysters, with their liquid
2 tablespoons butter
4 tablespoons chopped fresh chives

In a small pot, combine the half-and-half, clam juice, Worcestershire sauce, Tabasco, and salt and pepper, and bring to a boil. As soon as the mixture boils, turn off the heat and add the oysters and the butter. Stir until the butter is melted. Divide between 2 bowls, top with chives ,and serve.

Cardiac Arrest
This is a very rich dish, suffused with cream and butter. It should be enjoyed as an occasional treat, perhaps during the winter holidays or on New Year's Eve. You can vary the dish with almost any shellfish you like. It is excellent with clams and mussels.

Barbecued Oysters on the Grill

Grilling oysters is a great way to appreciate the taste of these delights hot rather than raw.

2 dozen oysters on the half shell
½ cup ketchup
1 tablespoon apple cider vinegar
1 teaspoon Worcestershire sauce
1 teaspoon honey

1. Place the oysters shell-side down on a hot grill.

2. In a small bowl, mix together the remaining ingredients.

3. When the juices in the oysters begin to get hot, spoon a bit of the sauce over each oyster. Turn off the grill and close the lid to allow the oysters to heat through without overcooking. Enjoy with a cold beer.

Oyster Etiquette

To eat oysters served on the half shell, you should pick one up in the shell, tip the oyster to your mouth, and work the oyster and its juice (called liquor) into your mouth. The small fork provided with oysters on the half shell is only there in case the oyster needs a little help sliding out of the shell.

Shrimp in Pesto Cream

This dish pairs pesto with the natural sweetness of shrimp and the richness of cream.

1 pound shrimp, peeled and deveined
¾ cup heavy whipping cream
¼ cup prepared pesto
Salt and pepper, to taste

Combine all the ingredients in a sauté pan and boil fairly hard for about 5 minutes, or until the shrimp turn pink and the sauce thickens. Serve immediately.

Beware the Pine Nuts!

It is important to remember that pesto almost always contains pine nuts, and that people with nut allergies may have an adverse reaction. Although most people with food allergies are quite vocal about their special needs, they sometimes forget or overlook them, especially after a few glasses of wine. Always announce the presence of nuts or nut oils when serving a dish to avoid any unpleasant accidents.

Hoisin-Glazed Shrimp

Look for hoisin sauce in Asian markets.

2 tablespoons peanut oil
1 pound jumbo shrimp, peeled and deveined
1 teaspoon chopped fresh gingerroot
1 tablespoon soy sauce
Juice of 1 lemon
1 tablespoon hoisin sauce

1. In a heavy sauté pan or wok, heat the oil on medium-high until barely smoking. Add the shrimp and ginger, and sauté for about 2 minutes.

2. Add the soy sauce and lemon juice, and cook for 1 minute.

3. Add the hoisin, and sauté for 1 more minute or until the shrimp are well coated and fully cooked. Serve hot over rice.

Stuffed Greek-Style Calamari

*Purchase cleaned squid. It is a bit more expensive than "dirty" squid,
but saves on cleanup time and mess.*

¾ pound cleaned squid, with
  tentacles and tubes
3 tablespoons olive oil
½ small white onion, minced
1 teaspoon dried oregano
Salt and pepper, to taste
1 cup cooked and cooled
  long-grain white rice
1 egg, lightly beaten
2 tablespoons lemon juice
1 recipe Quick Marinara
  Sauce (page 99)
1 cup dry red wine
6 black olives, minced
4 garlic cloves, minced

1. Separate the tentacles and tubes. Chop the tentacles finely and set aside.

2. Heat the olive oil in a small sauté pan on medium. Add the onion, chopped tentacles, oregano, and salt and pepper. Sauté for 1 minute. Transfer to a bowl.

3. Add the cooked rice, egg, and lemon juice to the onion-squid mixture. Mix well, and adjust seasoning to taste.

4. Stuff this mixture inside the squid tubes. Secure the open ends with toothpicks to prevent the stuffing from escaping when cooking.

5. Place the squid in a small pot. Pour the marinara and wine over the squid, and add the olives and garlic. Partially cover, and simmer gently for 45 minutes.

5. Remove the toothpicks and serve in plenty of the sauce.

Sticky Rice

Although the rice in this dish is very overcooked, it still retains a pleasant texture. It becomes very soft and soaks up the sauce and juices of the squid. It resembles a bread crumb stuffing, and the egg keeps it together. You could substitute bread crumbs or any cooked grain for the rice in this dish.

Grilled Octopus

1 (3-pound) octopus
½ cup extra-virgin olive oil
2 tablespoons dried oregano
Salt and pepper, to taste
1 lemon

Most octopuses are sold gutted, and frozen or thawed. If you have a Greek or Asian market near you, you may be able to find it fresh.

1. Simmer the octopus gently in a large pot of well-salted water for about 30 minutes or until the tentacles easily pull free from the body. Cool in ice water for 10 minutes, then drain.

2. Separate the tentacles from the body and peel off the suckers and skin with your hands. Rinse under water. Coat the octopus in the olive oil and oregano and let marinate for 30 minutes in the refrigerator.

3. Preheat grill on high.

4. Season the octopus with salt and pepper, and place on the grill. Grill for 1 or 2 minutes per side, just to char the surface and heat the octopus through. Transfer to plates, squeeze lemon over the top, and enjoy.

Octopus Lore
There are many theories on how to make an octopus more tender when cooking it. One is to add a wine cork to the pot while boiling. Another is to dip the octopus 3 times in the boiling water before cooking it, and another says to beat it no more than 20 times on a rock. Just simmer until tender, and that is all.

Chinese Clams with Black Bean Sauce

Look for prepared black bean sauce in the Asian section of your supermarket.

1. Heat a heavy pan or wok on high. Add the oil, ginger, garlic, and scallions, and stir-fry for 30 seconds. Add the clams, and toss well in the mixture.

2. Add the rice wine, black bean sauce, soy sauce, chicken broth, and sugar. Cover the pan and cook for about 3 minutes or until the clams are fully opened. Discard any clams that don't open.

3. Slowly drizzle in the cornstarch mixture, stirring constantly until the sauce thickens. Turn off heat and toss well. Serve in bowls.

Wok It

A wok is a wonder of ancient technology. The Chinese invented this perfect cooking vessel thousands of years ago and in turn developed a very complex and sophisticated cuisine around it. You can boil, steam, fry, smoke, stir-fry, and even roast in a wok. Do yourself a favor and invest in one.

3 tablespoons peanut oil
2 garlic cloves, minced
1 tablespoon grated fresh gingerroot
3 scallions, finely sliced
2 dozen live cherrystone clams, scrubbed of all sand
2 tablespoons Chinese rice wine or dry sherry
1 tablespoon prepared black bean sauce
1 tablespoon soy sauce
½ cup chicken broth
Pinch granulated sugar
2 tablespoons cornstarch dissolved in 2 tablespoons water

Sautéed Soft-Shelled Crabs in Tomato Sauce

*A great alternative to deep-fried crabs. The trick here is to crisp them up in
a hot pan, then to pour the sauce over them.*

All-purpose flour, as needed
Salt and pepper, to taste
4 soft-shelled crabs, cleaned
3 tablespoons butter, divided
2 tablespoons olive oil
¼ cup dry white wine
1 cup chopped ripe tomato
3 garlic cloves, minced
2 tablespoons chopped fresh
   parsley

1. Preheat oven to 200°F. Season the flour with salt and pepper, and dredge the crabs well. Shake off any excess flour.

2. Heat 2 tablespoons of the butter and the olive oil in a sauté pan large enough to hold all 4 crabs. Heat on medium-high until the butter stops bubbling. Add the crabs to the pan and cook for about 3 minutes per side.

3. When the crabs are crispy and hot in the center, transfer them to a plate and place in the oven to keep warm while you make the sauce.

4. Drain the fat from the pan, and heat on high. Add the wine and scrape the browned bits from the bottom of the pan into the wine. Bring to a boil.

5. Reduce heat and add the tomato, garlic, and the remaining butter. Cook until the butter is melted. Remove from heat, add the parsley, and stir to mix. Serve the sauce over the crabs

Getting Adventurous
For those who want to learn how to clean soft-shelled crabs: With a large scissors, cut off the front of the shell where the eyes and points are. Slightly squeeze the shell, and a greenish bubble will appear where you just made the incision. Remove this sack. Next, flip the corners of the shells up, exposing the feathery gills. Cut them out with the scissors. Finally, cut off the flap, or "apron," that is under the crab. Voilà, you're done!

Elegant Scallop Mousse with Caviar

*This simple and elegant dish is rich and luxurious. Serve it on special occasions.
It is also nice cold, sliced on toast.*

¾ pound fresh scallops, as
　cold as possible
1 egg white
1 teaspoon lemon juice
1 teaspoon chopped fresh dill
Salt and pepper, to taste
¾ cup heavy cream, as cold
　as possible
1 tablespoon softened butter
1 ounce high-quality caviar

1. Preheat oven to 325°F.

2. Place the scallops, egg white, lemon juice, dill, and salt and pepper in the bowl of a food processor. Purée the mixture for about 1 minute, then slowly drizzle in the cream with the processor running until it is fully incorporated in the mixture.

3. Grease two 6-ounce ramekins or muffin tins with the butter. Divide the scallop mousse between the ramekins. Place the ramekins in a shallow baking pan and fill the pan with water about 1 inch up the sides of the ramekins. Place the pan in the oven and bake until the center of the mousse reaches 140°F. Unmold the mousse onto serving plates, and serve hot topped with the caviar.

Is It Mousse?

This is not actually a mousse, but a "mousseline." The difference is that a mousse is normally served cold and contains whipped cream or egg whites. Also, a mousse is usually sweet. A mousseline, however, is usually a cooked dish made with a lean protein to which cream and eggs are added. You can substitute almost any lean protein for this dish, including chicken breast, fish, and so on.

Clams Broiled with Bacon and Bread Crumbs

24 cherrystone clams on the half shell
24 teaspoons bread crumbs
24 (1-inch) slices raw bacon

Similar to clams casino, this simple preparation
makes a great appetizer or main course.

Preheat broiler. Place the clams on a salt bed in a baking pan. Sprinkle the bread crumbs over the raw clams. Top each clam with a slice of bacon, and place under the broiler. Broil for about 3 minutes or until the bacon begins to crisp. Yum!

Seared Raw Scallops Sashimi Style

3 tablespoons peanut oil
1 pound large "dry" sea scallops (also called diver scallops)
¼ cup pickled sushi ginger
Soy sauce, for dipping

Fresh raw scallops are sweet as sugar and a real treat.
Look for them in November when the season is at its peak,
and ask your fishmonger for "dry" scallops.

1. Heat the oil to smoking in a very heavy pan. Carefully add the scallops to the pan. Do not overcrowd the pan. Sear the scallops for 30 seconds per side, and remove from the pan.

2. Slice each scallop in half so each half has a seared side and a raw side. Arrange artfully on 2 serving plates, and serve with the ginger and soy on the side to dip.

Japanese Simplicity
A dish like this is only great when the ingredients are superior. The Japanese cuisine relies on excellent ingredients without too much fuss. If you doubt the quality of the scallops or any product used in a dish like this, abandon the dish for another time.

chapter 11

one-dish meals—
casseroles and stews

Casablanca-Style Lamb Stew with Dried Fruits

Moroccan food usually has a touch of sweetness to it.
Here the dried fruits play this role in this "tagine," or stew.

1 pound lamb stew meat, cut
into 1-inch cubes
¼ cup all-purpose flour
8 tablespoons extra-virgin
olive oil, divided
Salt and pepper, to taste
1 large white onion, cut into
1-inch dice
2 carrots, peeled and cut into
¼-inch rounds
1 tablespoon grated fresh
gingerroot
2 tablespoons tomato paste
2 tablespoons ground
coriander
4 cups chicken or beef broth
1 (15.5-ounce) can chickpeas
6 dried apricots, cut into
small dice

1. Preheat oven to 400°F.

2. Toss the lamb with the flour, 4 tablespoons of the olive oil, and salt and pepper. Place on a baking sheet, and bake for 15 minutes. Drain off excess fat, and set aside.

3. Heat the remaining olive oil on medium-high in a pot large enough to accommodate all of the ingredients. Add the onions, carrots, and ginger, and sauté for about 2 minutes.

4. Add the tomato paste and coriander, and cook for another 2 minutes.

5. Add the meat, broth, chickpeas, and apricots. Partially cover and simmer gently for 1½ hours or until the meat is tender. Adjust seasoning to taste with salt and pepper, and serve over rice or couscous.

Prize-Winning Chili

This recipe won the Culinary Institute of America's annual Chili Cook-off in 1993.

1. Heat the oil in a heavy pot large enough to accommodate all the ingredients. Add the onion, garlic, and bell pepper. Sauté for about 5 minutes, until well softened.

2. Add the dry spices and flour, and sauté for another 2 minutes.

3. Add the meat, tomatoes, broth, beer, Worcestershire sauce, and sugar. Simmer gently for 1½ hours or until the meat is fork tender.

4. Turn off the heat and add the chocolate. Melt into the stew, stirring to mix. Serve with rice or cornbread.

Chocolate and Chili
Both chocolate and chili peppers share the birthplace of Mexico, and the flavors mix well. The original chocolate drink of ancient Mexico was not sweet at all and contained chili peppers, almonds, and cinnamon. The small amount of unsweetened chocolate added at the end of this chili adds a level of complexity that is sublime.

¼ cup vegetable oil or bacon fat
1 large white onion, cut into medium dice
4 garlic cloves, minced
1 green bell pepper, cut into medium dice
¼ cup all-purpose flour
1 heaping tablespoon ground cumin
1 heaping tablespoon ground coriander
1 heaping tablespoon chili powder
1 heaping tablespoon paprika
1½ pounds beef chuck, cut into ½-inch cubes
1 cup canned diced tomatoes
4 cups beef broth
¾ cup dark beer
2 tablespoons Worcestershire sauce
1 teaspoon brown sugar
¼ square unsweetened chocolate

Portuguese Clam and Sausage Stew

The Portuguese culture has a great love of anything from the sea as well as sausages. This is a classic combination that makes a great fall stew.

4 tablespoons extra-virgin
    olive oil
6 ounces linguica sausage
3 garlic cloves, minced
1 cup canned diced tomatoes
1 (15.5-ounce) can white
    beans, rinsed and drained
1 cup dry white wine
2 dozen cherrystone clams
3 tablespoons chopped fresh
    parsley
Salt and pepper, to taste
2 cups croutons

1. Heat the olive oil on medium-high in a pot large enough to accommodate the clams when they open. Add the sausage and garlic, and sauté for 2 minutes.

2. Add the tomatoes, beans, and wine, and simmer for 3 minutes.

3. Add the clams and cover the pot. Cook until all the clams open, about 4 minutes.

4. Turn off the heat and add the parsley. Season with salt and pepper. Place the croutons in the bottom of 2 serving bowls, and ladle the stew over the croutons.

Wet Bread
Adding dry bread or croutons to a bowl of soup is an age-old tradition that was meant to both extend the soups as well as provide a use for old bread. Try experimenting with different breads and seasonings as well as melted cheese. Dry bread is best, as the pores soak up the yummy broth and provide a pleasant texture.

Baby Vegetable Fricassee

Make this in the spring, when baby vegetables are abundant and fresh. You can leave out the bacon, but it adds a fantastic smoky note to the dish.

2 tablespoons butter
3 slices raw bacon, minced
½ cup peeled baby carrots
6 baby pattypan squash, cut in half
1 cup small white mushrooms
1 cup peeled pearl onions
1 cup baby turnips, cut in half, greens removed
1 cup chicken stock
1 tablespoon chopped fresh rosemary
Salt and pepper, to taste
¼ cup dry red wine

1. Melt the butter in a large pan, and add the bacon. Cook over medium heat until the bacon begins to crisp. Add all of the vegetables and cook over medium-high heat until the mushrooms release their juices and the juices evaporate.

2. Add the chicken stock and rosemary, and cover the pan. Cook over low heat for about 7 minutes.

3. Remove the lid, and season with salt and pepper. Cook over high heat until the stock is totally evaporated. Add the wine, and continue to cook until the wine has evaporated and the vegetables are glazed, stirring throughout. Serve hot.

Going Veggie

This dish can easily be made into a vegetarian dish. Leave out the bacon, substitute extra-virgin olive oil for the butter, and use vegetable stock instead of chicken stock. Use any small vegetables you can find, but avoid green vegetables, as they turn gray and soft with longer cooking times.

Polish Pork and Sauerkraut Stew (Bigos)

4 slices bacon
½ pound kielbasa, sliced into ½-inch rounds
½ pound pork shoulder, cut into 1-inch cubes
2 cups sauerkraut, rinsed
1 (12-ounce) bottle pilsner beer
2 tablespoons tomato paste
2 teaspoons caraway seeds
¼ cup granulated sugar
1 large white onion, thinly sliced
Salt and pepper, to taste

This is a dish from my childhood. Warming and satisfying, it takes humble ingredients and elevates them into a sum greater than their parts.

1. Preheat oven to 350°F.

2. Line a small casserole dish with the slices of bacon. Mix together the remaining ingredients and place in the casserole. Cover tightly with plastic wrap, then aluminum foil. Bake for about 3 hours. Serve.

Slow-Cooked Thai Long Beans with Pork

¼ cup peanut oil
½ pound ground pork
6 garlic cloves, minced
2 Thai chili peppers (also called bird peppers) or 2 jalapeño peppers, minced
1 pound Chinese long beans, cut into 4-inch pieces
2 cups chicken broth
3 tablespoons Thai fish sauce
¼ cup soy sauce
1 tablespoon granulated sugar

This is a spicy and garlicky dish from Thailand. It can be served as a main course or a side dish.

1. Heat the oil in a wok or heavy pan on high heat until barely smoking, and brown the meat well.

2. Add the garlic and peppers, and cook for 2 minutes.

3. Add all the remaining ingredients. Cover, and simmer gently for 15 minutes. Serve hot over rice.

Thai Fish Sauce
This stuff is potent! It smells awful straight from the bottle, with a scent resembling that of old socks. But used properly, it lends a complex saltiness that adds much to the dishes it seasons.

Fresh Soy Beans with Chinese Sausage

*Fresh soybeans are now available in the frozen vegetable section.
Look for them near the frozen peas. If you cannot find them,
baby lima beans are a good substitution.*

1. Heat the oil in a small saucepan on medium-high.

2. Add the sausage, ginger, and garlic, and sauté for about 3 minutes. Add the remaining ingredients and simmer gently, partially covered, for 15 minutes. Serve hot.

Beans and Sausage
The combination of beans and sausage is used in many cultures. The French have cassoulet; the Portuguese have feijoada; and the Mexicans have black beans with chorizo. Experiment with different bean and sausage combinations to come up with a new favorite.

2 tablespoons peanut oil
3 links Chinese sausage, cut into thin rounds
1 tablespoon grated fresh gingerroot
2 garlic cloves, minced
10 shiitake mushrooms, stems removed
3 cups defrosted fresh soybeans
3 tablespoons soy sauce
1½ cups chicken broth
1 teaspoon granulated sugar
Salt and pepper, to taste

Curried Chicken Hot Pot

This is a Malaysian-inspired curry. The cuisine of Malaysia is a unique blend of Indian, Chinese, and southeast Asian. Serve with white rice on the side.

1. Whisk together the red curry paste and the chicken stock to dissolve the paste.

2. In a small pot, combine all the ingredients except the tomato and cilantro. Bring to a simmer. Cover, and simmer gently for 25 minutes.

3. Season to taste with salt, then add the tomato and cilantro. Serve in bowls.

1 tablespoon prepared red curry paste
2 cups chicken broth
¾ pound skinless, boneless chicken thighs, cut into 1-inch chunks
1 cup coconut milk
1 tablespoon grated fresh gingerroot
10 scallions, white part only, trimmed but left whole
6 ounces fresh lotus root, cut into ½-inch slices
1 large ripe tomato, cut into 1-inch chunks
2 tablespoons chopped fresh cilantro
Salt, to taste

Hungarian Goulash

A classic stew. The trick here is to use an enormous amount of onions, which gives the stew a sweet complexity.

¾ pound beef stew meat, cut into 1-inch cubes
½ cup vegetable oil, divided
Salt and pepper, to taste
¾ pound white onions, sliced
4 tablespoons mild Hungarian paprika
4 cups beef broth or consommé
2 dollops sour cream, optional

1. Preheat oven to 450°F.

2. Toss the meat with half of the oil and salt and pepper. Place on a baking sheet and brown in the oven for about 10 minutes. Drain off excess fat.

3. Heat the remaining oil in a pot on medium-high. Add the onions and cook over medium heat for about 20 minutes, until the onions are deeply browned but not at all burned, stirring occasionally.

4. Add the paprika and continue to stir for 1 minute. Add the stew meat and broth. Simmer gently, partially covered, for about 1½ hours or until the meat is very tender. Adjust seasoning and skim off excess fat. Ladle the stew into bowls and top with a dollop of the sour cream, if desired.

Paprika
Most paprika is not very spicy. Paprika is made from sweet red peppers, similar to bell peppers, which are ripened in the sun, then dried and ground into a fine powder. It can be found hot or mild, and can be stored in an airtight container for up to 1 year before it starts to lose flavor.

Easy Beef Stroganoff

A great stew that benefits from the addition of sour cream, this version shows the Eastern European influence.

1. Preheat oven to 450°F.

2. Mix together the beef, oil, flour, and salt and pepper. Place on a baking sheet and bake for about 10 minutes to brown. Drain off any excess fat.

3. Place the beef, broth, and mushrooms in a pot. Simmer gently, partially covered, for about 1½ hours or until the meat is tender.

4. Skim off any excess fat and adjust seasoning with salt and pepper.

5. In a bowl, mix together the sour cream, dill, and lemon juice, and season with salt and pepper. Ladle a small amount of the broth from the pot into the bowl and quickly mix with the sour cream. Stir the mixture into the pot, and turn off the heat. Serve alone or over egg noodles.

Tempering Ingredients
The technique of adding the sour cream to a small amount of hot liquid and then returning it to the pot is called "tempering." This process allows the item, whether it is egg or sour cream, to adjust to a hot temperature gradually rather than all at once. This prevents the item from "breaking," or curdling.

1 pound beef stew meat, cut into 1-inch cubes
¼ cup vegetable oil
¼ cup all-purpose flour
Salt and pepper, to taste
4 cups beef broth or consommé
1 (10-ounce) package white mushrooms, quartered
¼ cup sour cream
2 teaspoons chopped fresh dill
2 teaspoons fresh lemon juice

Lamb Stew with Olives and Tomato

Wonderfully rich and satisfying, this stew gains interesting character from the addition of kalamata olives. Make sure to get the pits out!

¾ pound lamb stew meat, cut into 1-inch cubes
½ cup extra-virgin olive oil, divided
¼ cup all-purpose flour
Salt and pepper, to taste
3 garlic cloves, minced
1 white onion, cut into medium dice
1 carrot, peeled and cut into ¼-inch rounds
½ cup canned diced tomatoes
¼ cup pitted kalamata olives
3 cups chicken broth
1 cup dry red wine
2 teaspoons chopped fresh rosemary

1. Preheat oven to 450°F.

2. Mix together the lamb, half of the oil, the flour, and salt and pepper. Place on a baking sheet, and bake for about 10 minutes to brown. Drain off any excess fat.

3. In a pot, heat the remaining olive oil on medium-high and add the garlic, onion, and carrot. Sauté for about 3 minutes.

4. Add the lamb, tomatoes, olives, broth, wine, and rosemary. Simmer gently, partially covered, for about 1½ hours or until the meat is tender. Skim off excess fat, adjust seasoning with salt and pepper, and serve.

Searing in the Oven
There are several good reasons to sear meat in a hot oven instead of on the stovetop. There is no oil splattering all over the stovetop. You don't have to pay as careful attention to the product because the oven is doing all of the work. And you can start sautéing or cooking the other ingredients in your stew pot.

Old-School Tuna Casserole

The kicker here is the cornflakes on the top.

3 cups cooked and cooled
  egg noodles
2 cans tuna, drained
1 (14-ounce) can cream of
  mushroom soup
½ cup shredded Cheddar
  cheese
2 garlic cloves, minced
½ cup chopped scallion
Salt and pepper, to taste
1 cup crushed cornflakes
¼ cup melted butter

...nts except the butter and cornflakes. Place ...nproof casserole dish that will comfortably ...

... drizzle the butter over the top. Bake until ... the top is crispy and well browned (about ...

...aki—*all of these dishes are retro-chic and ...or cookbooks from the 1950s and 1960s, ...recipes. The comfort-food phenomenon is ...n treasures back into the spotlight.*

Chicken Fricassee with Biscuit Topping

This dish is kind of like a chicken potpie or chicken with dumplings. The use of store-bought biscuit dough makes this a snap.

2 tablespoons butter
1 white onion, cut into medium dice
1 celery stalk, cut into ¼-inch slices
1 carrot, peeled and cut into ¼-inch rounds
1 teaspoon fresh thyme leaves
¼ cup all-purpose flour
4 cups chicken broth
½ pound skinless, boneless chicken breast, cut into 1–inch chunks
Salt and pepper, to taste
1 package ready-bake frozen or refrigerated biscuits

1. Heat the butter in a large sauté pan and add the onion, celery, carrot, and thyme. Sauté for about 4 minutes over medium heat.

2. Add the flour and mix well. Slowly add the broth, stirring constantly, and bring to a simmer. Simmer gently for about 20 minutes, uncovered, skimming off any foam that rises to the top.

3. Preheat oven to 400°F.

4. Add the chicken and cook for 10 more minutes. Season with salt and pepper.

5. Transfer the mixture to a small ovenproof casserole with about 1 inch to spare from the top of the mixture to the top of the casserole dish. Place the individual biscuits evenly over the top of the chicken stew. Bake until the biscuits are cooked. (Check the package instructions on the biscuits.)

Semi-Scratch
It is a good idea to see what products are available in the supermarket that will allow you to simplify your cooking life but still come up with great results. Frozen dough, such as pizza, puff pastry, and biscuit, is excellent in quality and can enhance some homemade items from your kitchen.

Curried Lamb with Dried Mango

You can find dried mango in almost any market these days.
If you are having trouble, go to an Asian or Indian market.

1. Mix together the yogurt and curry powder, and coat the lamb in the mixture. Let marinate overnight in the refrigerator.

2. Heat the butter in a pot until it stops bubbling, then add the onions. Brown the onions slightly over medium heat. Add the marinated meat along with all the remaining ingredients except the cilantro.

3. Partially cover, and simmer gently for about 1 hour and 15 minutes or until the meat is very tender. Skim off excess fat and garnish with the cilantro.

The Many Cuisines of Cilantro

Cilantro, or coriander, is among the most popular herbs in the world. It is used in a host of cuisines, including Mexican, Chinese, Thai, Indian, Vietnamese, and Central American. It is usually added to dishes at the last minute or eaten raw in salads because of its delicate nature.

1 cup plain yogurt
2 tablespoons Madras curry powder
¾ pound lamb stew meat, cut into 1-inch cubes
3 tablespoons butter
1 large white onion, cut into medium dice
½ cup canned diced tomatoes
½ cup diced dried mango
1 cup store-bought gravy
3 cups chicken broth
Salt and pepper, to taste
¼ cup fresh cilantro leaves

1700s Layered Cod "Chowda"

"Chowda" is the proper pronunciation in New England.

1 cup heavy cream
½ cup clam juice
1 teaspoon fresh thyme
    leaves
2 Idaho potatoes, peeled and
    thinly sliced
4 strips bacon, finely chopped
1 pound chunk cod fillet,
    about 1½ inches thick,
    cut in half
Salt and pepper, to taste
1 bay leaf

1. Mix together the cream, clam juice, and thyme, and pour about ¼ cup of the mixture into a small pot.

2. Place a layer of the potatoes in the bottom of the pot and sprinkle some bacon over the top. Place 1 slice of the cod on top. Season each layer with salt and pepper. Repeat this process until all the ingredients are used. Pour the remaining cream mixture into the pot and set on low heat. Add the bay leaf, cover the pot, and cook very gently for about 25 minutes or until the potatoes are cooked.

3. Divide in 2 bowls and serve with oyster crackers or toast.

Tradition, Tradition

Tradition. Yes, it's a song from **Fiddler on the Roof,** *but this is a very traditional chowder dating back to the 1700s. One of the only differences is that they would have used salted pork fat instead of bacon. You can go this way if you want. There is a great reference to a chowder like this in the classic* **Moby Dick.**

Tuscan Beef Stew with Pumpkin

Butternut squash is used here in place of pumpkin for ease of preparation.

¾ pound beef stew meat, cut
    into 1-inch cubes
¾ cup all-purpose flour
Salt and pepper, to taste
½ cup extra-virgin olive oil
1 small white onion, small
    diced
1 bulb fennel, medium diced
2 garlic cloves, minced
1 teaspoon chopped fresh
    rosemary
1 cup dry red wine
1 cup cubed butternut squash
    (about 1-inch cubes)
4 cups beef broth

1. Toss the meat with the flour and salt and pepper. In a pot large enough to accommodate all of the ingredients, heat the oil on medium-high and brown the meat well. Remove the meat from the pan and set aside.

2. Add the onion, fennel, garlic, and rosemary to the same pot. Sauté over medium heat for 4 minutes. Add the wine, stirring and scraping to loosen any cooked-on bits from the bottom of the pot.

3. Return the meat to the pot. Add the broth, and bring to a boil. As soon as it boils, reduce to a gentle simmer and cook for 1 hour, uncovered.

4. Add the butternut squash and cook, uncovered, for 30 minutes more or until all of the ingredients are tender. Serve hot over pasta or bread.

Flouring Meat for Browning
There are 3 reasons that meat is floured before browning. First, the flour forms an attractive crust that helps the meat to brown effectively. Second, the flour adds a toasty flavor to the dish. And thirdly, the flour acts as a thickening agent and gives the finished sauce a nice consistency.

Andouille Sausage and Shrimp Bog

*The spicy andouille sausage adds a Cajun influence to this traditional southern
style of cooking, which is very hearty and comforting.*

¼ pound andouille sausage,
finely diced
1 medium-sized white onion,
finely diced
½ green bell pepper, finely
diced
1 celery stalk, finely diced
2 garlic cloves, crushed
½ cup uncooked long-grain
rice
4 cups chicken or fish stock, or
2 cups each
½ cup diced tomatoes,
drained
Dash Worcestershire sauce
½ pound medium shrimp,
peeled and deveined
Salt and pepper, to taste
3 scallions, green part only,
finely sliced

1. Heat a heavy-bottomed saucepan on medium. Add the andouille and
   cook gently for about 3 minutes, until the fat starts to render and the
   sausage begins to brown.

2. Add the onion, bell pepper, celery, and garlic. Sauté until the vegetables begin to soften, about 2 minutes. Add the rice and stir well to coat
   the grains with the fat.

3. Add the stock, tomatoes, and Worcestershire. Bring to a boil. Immediately reduce heat to a simmer, cover, and cook for 20 minutes. The rice
   should be cooked, and there should still be a bit of extra broth in the pot.
   If the bog seems dry, add a cup or so of stock and return to a simmer.

4. Add the shrimp and stir well. Cover and simmer for about 5 to 7 minutes, until the shrimp turn pink. Season to taste with salt and pepper.
   Serve in warm bowls and garnish with the chopped scallions.

Save Those Shells
*A nice trick here is to buy a good canned chicken broth and simmer it
along with the shrimp shells for 20 minutes. Strain out the shells and
you have a super stock to make Andouille Sausage and Shrimp Bog.
Always freeze any leftover shrimp or lobster shells for later uses.*

Chicken and Black Bean Stew

Never underestimate the power of beans.
They have an amazing way of extending a dish and carrying flavor.

2 chicken legs and thighs,
    skin on and bone in
2 tablespoons vegetable oil
1 white onion, small diced
1 teaspoon dried oregano
½ teaspoon ground cumin
½ teaspoon chili powder
2 teaspoons tomato paste
1 small can black beans, with
    their liquid
½ cup chicken stock
Salt and pepper, to taste
3 tablespoons chopped fresh
    cilantro
1 lime, cut in half

1. Using a cleaver, cut the chicken, through the bones, into 2-inch pieces. Heat the oil in a pot on medium-high, and brown the chicken well. Remove the chicken from the pot and set aside.

2. In the same pot, brown the onions over medium heat in the leftover oil. Add the dry spices and sauté for 1 minute. Add the tomato paste and cook for 1 more minute, stirring to coat the onions.

3. Add all the remaining ingredients except the cilantro and lime, and simmer, uncovered, gently for 30 minutes.

4. Adjust seasoning to taste, and ladle into 2 serving bowls. Sprinkle the cilantro on top, and squeeze the lime over the stew.

Lime and Cilantro
Adding lime and cilantro at the end of a cooking process has a way of "brightening" the dish as well as giving it a distinctly Mexican flavor. Try "Mexicanizing" some of your favorites like chicken soup or chili, or many other stews and soups, by adding these magical ingredients.

Polenta and Sweet Sausage Casserole

½ pound sweet Italian sausage, casings removed
3 tablespoons extra-virgin olive oil
2 garlic cloves, minced
½ cup cornmeal or polenta
2 cups cold chicken broth
Salt and pepper, to taste
2 tablespoons butter
1 cup grated Parmesan cheese
4 tablespoons chopped fresh parsley

Polenta is basically a porridge made from cornmeal. It is humble yet delicious.

1. In a skillet on medium-high heat, brown the sausage well in the olive oil. Add the garlic, and cook for 1 more minute. Drain off excess oil.

2. In a heavy saucepot, combine the cornmeal, cold chicken stock, and salt and pepper. Whisk well, and set heat on high. Whisk occasionally until the mixture begins to thicken. Switch to a wooden spoon, and continue to cook the polenta over low heat, stirring frequently, until the polenta begins to pull from the side of the pan (about 15 minutes).

3. Remove from the heat. Add the butter and half of the Parmesan cheese to the polenta, and stir to incorporate. Add the sausage and parsley, and adjust seasoning to taste with salt and pepper.

4. Transfer the entire mixture to a greased casserole dish. Top with the remaining cheese. Allow to firm up in the fridge for about 1 hour.

5. Preheat oven to 400°F.

6. Bake the casserole until the top is well browned. Be careful—this is hot!

Humble Luxury
Sometimes humble ingredients can become very luxurious. Polenta is the perfect example. It is basically porridge, but by adding copious amounts of butter and Parmesan cheese, and perhaps some truffles, polenta becomes something special.

Mixed Mushroom Stew

Mushrooms have an amazing ability to mimic meat in texture and flavor. They are also packed with protein.

1. In a pot, heat the butter on medium until it stops bubbling. Add the bacon, pearl onions, carrot, celery, and bay leaf. Sauté until the onions are golden brown. Add the flour and toss well.

2. Add the tomato paste, and cook for 1 minute. Add all the mushrooms, and cook for about 5 minutes or until the mushrooms have released a fair amount of liquid.

3. Add the wine, broth, and salt and pepper. Simmer gently for about 20 minutes, uncovered.

4. Add the potato, and cook for 15 more minutes over low heat, uncovered. Adjust seasoning with salt and pepper, and serve.

Mushrooms
If you can't find these specific mushrooms, don't let it stop you from making this dish. Look for any mushrooms that you can find, and experiment. Mushrooms such as cremini, porcini, hen of the woods, morels, chanterelles, and many others will all make an excellent stew.

3 tablespoons butter
4 slices bacon, finely chopped
1 cup peeled pearl onions
2 celery stalks, cut into ¼-inch slices
1 carrot, peeled and cut into ¼-inch slices
1 bay leaf
3 tablespoons all-purpose flour
1 tablespoon tomato paste
½ pound white mushrooms, quartered
½ pound oyster mushrooms, trimmed and torn
½ pound shiitake mushrooms, stems removed and cut in half
½ cup dry red wine
3 cups chicken stock
Salt and pepper, to taste
1 Idaho potato, peeled and cut into ½-inch cubes

Veal, Leek, and Mushroom Stew

This is an elegant and satisfying stew.

1 pound veal stew meat, cut in 1-inch cubes
1 cup all-purpose flour
Salt and pepper, to taste
½ cup extra-virgin olive oil
2 large leeks, white part only, washed and cut into 1-inch slices
1 (10-ounce) package white mushrooms, sliced
½ cup dry white wine
4 cups chicken broth

1. Toss the veal with the flour and salt and pepper. Heat the oil on medium-high in a pot large enough to hold all the ingredients. Brown the veal well. Remove the meat from the pot and set aside.

2. Add the leeks and mushrooms to the same pot, and sauté for 5 minutes over medium heat.

3. Add the wine to the pot, stirring and scraping to loosen the cooked-on bits from the bottom of the pan. Return the meat to the pan along with any juices.

4. Add the broth to the pot, bring to a boil, and immediately reduce to a gentle simmer. Simmer, uncovered, for 1½ hours or until the meat is very tender. Adjust seasoning with salt and pepper, and serve.

Leek 101
Leeks are members of the onion family and resemble large scallions or green onions. They are essential to many French dishes and are used often in soups and stews. They require careful cleaning because they tend to be very dirty and sandy, but they are worth the trouble. They have a subtle onion flavor that is hard to beat.

chapter 12
simple sides

Cheesy Twice-Baked Potatoes with Chives

2 large baking potatoes
3 tablespoons sour cream
½ cup shredded Cheddar
cheese
2 tablespoons grated
Parmesan cheese
2 tablespoons chopped fresh
chives
Salt and pepper, to taste
Cooking spray

*Always a favorite and easy to make,
these potatoes will warm the heart of any hungry person.*

1. Preheat oven to 375°F.

2. Wash the potatoes and wrap in foil. Bake for about 30 minutes or until the potato is fork tender. Let cool slightly.

3. Cut off a thin slice from the top of each potato, lengthwise, and discard. Being careful not to damage the potato shells, scoop out most of the potato flesh into a bowl. Mix with the sour cream, cheeses, chives, and salt and pepper. Spoon the potato mixture into the potato shells.

4. Place the potatoes on a baking sheet and spray the tops with the cooking spray. Bake until tops are browned.

Mix It Up
Experiment with these potatoes. Add any cheese of your choice. They are also a great way to use leftover vegetables or tomato sauce, or mushrooms, or sausage, or anything! Play with these potatoes and find your own favorite.

Easiest Scalloped Potatoes Ever

*Scalloped or au gratin potatoes are easier than you think.
Use the same ratio if you want to make a bunch for a crowd.*

2 large Idaho potatoes,
   peeled and cut into thin
   slices
2 cups heavy cream
1 garlic clove, minced
1 teaspoon chopped fresh
   rosemary
Salt and pepper, to taste

1. Preheat oven to 400°F.

2. Mix together all the ingredients and place in a small ovenproof casserole dish so the mixture is about 2 inches thick.

3. Bake for about 45 minutes. The potatoes will be fork tender and the top will be well browned. Rest the casserole in a warm place for about 15 minutes before serving to allow the cream to settle back into the potatoes.

String Beans with Toasted Bread Crumbs

This is a very simple and tasty way to serve green beans. Kids love this!

2 tablespoons butter
1 garlic clove, minced
½ cup plain bread crumbs
4 cups snipped green beans
Salt and pepper, to taste

1. Melt the butter in a pan and add the garlic and bread crumbs. Cook slowly over low heat, stirring occasionally, until the bread crumbs are well toasted and the butter releases a nutty aroma. Keep warm.

2. Boil the green beans in plenty of salted water until tender. Drain, and toss with the buttered bread crumbs. Season with salt and pepper, and serve.

Roasted Potatoes with Lemon and Garlic

These potatoes are evocative of the flavors of Greece.
Use as a side dish for lamb or other roasted meats.

3 cups quartered red bliss potatoes
3 garlic cloves, minced
3 tablespoons extra-virgin olive oil
Juice of 1 lemon
½ teaspoon dried oregano
Salt and pepper, to taste
2 tablespoons chopped fresh parsley

1. Preheat oven to 425°F.

2. Toss together the potatoes, garlic, oil, lemon juice, oregano, and salt and pepper. Spread out the potatoes in an even layer on a baking sheet or in a pan. Roast until well browned and tender, about 20 minutes. Toss with the parsley, and serve.

Potato Croquettes with Smoked Gouda

This is a great way to use leftover mashed potatoes,
and the recipe is written to reflect this.

2 cups leftover mashed potatoes
1 egg, lightly beaten
2 tablespoons all-purpose flour
Salt and pepper, to taste
2 cubes smoked Gouda, about 1 inch each
Olive oil, for frying

1. Mix together the potato, egg, flour, and salt and pepper. Divide into 4 piles and form into loose balls.

2. Press a cube of cheese into the center of each ball and form into patties.

3. Heat about 1 inch of olive oil in a heavy pan until almost smoking. Fry the patties for about 2 minutes per side. Serve hot.

Wild Mushroom Mashed Potatoes

*The basic mashed potato recipe here is simply spruced up
with the addition of wild mushrooms.*

2 large Idaho potatoes,
 peeled and cut into
 2-inch cubes
1 tablespoon kosher salt
3 tablespoons butter, divided
½ pound mixed wild
 mushrooms, trimmed
 and sliced
1 garlic clove, minced
Salt and pepper, to taste
½ cup half-and-half
1 tablespoon chopped fresh
 parsley

1. Place the potatoes in a pot and cover with cold water by 1 inch. Add the kosher salt, and bring to a very gentle simmer. Cook very slowly for about 20 minutes or until the potatoes are fork tender.

2. Meanwhile, heat 1 tablespoon of the butter in a pan until it stops bubbling. Add the mushrooms, garlic, and salt and pepper, and sauté until the water that releases from the mushrooms evaporates. Remove from heat.

3. Drain the potatoes very well. Mash the potatoes with the remaining butter and the half-and-half. Season with salt and pepper, and fold in the mushrooms and parsley. Keep hot, and serve.

Keeping Mashed Potatoes Hot

There are some great tips for keeping mashed potatoes hot for long periods of time. After the potatoes are finished, transfer them to a heat-proof container and cover well. Place the container in a pot filled with a few inches of water. Place the pot over a burner and heat the water until very hot, but don't let it boil. This will keep your potatoes hot without dirtying a pan.

Sweet Potato Mash with Sour Cream and Rosemary

2 medium-sized sweet
  potatoes
3 tablespoons sour cream
1 tablespoon chopped fresh
  rosemary
Salt and pepper, to taste

A great departure from those too-sweet potatoes that taste more like dessert.

1. Preheat oven to 350°F.

2. Wrap the potatoes in foil and place them directly on the oven rack. Bake the potatoes until a knife inserted in the deepest part comes free with no resistance. Let cool for about 5 minutes, until cool enough to handle.

3. Peel off the skin and place the potatoes in a bowl. Mash the potatoes with the sour cream, rosemary, and salt and pepper. Serve hot.

Roast Instead of Boil
Roasting the sweet potatoes as opposed to boiling them has a few advantages. The first is that there is no chance of the potatoes spending too much time in the water and becoming waterlogged and soggy. Second, the sugar in the potato remains in the potato instead of dissipating into the water.

Pesto Rice with Tomato

A great way to liven up plain old rice.

1 cup long-grain white rice
½ cup store-bought pesto
Salt and pepper, to taste

1. Place the rice and 2 cups of cold water in a small pot. Bring to a simmer, then reduce heat to the lowest setting. Cover, and cook for exactly 18 minutes. Remove from heat and let sit for 5 minutes, covered.

2. Add the pesto to the rice and season with salt and pepper. Serve.

Condimento

Pesto is among the many condimentos, or condiments, from the Italian table. Look for other products to add to rice or potatoes or pastas that will make life easier. Olive pastes, sun-dried tomato spreads, artichoke pastes, and many others are readily available in many supermarkets. Get creative!

Savory Marinated Mushrooms

These mushrooms are great as a simple side with a cold lunch or picnic.

1 pound assorted mushrooms
1 cup sherry vinegar
½ cup granulated sugar
¼ cup extra-virgin olive oil
Salt and pepper, to taste
1 tablespoon chopped fresh savory

Place everything in a small pan except the savory. Bring to a boil, then turn off heat and let cool to room temperature. Drain and toss with the savory.

Pickle It

This simple technique of boiling a vegetable in vinegar and sugar is a very simple pickling process. You can try this with almost any vegetables and add any seasonings you wish. This is a great way to preserve vegetables that are overabundant in the garden. Pick up a book on preserving and pickling, and have a ball!

Dominican Rice with Sofrito and Pigeon Peas

½ a small white onion, roughly chopped
½ red bell pepper, roughly chopped
3 scallions, roughly chopped
3 garlic cloves
3 tablespoons fresh cilantro leaves, chopped
1 teaspoon dried oregano
2 cups water
1 cup long-grained white rice
1 15-ounce can pigeon peas
1 tablespoon butter
Salt and pepper, to taste

The Dominican Republic plays host to a very flavorful cuisine, and rice is served with most meals.

1. Place the onion, pepper, scallions, garlic, cilantro, and oregano in a blender with 1 cup of the water. Purée until smooth.

2. Combine the onion purée, rice, peas, and the remaining water in a small pot. Bring to a boil, then reduce to a very low simmer. Cover, and cook for exactly 18 minutes. Let rest for 5 minutes, covered, then add the butter and salt and pepper.

Adding Flavor
The "sofrito" made in the blender in this recipe is one of many types. Create your own by using what you have in the fridge. This is a great way to utilize vegetable scraps as well as small scraps of sausage, bacon, or ham. You can also substitute broth for water anytime.

Cumin and Sweet Pea Basmati Rice

*Seek out basmati rice. The flavor is incredible,
and the perfume resembles popcorn. Very cool.*

1 cup Basmati rice
2 tablespoons butter, divided
1 small white onion, finely dice
1 garlic clove, minced
1 teaspoon cumin seeds
½ cup frozen baby peas, defrosted
1½ cups chicken stock
Salt and pepper, to taste

1. Wash the Basmati rice under cold running water until the water runs clear. Soak the rice in cold water for 30 minutes.

2. In a small saucepot, heat 1 tablespoon of the butter on medium, and sauté the onion, garlic, and cumin seeds for about 3 minutes or until the onions are lightly golden.

3. Drain the rice, add it to the pan, stir well. Add the peas and broth, and bring to a simmer. Immediately reduce the heat to the lowest setting, and cover the pot.

4. Cook for exactly 15 minutes. Remove from heat, and add the remaining butter and salt and pepper. Stir gently, to avoid breaking the grains of rice. Serve immediately.

Cumin

A very characteristic seasoning popular in Indian, Arabic, and Mexican cuisines, cumin is usually used ground. Here the whole seeds add a gentler perfume than if the ground seeds were used. You can also buy the seeds, toast them in a dry pan, and then grind them in a spice mill.

Roasted Caramelized Cauliflower

An amazing way to turn a rather mundane and unpopular vegetable into a crowd-pleaser. Try this recipe even if you think you do not like cauliflower.

1 small head cauliflower
3 tablespoons extra-virgin olive oil
Salt and pepper, to taste

1. Preheat the oven to the highest possible temperature.

2. Cut the cauliflower off of its core and separate the florets into roughly 2-inch pieces. Toss will the oil and a good amount of salt and pepper.

3. Place the florets on a baking sheet, well spaced. Roast until the florets are well browned, about 15 minutes. Serve at any temperature.

Caramelizing

The word caramelize comes from the great French chef Careme. It refers to any cooking process that allows the sugars in an ingredient to brown. The candies known as caramels are simply browned sugar with milk. Our cauliflower caramelizes because the natural sugars present turn brown on the surface of the vegetable.

Oven-Roasted Baby Artichokes

*A great way to enjoy this summer treat,
roasting is an easy and flavorful way to maximize the flavor
as well as ease the tedious process of cleaning the artichokes.*

½ cup dry white wine
¼ cup extra-virgin olive oil
Juice of 1 lemon
2 teaspoons dried oregano
Salt and pepper, to taste
About 2 pounds baby
    artichokes (the smallest
    you can find)

1. Preheat oven to 425°F.

2. Mix together the wine, oil, lemon juice, oregano, and salt and pepper. Pour the mixture onto a baking sheet.

3. Cut the artichokes in half through the stem and place them cut-side down on the baking sheet. Bake for about 25 minutes, or until the outer leaves are crispy and the innards are tender. Let cool slightly.

4. When the artichokes are cool enough to handle, grasp the crispy leaves and pull them back toward the stem. You will be left with a tender inner core that can all be eaten. The choke does not need to be removed from the small artichokes.

It Might Choke Arty, But It Won't Choke Me
The artichoke is the largest member of the thistle family. It is widely cultivated in California, and is very popular in all Mediterranean cultures. The edible parts are the stem, heart, and fleshy bases of the leaves. The "choke," or fibrous center, needs to be removed from the mature artichokes, but is unnoticeable in the baby ones.

Roasted Napa Cabbage

6 tablespoons vegetable oil
2 garlic cloves, crushed
6 cups roughly shredded
napa cabbage
Salt and pepper, to taste

Napa cabbage is much more delicate and sweeter than green or Savoy cabbage.
This is another surprising way to make an unpopular vegetable very popular.

1. Heat the oil in a skillet on low. Add the garlic cloves and cook very gently for 15 minutes. Discard the garlic, and toss the cabbage with the oil and salt and pepper.

2. Preheat the oven to 450°F.

3. Place the cabbage on a baking sheet and bake for about 15 minutes or until the tops of the cabbage pieces are browned. Serve hot.

Roasting Vegetables
Roasting vegetables in a very hot oven lightly coated with oil yields extraordinary results. The sugars caramelize and the rich deep flavors develop, which are lost in boiling or braising. Try roasting everything from asparagus to winter squash, and experiment with different oils and seasonings.

Savory Asparagus Custard

A simple and different way to serve asparagus, the egg flavor of the custard complements the asparagus perfectly.

1. Preheat the oven to 325°F.

2. Blanch the asparagus in boiling salted water for about 3 minutes or until barely tender. Shock in cold water and drain.

3. Mix together all the ingredients and divide between two 6- to 8-ounce ramekins. Place the ramekins in a baking pan, and fill the pan with water to about 1 inch up the sides of the ramekins. Place the pan in the oven, and bake until a toothpick inserted in the center of the custard comes out clean (about 30 minutes). Serve hot in the ramekins.

Asparagus and Eggs
Asparagus and eggs have a natural affinity for each other. In Italy and Spain, wild asparagus is picked in the spring, sautéed in butter or olive oil, and made into omelets. The Chinese have a soup with asparagus and eggs, and some adventurous chefs even make asparagus ice cream as a dessert, which is incredibly good.

1½ cups asparagus, cut into
  ½-inch pieces
4 eggs, lightly beaten
2 cups heavy cream
¼ cup grated Parmesan
  cheese
Salt and pepper, to taste

Creamed Spinach with Nutmeg and Parmesan

The secret to this recipe is long and slow cooking to achieve the depth and silky texture that good creamed spinach has.

2 tablespoons butter
2 tablespoons all-purpose flour
2 cups milk
1 pound frozen chopped spinach, defrosted and squeezed dry
2 garlic cloves, minced
Freshly grated nutmeg, to taste
Salt and pepper, to taste
¼ cup grated Parmesan cheese

1. In a saucepan, melt the butter over medium heat and add the flour, stirring well to make a smooth paste. Slowly stir in the cold milk, whisking constantly.

2. Add the spinach, garlic, nutmeg, and salt and pepper. Bring to a gentle simmer. Cook very slowly, uncovered, for about 1½ hours, stirring occasionally. If the mixture becomes too dry, add a bit of milk to it.

3. Add the Parmesan cheese and stir to mix. Adjust seasoning with salt and pepper. Serve hot.

Time Is of the Essence
Spinach is a vegetable that, in general, is almost always served undercooked. Sautéing spinach properly requires at least 7 or 8 minutes of cooking to ensure that all of the water evaporates and the spinach develops the most flavors. Also, cooking creamed spinach requires at least 1 hour to fully achieve the best texture and flavor. Seek out curly spinach. Avoid the so-called "flat-leaf" spinach, which is not spinach at all, but a relative with inferior flavor.

Orange-Glazed Baby Brussels Sprouts with Walnuts

*If you cannot find the marble-sized baby Brussels sprouts,
cut regular sprouts in half through the core.*

1 pound baby Brussels sprouts
2 tablespoons melted butter
2 tablespoons extra-virgin olive oil
Salt and pepper, to taste
2 cups fresh-squeezed orange juice
½ cup toasted walnuts

1. Preheat oven to 375°F.

2. Score the stems of the Brussels sprouts with a small knife in an X shape to ensure even cooking. Toss with the melted butter, oil, and salt and pepper. Place on a baking sheet and bake for about 25 minutes or until the sprouts are browned and tender.

3. Meanwhile, boil the orange juice in a small pan until about ½ cup remains. Set aside.

4. Toss the Brussels sprouts with the orange juice and return to the oven for 5 more minutes. Place on a platter and sprinkle the walnuts over the top.

Score!

Because the Brussels sprout has such a tough stem, it is very important that a small X be made deep into the stem to allow heat to penetrate into the core. If this step is not followed, the stem will be tough when the rest of the sprout is cooked through. This holds true for any cooking method, especially boiling.

Braised Red Cabbage

This recipe is always a favorite. Complex, sweet, rich, and creamy,
you'll get a lot of requests for this dish.

4 tablespoons butter, divided
1 large white onion, thinly
   sliced
6 cups shredded red cabbage
1 Granny Smith apple, peeled,
   cored, and roughly
   chopped
2 tablespoons red wine
   vinegar
¼ cup granulated sugar
1 cup dry red wine
½ cup water
1 whole clove
1 small cinnamon stick
Salt and pepper, to taste

1. Melt half of the butter in a pot and add the onion. Sauté the onion until it begins to soften. Add the remaining ingredients except the remaining 2 tablespoons butter.

2. Bring to a boil, then reduce heat to low. Cook very gently for 1 hour and 15 minutes, covered. Turn off heat and add the remaining butter. Adjust seasoning with salt and pepper, and serve.

Keep It Red
Foods with red pigments such as red cabbage and beets will keep their brilliant red color during cooking if a small amount of acid is present. Add a bit of vinegar, wine, or lemon juice to these vegetables and their color will fix. This is important for presentation purposes.

Broccoli di Rape

Broccoli di Rape, or broccoli raab, is a member of the broccoli family with a bitter edge.

1 bunch broccoli raab
2 tablespoons extra-virgin olive oil
1 garlic clove, minced
Pinch dried red pepper flakes
2 tablespoons toasted pine nuts
2 tablespoons golden raisins
Salt and pepper, to taste

1. Boil the broccoli in plenty of salted water for 3 minutes. Cool in ice water and drain.

2. Heat the olive oil on medium in a sauté pan and add the garlic and red pepper flakes. Sauté until the garlic is golden. Add the pine nuts, raisins, and broccoli. Sauté until the broccoli is hot. Season with salt and pepper, and serve.

Culinary History
The combination of raisins and nuts was brought to Southern Italy by Arabs during the spice trade. This combination of sweet and savory is very popular in North Africa and most Arabic countries. This same influence brought the widespread use of nutmeg to many Italian dishes.

Barley Risotto with Caramelized Onions

Although not a true risotto, the high starch content of barley gives this dish the texture of the true dish. If it's too thick, add a bit more broth and butter.

2 tablespoons butter
1 large white onion, finely diced
½ cup pearl barley
½ cup dry white wine
4 cups chicken broth
½ cup grated Parmesan cheese
3 tablespoons chopped fresh parsley
Salt and pepper, to taste

1. Heat the butter in a pot on medium and cook the onion until well browned. Add the barley and the wine, and cook until the wine evaporates.

2. Add the broth and simmer very gently until the barley is done, about 35 minutes.

3. Turn off the heat and stir in the cheese and the parsley. Season to taste with salt and pepper, and serve.

Thanksgiving Stuffing with Sweet Sausage

This is a treat even when it's not Thanksgiving.
Serve it alongside roast chicken anytime.

2 tablespoons butter
6 ounces sweet sausage, casing removed
½ cup small-diced white onion
½ cup peeled and small-diced carrots
½ cup small-diced celery
1 teaspoon fresh thyme leaves
2 cups stale bread cubes
1 egg, lightly beaten
1 cup chicken broth
Salt and pepper, to taste

1. Heat the butter in a pan on medium-high, and brown the sausage until it crumbles. Remove the sausage, but keep the fat in the pan.

2. Preheat oven to 375°F.

3. Sauté the onion, carrot, celery, and thyme in the fat until the vegetables begin to soften, about 5 minutes).

4. In a bowl, combine the sausage, sautéed vegetables, bread, egg, chicken stock, and salt and pepper. Place in a small casserole dish and bake for 35 minutes or until the top is well browned and the middle is piping hot.

Stale Is Better
The reason stale bread makes the best stuffing is that most of the moisture in the bread has evaporated slowly, leaving the bread as a virtual sponge for the broth and flavors. Another option is to make toasted croutons, but the texture is not as pleasant as the stale bread.

Parsnip Gratin

Parsnips are sometimes called white carrots, and look as though they should be.

3 cups peeled and sliced parsnips (about ¼ inch thick)
1½ cups heavy cream
2 tablespoons grated Parmesan cheese
Salt and pepper, to taste

1. Preheat oven to 400°F.

2. Mix together all the ingredients and place in a small ovenproof dish. Bake for about 40 minutes or until the top is well browned and the parsnips are tender. Remover from the oven and let stand for 10 minutes before serving.

Can All Vegetables Go in a Gratin?
Vegetables that do well in a gratin are sturdy and starchy vegetables such as turnips, winter squash, potatoes, carrots, and the like. The starch helps thicken the cream as well as to hold the gratin together. Experiment with different vegetables and herbs to come up with your own signature gratin.

Butternut Squash Soufflé

With such a sweet pumpkinlike flavor,
butternut squash has become a fall favorite.

3 cups peeled and diced
  butternut squash
½ cup half-and-half
2 eggs, lightly beaten
¼ cup grated Parmesan
  cheese
2 tablespoons butter
Salt and pepper, to taste
12 sage leaves

1. In a pot, simmer the butternut in salted water until very tender, about 15 minutes. Drain, and whisk until smooth.

2. Preheat oven to 400°F.

3. Add all the remaining ingredients except the sage and butter to the squash, and whisk well. Bake in a casserole dish for 15 minutes or until browned and bubbly.

4. Heat the butter in a small pan on medium heat until it stops bubbling. Add the sage leaves and fry until crispy, about 1 minute. Arrange the sage leaves on top of the soufflé, and pour the sage-flavored butter over the top.

The Flavors of Fall
Sage is often used in the fall to complement poultry, game, and vegetables. Other flavors of fall include pumpkin, mushrooms, thyme, wild game, apples, pears, and rosemary. Play with these combinations. Who says rosemary and apples don't work? Try it!

chapter 13
sandwiches

Chipotle Chicken Club Sandwich

A chipotle is a smoked and dried jalapeño pepper.
This flavor is quickly gaining popularity in the United States.

4 tablespoons mayonnaise
1 teaspoon store-bought
    chipotle pepper purée
6 slices whole-wheat bread,
    toasted
½ ripe avocado, mashed into
    a paste
½ pound cooked chicken
    breast, thinly sliced
8 slices slab bacon, cooked
    until crispy
1 large ripe tomato, thinly
    sliced
Several lettuce leaves

1. Mix together the mayonnaise and chipotle pepper purée. Spread the spicy mayonnaise on 4 slices of the bread.

2. Spread the avocado on the remaining 2 slices of bread.

3. Build the sandwiches: Top 2 of the mayo-spread bread slices with the chicken. Place an avocado-spread bread slice, avocado side down, on top of each. Divide the bacon, tomato, and lettuce on top of each sandwich. Finish by placing 1 of the remaining mayo-spread slices of bread on top of each sandwich.

4. Place 4 toothpicks in each sandwich and slice into quarters.

Join the Club

A club sandwich is a triple-decker sandwich with a BLT component. Basically you can make anything into a club sandwich by putting a BLT on top of it. The classics are turkey or roast beef, but do not be confined to these basics. Any grilled fish, cold cut, or even vegetable works great.

Smoked Turkey and Brie

This is a simple and elegant sandwich with a twist.

2 tablespoons prepared cranberry sauce
4 tablespoons Dijon mustard
4 slices multigrain bread, toasted
½ pound thinly sliced smoked deli turkey
6 ounces soft Brie cheese, thinly sliced
2 large lettuce leaves

1. Mix together the cranberry sauce and mustard. Spread on one side of each slice of bread.

2. Build the sandwiches with the turkey, cheese, and lettuce, and enjoy.

Dijon Mustard
Dijon mustard is from the town of Dijon in France. This region has been famous for its smooth and light mustards, which are sometimes made with the local white wine. There are countless varieties of mustards from all over the world, and you should try many of them.

Grilled Kielbasa Sandwiches

Try to seek out a Polish market for the best kielbasa.

¾ pound kielbasa, sliced into 4-inch-long pieces about ¼ inch thick
4 slices good rye bread with seeds
1 cup hot sauerkraut
3 tablespoons Polish-style mustard

Grill or sauté the kielbasa for 1 minute per side. Place on the bread and top with the kraut and mustard. Serve with plenty of cold beer and pickles for a Polish treat.

Flavors of Poland
The Poles are known for being expert sausage makers and meat smokers. Also popular in their cuisine are mustards, cabbages, caraway seeds, mushrooms, poppy seeds, and all manner of pork products. Try to seek out a Polish market and explore the rich and delicious foods of this nation.

True Cuban Sandwich

2 (8-inch) soft hero rolls, split
¼ pound Swiss cheese, sliced
½ pound cooked roast pork,
thinly sliced
4 slices smoked ham
2 garlicky dill pickles, very
thinly sliced
2 tablespoons melted butter
1 garlic clove, minced

The trick to this sandwich is the pressing and grilling.
This is a perfect use of leftover pork chops.

1. Assemble the sandwiches by lining both sides of the bread with the sliced cheese. Then pile on the pork, ham, and pickles. Close up the sandwiches.

2. Mix together the butter and garlic. Brush the garlic butter on both sides of the bread.

3. Heat a large, heavy skillet on medium-low and place the sandwiches in the pan. Take another heavy pan and press it on top of the sandwiches to press them down while they grill. Turn them over when one side is well browned and the cheese begins to melt. Grill the other side, and press again to really flatten out the sandwich. Serve hot.

Finding Cubanos in the USA
Anywhere that there is a Cuban neighborhood, you can find Cuban sandwiches, or Cubanos. The small local shops that cater to the working class are the best places to find these treats. Look for the telltale sandwich press, usually coated with aluminum foil, to tell you this treat is available. Order a Cubano with a café con leche, and enjoy a truly Cuban delicacy.

Roasted Portobello Mushroom Burger

These meaty mushrooms do a great stand-in for the traditional burger. Use the largest you can find.

2 large portobello
    mushrooms, caps only
2 tablespoons Worcestershire
    sauce
2 tablespoons olive oil
2 hamburger buns, toasted
A few slices red onion
1 ripe tomato, thinly sliced
Several iceberg lettuce leaves
2 slices American cheese

1. Preheat oven to 400°F.

2. Using a spoon, scrape out the black "gills" on the bottom of each mushroom cap. Peel off the "skin" from the top of the caps. (This is easily done with your hands.)

3. Mix together the Worcestershire sauce and olive oil, and brush over the top and bottom of the mushroom caps. Place the mushrooms stem-side up on a lightly greased baking sheet. Bake for 15 minutes.

4. Assemble the burgers as you would a traditional hamburger.

Worcestershire Sauce
This complex sauce, developed in England, has a host of unusual ingredients including tamarind and anchovy. Some strict vegans and vegetarians will not eat this sauce because of the anchovy component. Using Worcestershire sauce in marinades and sauces adds an unusual "meaty" or "beefy" quality to the product.

Curried Tuna Salad Sandwich

The water chestnuts in this tuna salad replace the traditional celery crunch.

2 (6-ounce) cans tuna packed
    in water, drained
¼ cup chopped canned water
    chestnuts
2 scallions, finely minced
3 tablespoons mayonnaise
2 teaspoons sweet relish
1 tablespoon curry powder
Salt and pepper, to taste
4 slices sourdough bread,
    toasted
1 cup shredded lettuce

1. Prepare the tuna salad by mixing together the tuna, water chestnuts, scallions, mayonnaise, relish, curry powder, and salt and pepper.

2. Divide the shredded lettuce between 2 slices of the bread and pile the tuna salad on top. Top with the remaining bread, and serve.

Bologna with Crumbled Potato Chips

This is a very playful sandwich that harkens back to childhood after-school treats.

3 tablespoons mayonnaise
1 tablespoon Dijon mustard
4 slices white bread
1 cup shredded iceberg
    lettuce
½ pound bologna, thinly
    sliced
1 (1-ounce) bag potato chips,
    crushed
1 ripe tomato, sliced

1. Mix together the mayonnaise and mustard, and spread on all the bread slices.

2. Top 2 slices with the shredded lettuce and bologna. Crumble potato chips all over the bologna and top with the tomato and the remaining bread.

Nothing but Bologna
American bologna is inspired by the famous cold cut from the town of Bologna in Italy called mortadella. Mortadella is very similar to bologna, but it is garnished throughout with pistachios, black pepper, and pieces of pork fat. This is the real Bologna and is a very special cold cut.

Smoked Salmon and Cucumber Sandwich

This sandwich works well for any meal, breakfast, lunch, or dinner!

1 small peeled cucumber,
    very thinly sliced
1 teaspoon salt
1 tablespoon white wine
    vinegar
1 teaspoon granulated sugar
¼ cup minced red onion
½ cup cream cheese, softened
4 slices pumpernickel bread,
    toasted
½ pound smoked salmon
    (lox)
1 teaspoon chopped fresh dill
1 large ripe tomato, thinly
    sliced

1. Toss the sliced cucumber with 1 teaspoon of salt and let purge for 10 minutes. Squeeze the cukes dry and toss with the vinegar and sugar.

2. Mix together the onion and cream cheese, and spread on all 4 slices of bread. Top 2 slices with tomato, then the salmon, then the cucumbers. Top off with the remaining bread, and serve.

Cold Vs. Hot Smoking
Smoked salmon (lox) is a cold smoked product. This means that the temperature in the smoker does not reach a high enough temperature to cook the meat of the fish. Hot smoking is a process when the smoker is well over 140°F and the product gets fully cooked.

Boneless Barbecue Ribwich

The trick here is to cook the ribs long enough so the bones slide out.

1 rack baby back ribs
Salted water to fill a pot
½ cup store-bought barbecue
    sauce
2 (8-inch) soft hero rolls
1 cup store-bought or
    homemade coleslaw

1. Cut the rack of ribs in half and place in a pot of water with the salt. Simmer very gently for about 2 hours or until the bones pull free but the meat is not falling apart. Remove the ribs from the water and use a paper towel to pull the bones straight out.

2. Preheat broiler.

3. Place the ribs on a baking sheet and brush with the barbecue sauce. Broil until the tops are bubbling and browned.

4. Fill each roll with the rib meat and top with the coleslaw. Eat at any temperature.

Different Kinds of Ribs
A few different ribs are available in today's market. Spare ribs are the most popular. They are affordable and meaty, and have a fair amount of fat and cartilage. Country-style ribs are much meatier, but they contain meat from the loin and are not as tender and unctuous as spare ribs. Baby backs are the most refined, with a nice bone-to-meat ratio, and are very easy to eat. They are the most expensive.

Warm Mortadella on Focaccia

This is a classic Italian treat. Italy is famous for its sandwich bars, which are filled to capacity each day.

1. Preheat oven to 400°F.

2. Split the focaccia and drizzle the inside of each with the olive oil. Add basil leaves, mortadella, and mozzarella. Place on a baking sheet, and bake for 6 minutes. Eat hot.

The European Sandwich
In Europe, particularly Italy, sandwiches are more modest than their American cousins. There is almost never an overabundance of meats and cheeses; instead, the sandwiches rely on a simple ratio of a little bit of meat, some great bread, and a small amount of condiments. Rarely will lettuce or tomato be featured, as many sandwiches are served warm.

Focaccia bread (enough to make 2 sandwiches)
¼ cup extra-virgin olive oil
8 ounces mortadella, thinly sliced
6 ounces fresh mozzarella cheese, cut into ¼-inch-thick slices
12 basil leaves, washed and dried

Thanksgiving on a Roll

*This is best made the days following Thanksgiving using leftovers,
but is great anytime.*

½ cup cranberry sauce
1 tablespoon mustard
2 large soft rolls, split
2 tablespoons butter
2 cups prepared stuffing
½ pound fresh cooked turkey breast
½ cup prepared brown gravy

1. Mix together the cranberry sauce and mustard, and spread on the rolls.

2. Melt the butter in a sauté pan and heat the stuffing well, slightly browning it. Pile it on the roll.

3. Heat the turkey in the gravy and pile on top of the stuffing. Get a large napkin and a beer, and enjoy!

Turkey and Tryptophan

Tryptophan is a chemical present in turkey that promotes sleep. Besides the fact that you have eaten a load of food and then sat down on the couch, another reason you are tired after Thanksgiving may be your reaction to this chemical. (Or perhaps you are just exhausted from your crazy relatives and hectic cooking!)

Peanut Butter and Bacon

This is an incredibly delicious combination that needs to be tried to be believed. Have faith!

ℰ

Spread the peanut butter on the bread, and top with the bacon. Close up the sandwiches, and revel in the complex play of flavors and textures.

Why It Works
Peanut and peanut-based sauces are common in many cultures and are often served in a savory and not sweet style. The famous satays of Asia, the African peanut soups, and the Chinese peanut-flavored dishes are just a few examples of the savory use of peanuts. If this doesn't convince you to try this sandwich, nothing will!

1 cup peanut butter (preferably natural)
4 slices white bread
8 slices bacon, cooked until crisp

Grilled Cheese with Mayonnaise

This is an excellent grilled cheese sandwich!

ℰ

Assemble the cheese sandwiches. Spread the outsides of the bread with the mayonnaise and place in a nonstick pan over medium heat until both sides are crispy and brown. Eat hot, but don't burn your mouth!

Unconventional Uses of Mayonnaise
Mayonnaise is made from oil and eggs, with oil being the dominant ingredient. Other uses for mayo are as a basting for a thanksgiving turkey, or even as an oil substitute in Caesar dressing. It's not just for sandwiches!

4 slices white bread
½ pound yellow American cheese
Mayonnaise, to taste

Mexican-Style Beef "Torta"

*The torta is a classic Mexican street food that is
a sandwich piled on a soft roll with avocado.*

¾ pound trimmed skirt steak
2 tablespoons olive oil
1 teaspoon ground cumin
Salt and pepper, to taste
2 large soft rolls
2 cups shredded iceberg
    lettuce
1 large ripe tomato, sliced
Several slices red onion
1 ripe Haas avocado, sliced
1 lime
Mexican hot sauce, to taste

1. Rub the steak with the oil, cumin, and salt and pepper. Sear in a hot pan for 3 minutes per side. Allow the meat to rest while you assemble the rest of the sandwich.

2. Pile the rolls with the lettuce, tomato, onion, and avocado. Squeeze the lime over the avocado.

3. Slice the meat across the grain into ¼-inch slices and pile on the rolls. Sprinkle with hot sauce and enjoy.

Viva Mexico!
Street food in Mexico is elevated to an art form. The streets are filled with all manner of carts and stalls offering everything from goat's head tacos to fresh fruit shakes. The most popular foods are the tacos and tortas. You will see many signs reading "Ricos Tacos" or "Ricos Tortas" all over Mexico. Here you can choose toppings and different meats to make your sandwich original.

Souvlaki-Style Lamb Sandwich

The key to the sauce is to drain the yogurt overnight to make it thick and delicious.

1 cup plain, whole yogurt
2 garlic cloves, minced
Salt and pepper, to taste
¾ pound cooked leg of lamb, thinly sliced
Juice of 1 lemon
2 tablespoons olive oil
2 teaspoons dried oregano
2 cups shredded lettuce
1 ripe tomato, diced
1 small red onion, finely minced
2 large pocketless pita bread rounds

1. Place the yogurt in a strainer lined with a coffee filter, set inside a bowl, and drain overnight in the refrigerator. Discard the liquid and mix the yogurt with the garlic and salt and pepper.

2. Toss the sliced lamb with the lemon juice, olive oil, oregano, and some salt and pepper. Heat the lamb gently in a pan just to warm.

3. Toss together the lettuce, tomato, and onion with the yogurt sauce and pile on the bread. Top with the warm lamb and fold each pita over itself. Serve immediately.

Curds and Whey
Draining the yogurt separates the curds of the yogurt from the whey, or liquid. This step allows the yogurt to concentrate in flavor as well as to thicken nicely into a great sauce.

Fried Calamari Po' Boy

Make sure the oil you fry the calamari in is clean and hot.

1 pound calamari tubes and
  tentacles, cut into ½-inch
  pieces
3 cups all-purpose flour
2 tablespoons garlic powder
2 teaspoons cayenne pepper
Salt and pepper, to taste
Peanut oil, for deep-frying
2 long, soft hero rolls, split
2 cups shredded iceberg
  lettuce
1 large tomato, thinly sliced
1 lemon
Tabasco sauce, to taste
½ cup tartar sauce

1. Toss the calamari with the flour, garlic powder, cayenne, and salt and pepper. Shake off excess flour and deep-fry in 3 batches in 375°F oil for 1 minute each. Drain on paper towels and season with salt while still hot from the fryer.

2. Fill each roll with the lettuce and tomato. Pile on the fried calamari, squeeze lemon over the top, and sprinkle with Tabasco sauce. Top with the tartar sauce, and serve.

The Big Easy
A po' boy or "poor boy" is a style of sandwich made famous in New Orleans. It can be anything from fried oysters to fried fish, but is always on a long, soft roll and usually has a mayonnaise-type sauce such as tartar or remoulade. This works well with any seafood, and even some vegetables such as eggplant and mushrooms.

Sliced Steak Sandwich with Horseradish Sauce

Hanger steak is the key to this affordable and delicious sandwich.

1. Marinate the steak in the Worcestershire sauce, red wine, and garlic powder for 2 hours.

2. Preheat oven to 425°F.

3. Roast the steak in the oven for about 13 minutes or until the internal temperature reaches 145°F (for medium).

4. Heat a large skillet and add the oil. Sauté the onions and mushrooms for about 5 minutes or until the liquid that releases from the mushrooms evaporates. Season with salt and pepper, and set aside.

5. Mix together the horseradish, sour cream, mayonnaise, and salt and pepper.

6. Slice the steak thinly across the grain of the meat. (Ignore the tendon that runs through this cut of meat; it is tender as long as it is sliced well.) Pile the meat on the rolls, top with the mushrooms and onions, and spoon the sauce over the top. Serve immediately.

1½ pounds trimmed hanger
   steak
3 tablespoons Worcestershire
   sauce
½ cup red wine
1 teaspoon garlic powder
4 tablespoons olive oil
1 large white onion, sliced
10 white mushrooms, sliced
Salt and pepper, to taste
2 tablespoons sour cream
2 tablespoons mayonnaise
2 teaspoons horseradish
2 crusty hero rolls, split

Decadent Pâté Sandwich with Spicy Asian Slaw

This is a twist on a classic Vietnamese sandwich that was originally influenced by the French occupation of Vietnam.

3 cups shredded napa cabbage
1 jalapeño pepper, minced
1 teaspoon minced fresh gingerroot
2 tablespoons granulated sugar
¼ cup rice vinegar
2 tablespoons fresh cilantro leaves, chopped
Salt, to taste
2 long, soft rolls, split
8 ounces liver pâté or braunschweiger liverwurst

1. Mix together the cabbage, jalapeño, ginger, sugar, vinegar, cilantro, and some salt. Let stand for 30 minutes, then drain.

2. Toast the insides of the rolls, spread with the pâté, and top with the slaw. Enjoy!

Choosing Pâté
Pâté is usually made from a combination of pork and duck livers. It is a very elegant item that exudes luxury. Look for pâtés that are smooth in texture, not the rough "country-style" pâtés, which are better suited to be eaten alone or on crackers. The silky texture of a fine pâté is what makes this sandwich so special.

Sautéed Salmon Club with Spicy Mayonnaise

This sandwich is a winner. The rich salmon and bacon are perfectly offset by the spicy mayo and crispy lettuce.

2 thin salmon fillets (about 6 ounces each)
1 tablespoon olive oil
Salt and pepper, to taste
4 tablespoons mayonnaise
1 teaspoon Tabasco sauce
6 slices rye bread, toasted
6 slices bacon, cooked until crispy
4 romaine lettuce leaves
1 ripe tomato, thinly sliced

1. Rub the salmon with the oil and season with salt and pepper. Sauté in a hot pan for about 3 minutes per side or until the fish is just cooked. Set aside.

2. Mix together the mayonnaise and Tabasco, and spread on all the bread slices. Top 2 of the slices of bread with the bacon, lettuce, and tomato. Top each with another slice of bread, then the salmon, and another slice of bread. Slice the triple-decker in quarters and serve.

The Fuss about Salmon

Salmon has gotten a lot of press recently, both negative and positive. The crux seems to be that salmon is rich in omega-3 fatty acids, which are a very healthy form of fat. However, the majority of salmon served in the United States is farm raised, and may contain higher than desirable levels of toxins because of conditions in the farms. Continue to enjoy salmon, but in moderation, perhaps 2 or 3 times a month.

NY-Style Italian Combo Submarine

This is a classic in the New York area.
The key is finding the authentic Italian-style cold cuts.

6 tablespoons extra-virgin olive oil

4 tablespoons red wine vinegar

2 teaspoons dried oregano

2 long submarine rolls, split almost all the way through

3 cups shredded iceberg lettuce

1 ripe tomato, thinly sliced

½ cup roasted red peppers, drained and rinsed

4 ounces prosciutto, thinly sliced

4 ounces mortadella, thinly sliced

4 ounces capicola ham

4 ounces provolone cheese, sliced

1. Mix together the oil, vinegar, and oregano, and drizzle on the insides of the rolls. Pile the lettuce, tomato, and roasted peppers in the roll.

2. Add the meats and cheese to the sandwich by folding each slice to make the sandwich more full and less dense.

What's in a Name?

Different parts of the country have different names for the long, rolled sandwich referred to as a submarine. In New England, the term is grinder. In many parts of the country the term is hero, and in Philly and New York, the term is submarine. Whichever name you use, the sandwiches are still all delicious.

Rotisserie Chicken Salad Panini

Make this sandwich when you have leftover roast chicken.

½ pound cooked chicken meat, pulled apart roughly
2 tablespoons mayonnaise
1 teaspoon paprika
1 teaspoon garlic powder
1 teaspoon onion powder
Salt and pepper, to taste
4 slices good white or wheat bread
Cooking spray

1. Mix together the chicken, mayonnaise, and all the spices. Pile on the bread and make 2 sandwiches.

2. Spray the outside of the bread with cooking spray and toast in a hot pan or in a clamshell grill for 2 minutes per side.

Dry Spices Vs. Fresh
In this recipe, onion and garlic powders are used instead of fresh onion and garlic. The reason this is sometimes done is that the flavor is desired but the texture of the ingredient is not. Do not substitute these items for fresh vegetables in soups or main dishes, but do experiment with them in spice blends and rubs.

Grilled Peanut Butter and Banana Sandwich

4 thick slices white bread
½ cup peanut butter
1 large banana, thinly sliced
3 tablespoons softened butter

Already an American classic, this sandwich benefits greatly from a crispy grilling.

1. Make 2 peanut butter and banana sandwiches. Spread the outside of all the bread slices with the softened butter.

2. Place each sandwich in a nonstick pan over medium heat. Fry on both sides until well browned and the peanut butter is oozy and hot.

Go USA!

Peanut butter was invented in the United States and was originally used as a high-protein/calorie food for our troops in their rations. It gained much popularity when the troops returned home and has been a favorite ever since. Try to seek out natural peanut butter, which has less salt, sugar, and fat than most commercial brands.

chapter 14
sweets and desserts

Pears Poached in White Wine and Vanilla

2 cups water
2 cups dry white wine
Juice of 1 lemon
2 firm pears, peeled and
    cored
1 cinnamon stick
2 cups granulated sugar
1 vanilla bean, split

Simple and elegant, poached pears are always a treat. Make them ahead and keep them in the fridge; they will last for 2 weeks.

1. In a small pot, mix together the water, wine, and lemon juice. Add the pears, cinnamon, sugar, and vanilla, and heat to just below a simmer.

2. Place a clean dish towel on top of the pears to keep them from floating too high. Allow the towel to totally soak.

3. Cook very gently for about 13 minutes or until a small knife inserted in the bottom of the pear comes free with no resistance. Pour the pears and liquid into a shallow dish and place in the refrigerator to cool, uncovered. Serve the pears in bowls with some of the liquid poured on top.

Poaching Vs. Boiling
The difference between boiling and poaching is the temperature and movement of the water. Poach items that are delicate and risk falling apart if cooked too fast, such as fruit or fish. The temperature of the liquid should be between 185 and 200°F so the water does not move fast or boil.

Baked Apples with Pecan Butter

This makes a nice and simple fall dessert.
These also make a homey addition to the Thanksgiving dessert table.

2 tablespoons butter
½ cup toasted pecan pieces
2 tablespoons brown sugar
1 teaspoon ground cinnamon
2 teaspoons bourbon
2 cooking apples (such
   as Granny Smith or
   Cortland), cored but left
   whole

1. Preheat oven to 350°F.

2. Mix together all the ingredients except the apples. Stuff the mixture into the cavity in the apples. Place in a baking dish and bake for about 20 minutes or until the apples are soft. Place the apples on a plate and pour all the juices in the pan over the tops.

Apple Trees

Apple trees are actually bushes that people have trained to grow upright as trees. The other interesting thing about apples is that each time a seed is planted, a different kind of apple will grow, not necessarily the same kind that was planted. Because of this fact, apples are always grown from cuttings or "clones" to ensure that the same type of apple grows.

Grilled Pineapple with Caramel Ice Cream

This is a great summertime dessert when the grill is already in use.
Try with peaches too!

½ medium pineapple, cored
  and cut into ½-inch-thick
  slices
2 tablespoons vegetable oil
Salt and pepper, to taste
3 cups caramel or dulce de
  leche ice cream

1. Preheat grill. Toss the pineapple with the oil and salt and pepper. Grill over high heat until both sides are well browned. Place on a cutting board and chop into bite-sized pieces.

2. Place the ice cream in bowls and top with the warm pineapple chunks.

Salt and Pepper on Dessert?
Most desserts have a salt component because salt helps the human palette to better recognize different tastes. The desserts are not "salty" but just plain taste better. Adding pepper to this and other desserts adds an interesting note that is hard to pinpoint, but adds a level of complexity and surprise.

Figs Roasted with Sweet Cheese and Licorice

This is a sophisticated and elegant dessert. Serve after an Italian-style meal.

½ cup cream cheese
1 tablespoon granulated
  sugar
1 egg yolk
½ teaspoon ground fennel
¼ teaspoon ground
  cinnamon
8 ripe figs, stems removed
1 tablespoon melted butter
Salt and pepper, to taste

1. Preheat oven to 400°F. Cut a small X into the bottom of each fig.

2. Mix together the cheese, sugar, egg yolk, fennel, and cinnamon. Place in a piping bag and pipe the mixture into the bottom of each fig.

3. Place the figs on a baking sheet. Brush the figs with the butter, and season with salt and pepper. Bake for 7 minutes. Serve warm.

Piping Bag Basics
Properly fill a piping bag by folding the sides over a few inches and filling the bag no more than halfway with your mixture. Squeeze the top of the bag gently to push out the product smoothly.

Ice Cream Sandwiches with Toasted Almonds

This is a fun way to get kids involved with food preparation.

½ cup toasted almonds
2 (6-ounce) scoops vanilla ice
  cream
4 large Chocolate Chunk
  Cookies with Sweet Milk
  Sauce (page 267)

1. Grind the almonds in a food processor until fine.

2. Place the ice cream between the cookies and squeeze down to make 2 sandwiches. Roll the edges in the toasted almonds and serve.

Interesting Almonds
Almonds are the seed of a fruit that is related to peaches and apricots. The fruit is quite small and bitter and is rarely eaten. The almonds are extracted from the fuzzy little fruits and dried. Almonds are full of healthy fat and are a nutritious snack.

Roasted Peach Crisp

*Simple and heartwarming, this dish is best to make
when peaches are at their peak in late summer.*

2 ripe peaches, cut in half and
    seed removed
3 tablespoons melted butter,
    divided
½ cup granola
¼ cup all-purpose flour
1 tablespoon brown sugar
Pinch salt
Juice of 1 lemon

1. Preheat oven to 400°F.

2. Place the peaches skin-side up on a baking sheet and brush them with
   1 tablespoon of the butter. Roast for 10 minutes. Remove from oven and
   let cool. Reduce oven temperature to 375°F.

3. Grease two 6-ounce ramekins. Peel off the skins from the peaches and
   cut the flesh into 1-inch chunks. Place the peaches in the ramekins.

4. Mix together all the remaining ingredients. Add the granola topping to
   the ramekins, and bake for 12 minutes. Serve with vanilla ice cream.

Crisps, Crumbles, and Cobblers
*These terms are often used interchangeably. A cobbler is a deep-dish
fruit dessert with a dough topping. A crisp is what we have made here,
which is fresh fruit with a crumb topping of some sort. A crumble is the
British term for our crisp.*

Chocolate Chunk Cookies with Sweet Milk Sauce

Cookies and milk are a classic.
Here we put a twist on this dish with a caramelized milk sauce.

½ pound sweet butter
¾ cup granulated sugar
1 cup light brown sugar
½ teaspoon vanilla extract
1 egg, plus 1 egg yolk
3 cups all-purpose flour
½ teaspoon salt
1 teaspoon baking soda
6 ounces chocolate chunks
1 can sweetened condensed
milk

1. Preheat oven to 325°F.

2. Mix together the butter, both sugars, and vanilla until smooth. Slowly add the eggs, and mix well.

3. In a separate bowl, mix together the flour, salt, and baking soda. Mix this into the sugar mixture. Fold in the chocolate.

4. Form the dough into 6 large balls. Place these balls on a cookie sheet lined with parchment paper. Bake for 20 minutes or until lightly browned all over. Remove from oven and let cool. Increase oven temperature to 425°F.

4. Pour the sweetened condensed milk into a standard 9-inch pie tin. Place the pie tin in a baking pan and fill the pan with water to about ½ inch up the sides of the tin. Cover the baking pan with foil, and bake for 1 hour. The milk will thicken and turn a caramel brown. Cool to room temperature, and serve over the cookies.

Caramelized Milk
In Mexico this sauce is known as dulce de leche, which translates as "sweet milk." It is traditionally made with goat milk that is slowly cooked for hours to allow the milk sugars to brown. This recipe uses a shortcut and makes a nice sauce. Just don't forget about it in the oven!

Dark Chocolate "Salami" with Biscotti Chunks

7 ounces sweetened
    condensed milk
10 ounces semisweet
    chocolate morsels
1 tablespoon butter
½ cup toasted hazelnuts
2 biscotti cookies, broken into
    ¼-inch pieces

This is a fun dessert with a play on words.
The "salami" is really just the shape of this dessert.

1. In a small saucepan, heat the condensed milk, chocolate, and butter until smooth. Remove from heat and add the nuts and biscotti pieces.

2. Pour out onto a cookie sheet lined with plastic wrap and let cool for 10 minutes.

3. Roll the plastic wrap around the mixture and form into a long tube. Tighten the ends down and refrigerate until firm. Slice and serve.

Sweetness in Chocolate

Chocolate has many levels of sweetness. Milk, semisweet, bitter, and unsweetened are just a few. The recipe here can be made with any kind of chocolate, but semisweet is recommended because the milk is so sweet. Americans tend to like milk chocolate while Europeans prefer more bitter chocolates. Experiment and see which type you like the best.

Chocolate and Coffee Semifredo

Don't eat this dish late at night; the caffeine will keep you up!

ℰ

1. Whip the cream with the brewed coffee until soft peaks form. Chill in the refrigerator.

2. Place the sugar and corn syrup in a small pan and slowly add the water. Cook over medium-high heat until the sugar has dissolved. Stop stirring, and cook until the mixture reaches 240°F.

3. Whip the egg whites until stiff peaks form. Add the salt, and pour the corn syrup mixture into the bowl. Whip for about 5 minutes, until it reaches room temperature.

4. Fold in the chocolate, butter, ground coffee, and the chilled whipped cream. Pour into two 6-ounce ramekins, and freeze overnight.

Semifredo
This translates literally as "half frozen." This is not an ice cream, yet not a mousse. It is almost a frozen mousse. Semifredos are a popular dessert in Italy, especially during the warmer months. They can be made with fruit and a myriad of other flavors.

½ cup heavy cream
2 teaspoons cold brewed coffee
½ cup granulated sugar
2 teaspoons light corn syrup
3 tablespoons water
3 egg whites
Pinch kosher salt
3 ounces bittersweet chocolate, melted and cooled to room temperature
1 tablespoon sweet butter, melted
1 tablespoon finely ground coffee

Mexican Hot Chocolate Float

4 squares Mexican chocolate
3 cups milk
2 scoops coffee ice cream
Ground cinnamon, for
    dusting

Mexican hot chocolate can be purchased at any Mexican grocery.
Look for the Ibarra brand.

Place the chocolate and milk in a small pot. Heat to just under a boil, then transfer to a blender. Blend on high for 30 seconds, and pour into large coffee mugs. Top with a scoop of ice cream and dust with cinnamon.

Mexican Chocolate

Mexican chocolate is an interesting mix of chocolate, ground almonds, sugar, and cinnamon. It has a uniquely light and nutty flavor quite different from American and European chocolates. The original chocolate drink that was served by the Mayan people was not sweetened and contained hot chili peppers!

Saffron Crème Brûlée

This is a very interesting way to flavor a classic dessert.

1. Preheat oven to 250°F.

2. Heat the cream and saffron to just under a simmer. Keep warm.

3. Mix together the egg yolks and sugar. Slowly stir the cream mixture into the sugar mixture. Strain through a fine-meshed sieve.

4. Pour into two 6-ounce ramekins and place the ramekins in a baking pan. Fill the pan with water to about 1 inch up the sides of the ramekins. Place the baking pan in the oven and bake for 1 to 1½ hours, until lightly set. Let cool at room temperature for 1 hour, then cool in the refrigerator overnight.

5. Preheat broiler. Sprinkle each ramekin with a ¼-inch layer of sugar and place under the broiler, as close to the heat as possible, until the tops are very brown. Allow the sugar to cool for 1 minute, and then serve.

Custard 101

This dessert is a very simple custard. A custard is a mixture of milk or cream and eggs that is cooked into a creamy consistency. Ice cream is a frozen custard, and quiches are made with savory custards. The trick is to cook them gently so you don't wind up with sweet scrambled eggs!

1 cup heavy cream
1 small pinch saffron
4 egg yolks
¼ cup granulated sugar, plus extra for sprinkling

Crustless Ricotta Cheesecakes

Simple and satisfying, these little "cakes" are a breeze to make.

*2 cups whole-milk ricotta
cheese*
2 eggs
½ cup granulated sugar
¼ cup all-purpose flour
1 tablespoon lemon zest
Pinch salt
Pinch ground nutmeg
1 tablespoon butter

1. Preheat oven to 300°F.

2. Place all the ingredients except the butter into a food processor and process until smooth.

3. Grease two 8-ounce ramekins with the butter and divide the cake mix between the ramekins. Bake for 20 minutes or until a toothpick inserted in the center comes out clean. Cool to room temperature before serving.

New York Vs. Italian Cheesecake
New York cheesecake is usually made from cream cheese and is very fine and creamy in texture. Italian cheesecake is usually made from ricotta cheese and has a more coarse texture. Both styles have their fans and defenders, and both have their virtues. You could make the recipe here with cream cheese in place of the ricotta.

Pumpkin Gratin with Marshmallows

Sort of like sweet potatoes with marshmallows, this is a playful dessert.

1 15-ounce can pumpkin pie filling
3 eggs
1 tablespoon butter
1 small bag mini marshmallows

1. Preheat oven to 375°F. Grease a small casserole dish with the butter.

2. Mix together the pumpkin pie filling and the eggs. Grease a small casserole dish with the butter. Spoon the pumpkin filling into the dish, spreading it out in an even layer.

3. Top with the marshmallows, and bake for about 18 minutes or until the marshmallows are browned and the center is piping hot. Let cool slightly, and serve warm.

Is It Really Pumpkin?
The large pumpkins that are used for jack-o'-lanterns are never eaten. It is the small "sugar pumpkins" that are typically eaten. Ironically, pumpkin pie filling and canned pumpkin are often made with all manner of winter squash, such as hubbard, butternut, acorn, and cheese pumpkin.

Broiled Banana Custard with Peanut Butter Sauce

1 large or 2 small ripe bananas
½ cup heavy cream
2 eggs
2 tablespoons granulated sugar
1 tablespoon dark rum
1 tablespoon butter
3 tablespoons creamy peanut butter
1 tablespoon milk

Peanut butter and bananas make a fantastic (and delicious) combination.

1. Preheat oven to 350°F.

2. Place the bananas, cream, eggs, sugar, and rum in a food processor, and process until smooth.

3. Grease two 6-ounce ramekins with the butter and pour the banana mix in the ramekins. Place the ramekins in a baking pan, and fill the pan with water to about 1 inch up the sides of the ramekins. Place the baking pan in the oven, and bake for 25 minutes or until a toothpick inserted in the center comes out clean.

4. Heat the milk and peanut butter together until smooth and warm, and pour over the custards.

Bananas and Rum
Bananas and rum have a natural affinity for each other. Try putting some rum in banana bread or muffins for a nice twist. Also, sautéing bananas in butter and then flaming with a little rum is a great ice cream topping or crepe filling.

Apple Tart Tatin with Puff Pastry

This is the classic apple upside-down torte. It's a winner.

1. In an 8- or 10-inch ovenproof sauté pan, melt the butter with the sugar. Arrange the apples in an attractive pattern in the melted butter and sugar mixture.

2. Keep the heat on medium and cook slowly for about 15 minutes or until the sugar starts to brown.

3. Preheat oven to 400°F.

4. Cut the puff pastry to fit the pan and place directly on top of the apples. Place the pan in the oven and bake for about 20 minutes or until the pastry is brown and the mixture is bubbling.

5. Remove from the oven and turn out onto a large serving dish. Let cool slightly, and serve warm.

Sweet History
Legend has it that a young French woman named Tatin invented this tart after flirting with a hunter who was staying at the family inn. Whatever the provenance of this tart, the results speak for themselves, with a melting texture and rich flavor. Try this.

½ cup butter
½ cup granulated sugar
2 tart apples, peeled, cored, and sliced ½ inch thick
1 sheet puff pastry

Strawberry Shakes with Orange Liqueur

4 scoops strawberry ice cream
2 cups milk
3 ounces orange liqueur
2 fresh strawberries

Yet another playful dessert, this shake is a bit grown-up with the addition of the liqueur.

In a blender, combine the ice cream, milk, and liqueur. Blend well and pour into tall, chilled glasses. Top with a fresh strawberry on the rim of the glass.

Strawberry Safety

Since strawberries are sweet, soft, and vulnerable, everything on earth likes to eat them, including bugs. For this reason, the strawberry crop has one of the highest concentrations of pesticides. It is important to always thoroughly wash strawberries under plenty of running water to get rid of most of these chemicals.

Strawberries with Balsamic Syrup

1 cup balsamic vinegar
¼ cup granulated sugar
1 quart washed strawberries

Strawberries and balsamic vinegar are a classic combination. Don't knock it till you try it.

In a small saucepan, combine the vinegar and sugar, and simmer until about 1/3 of a cup remains. Let cool to room temperature. Drizzle all over the berries, and enjoy.

Persimmon Split in Warm Honey Sauce

If you haven't had a persimmon, seek it out. They are available in the fall, and are a fantastic fruit. They are ripe when quite soft.

2 ripe persimmons, tops trimmed and split in half
2 scoops of your favorite ice cream
½ cup honey
1 tablespoon lemon juice
3 tablespoons crushed walnuts
1 cup whipped cream

1. Place the persimmons in a bowl and put the ice cream in the middle of the split fruit.

2. In a saucepan, combine the honey, lemon juice, and nuts. Heat until warm, and pour over the split. Top with the whipped cream and enjoy.

Persimmons

Persimmons are native to China and are cultivated throughout the East. Also known as the Japanese persimmon, there are 2 varieties available in the United States. There is a short, squat, and round fruit and an elongated larger fruit. They are both suitable for this dish if ripe.

Coconut and Ice Cream Snowballs

A great ending for a Caribbean or Hawaiian meal, or just fun in general.

2 cups vanilla ice cream
½ teaspoon coconut extract
3 cups shredded sweetened
  coconut

1. In a blender, combine the ice cream, coconut extract, and half of the coconut. Place in the freezer to harden.

2. Divide the frozen ice cream into 4 equal parts and roll into balls with gloved hands. Roll the balls in the remaining coconut and refreeze before serving.

Cuckoo for Coconuts
The coconut is an amazing fruit. It can travel hundreds of miles across open ocean and then send out roots through pure sand. It has colonized so many warm environments that they seem ubiquitous in many locales. They are full of a sweet liquid, which is called coconut water, not milk. The milk is gathered by shredding the flesh and then squeezing it out.

Easy Apple Strudel

Frozen phyllo dough and cooking spray make this dessert a pleasure to make.

¼ cup raisins
¼ cup brandy
2 green apples, peeled, cored, and diced
3 tablespoons butter
6 sheets phyllo dough, defrosted
Powdered sugar, for dusting

1. Soak the raisins in the brandy for 10 minutes. Sauté the apples in the butter until softened. Add the raisins and brandy, and let cool to room temperature.

2. Preheat oven to 375°F.

3. Lay out 1 sheet of dough and spray with the cooking spray, and repeat the process until all 6 sheets are stacked on top of one another.

4. Place the apple mixture at the bottom of the sheets, and roll up the sheets like a jelly roll. Tuck in the edges and place on a cookie sheet lined with parchment paper.

5. Spray the top of the strudel and place in the oven for about 20 minutes or until the pastry is golden. Let cool, and dust with the powdered sugar.

S'more Crisp Pie

6 graham crackers, crushed
2 tablespoons softened butter
2 standard Hershey's milk chocolate bars
6 large marshmallows

This is a fun and playful dessert, sure to remind you of childhood.

1. Preheat broiler. Mix together the graham crackers and butter and pack into a 6-inch tart shell or pie tin.

2. Melt the chocolate in the microwave on low, and pour on top of the crust.

3. Slice the marshmallows in half and place on top of the chocolate.

4. Place under the broiler for about 1 minute until the marshmallows brown. Let cool to room temperature, and serve.

Some More, Please
Of course, s'mores got their name because children were always asking for "some more." The classic campfire treats are nothing more than a toasted marshmallow on a gram cracker with a piece of chocolate. Eaten like a sweet sandwich after a hard day of hiking and tent pitching, these treats are hard to beat.

chapter 15
breakfast and brunch

"Lost Bread" (True French Toast)

This is the real deal. You haven't had French toast until you have had this recipe.

2 thick slices crusty bread,
    about 2 inches thick
2 cups milk
8 eggs, beaten
Pinch salt
3 tablespoons butter

1. Allow the bread to sit out, uncovered, for 24 to 36 hours to go completely stale. Place in a small dish just wide and deep enough to hold slices.

2. Mix together the milk, eggs, and salt, and pour over the bread. Cover with plastic wrap, and place a small dish on the top to prevent the bread from floating. Refrigerate overnight.

3. Remove the bread from the dish and cook over medium heat in the butter until very brown on all sides and no liquid escapes when the bread is squeezed (about 5 minutes per side). Serve warm.

Sour Cream Pancakes

These very delicate pancakes are exquisite in texture and flavor.

1 cup sour cream
2 eggs
¼ cup all-purpose flour
2 teaspoons granulated sugar
Pinch salt
Butter, as needed

1. Mix together all the ingredients except the butter and let rest for 10 minutes.

2. Lightly coat a nonstick pan with the butter. Pour about ¼ cup of the batter into the pan and cook for about 1 minute or until the up side is peppered with small bubbles. Flip very gently, and cook for about 1 more minute, until nicely browned. Repeat with the remaining batter. Serve hot.

Oatmeal, Buttermilk, and Banana Pancakes

These pancakes are very hearty. The bananas are a perfect addition.

¼ cup instant oatmeal
½ cup buttermilk
1 egg, beaten
Butter, as needed
¼ cup all-purpose flour
2 teaspoons granulated sugar
½ teaspoon baking powder
1 banana, sliced

1. Mix together the oatmeal and the buttermilk, and let stand for 1 hour.

2. Add the oatmeal mixture to the egg, 1 tablespoon melted butter, the flour, sugar, and baking powder. Let stand for 10 minutes.

3. Sauté the banana in 1 tablespoon butter for 1 minute over medium-high heat. Set aside and keep warm.

4. Coat a nonstick pan with butter and pour ¼ cup of the batter into the pan. Cook over medium heat until the top side is evenly peppered with bubbles. Flip over and cook for another 2 minutes. Repeat with the remaining batter. Serve with the bananas on top.

Cooked Bananas

Cooking bananas is a simple and effective way to change their flavor and texture. Bananas can be sautéed, fried in batter, broiled with sugar, grilled on a hot grill, and even boiled in their skins. Sugar, liqueur, and any manner of flavorings can be added. Some cultures even eat cooked bananas in a savory manner by adding garlic or even curry.

Maple-Apple-Brandy-Cranberry Sauce

Pour it over pancakes, French toast, or even ice cream! Yum!

2 tablespoons butter
1 large Granny Smith apple, peeled, cored, and sliced
2 tablespoons dried cranberries
¼ cup brandy
1 cup pure maple syrup

Melt the butter and sauté the apple until golden brown and softened. Add the remaining ingredients and cook over low heat for 5 minutes. Keep warm, and serve.

Cooking with Alcohol
When alcohol boils, 99 percent of the alcohol burns off. There are very small traces that remain, and this is important to know for people who have allergies. Always be cautious when adding alcohol to a hot pan, as it may burst into flames and cause some damage to either you or your kitchen.

Mushroom and Parmesan Frittata

This is a great breakfast for the mushroom lover.

2 tablespoons butter
1 (10-ounce) package white mushrooms, sliced
Salt and pepper, to taste
3 tablespoons extra-virgin olive oil
5 eggs, beaten
½ cup grated Parmesan cheese
1 tablespoon chopped fresh parsley

1. Preheat broiler.

2. Heat the butter on medium-high in a large skillet until it stops bubbling. Add the mushrooms, season with salt and pepper, and sauté for about 6 minutes or until the water releases from the mushrooms and evaporates.

3. Add the oil to the pan, then pour in the eggs and half of the Parmesan cheese. Cook the frittata by constantly stirring the eggs over medium-high heat until the eggs have set but are still quite moist.

4. Top the frittata with the remaining cheese and place under the broiler for about 3 minutes or until the top is very brown and the eggs are dry. Slide onto a platter and serve.

Perfect Poached Eggs

Many people complain about the trouble they have poaching eggs.
This is a good method.

4 eggs
2 quarts water
1 tablespoon white vinegar
Pinch salt

1. Place the water in a small saucepot. Bring the water to just under a boil and add the vinegar and salt.

2. Swirl the water in the pot with a large spoon very rapidly to form a fast-moving "whirlpool." Crack each egg into a bowl and drop in one at a time in the center of the whirlpool. Do not allow the water to boil. Cook for exactly 3 minutes for medium-soft yolks. Remove from the water with a slotted spoon, and drain on paper towels. Serve hot.

Poaching in Advance
You can prepoach eggs in anticipation of a large group of people. Simply follow the directions in this recipe, and when the eggs are almost done, place them in a bath of ice water. This will stop the eggs from cooking. You can store the eggs in the cold water in the fridge for up to 24 hours. When you are ready to serve them, simply drop them into the hot water for about 30 seconds to reheat. It works great!

Creamy Goat Cheese Scramble

*Goat cheese has a natural tanginess that goes great with eggs.
You can substitute cream cheese if you wish.*

6 eggs
4 ounces soft fresh goat
  cheese
2 tablespoons minced fresh
  chives
2 tablespoons butter
Salt and pepper, to taste

1. Melt the butter in a skillet over medium heat.

2. Mix together all the remaining ingredients well. Add to the warm butter and cook slowly, constantly stirring to make the smallest "curds" possible. Stop cooking the eggs when they are still very moist, but not watery. (This takes practice.) Serve in warm bowls and eat with a spoon.

Eggs and Salmonella

It is true that undercooked eggs can carry salmonella. The bacteria are commonly found on the outside of the shell, and a careful washing may prevent transmission. The other way to prevent infection is to always cook eggs to at least 165°F. The problem with this is that it eliminates all sunny-side, overeasy, poached, and soft-scrambled eggs. Buy eggs from refrigerated cases and in stores that do a brisk business and have lots of turnover of products on the shelf.

Chorizo and Eggs in Tortillas

A great Mexican-style breakfast; add guacamole and salsa if you wish.

❧

4 ounces chorizo sausage,
    minced
6 eggs, beaten
Salt and pepper, to taste
4 (6-inch) flour tortillas

1. Place the chorizo in a small pan over medium heat and allow the fat to slowly render and the sausage to become crispy (about 4 minutes).

2. Add the eggs and cook as you would scrambled eggs. Season with salt and pepper, and keep warm.

3. Warm the tortillas by holding them over a hot burner for a few seconds per side. Roll up the eggs in the tortillas, and eat like a taco with your hands.

Differences in Tortillas

The basic types of tortillas are flour and corn. Most Americans are familiar with the crispy fried yellow corn tortillas used for hard tacos. However, in Mexico the soft white corn tortillas are much more popular. Flour tortillas are used more for wrapping burritos and soft tacos. Experiment with different tortillas and find your favorite.

Separated Fluffy Omelet with Jam

4 eggs, separated
3 tablespoons butter
3 tablespoons jam
Powdered sugar, for dusting

This is an interesting take on the omelet, part breakfast, part dessert.

1. Preheat oven to 400°F.

2. Beat the egg whites with a mixer until stiff peaks form.

3. Beat the yolks until smooth.

4. Fold the yolks gently into the egg whites.

5. Heat the butter in a large ovenproof skillet until it stops bubbling. Pour the egg mixture into the pan, then immediately place the pan in the oven. Cook for about 7 minutes or until a toothpick inserted into the center comes out clean.

6. Slide the omelet onto a platter and top with the jam and powdered sugar. Serve hot.

Types of Omelets

There are several types of omelets. There are French omelets, which are rolled around a filling and are moist inside. There are country-style omelets, which are more like scrambled eggs with garnish cooked into a "pancake." And there are raised omelets like the one in this recipe. Egg cookery is complicated and requires practice. Many chefs ask perspective cooks to make an omelet as an audition.

Pastrami Hash

*This is a nice twist on the classic corned beef hash.
It's great for leftover pastrami sandwich meat.*

4 tablespoons butter, divided
½ pound pastrami, finely chopped
½ cup finely diced white onion
½ cup finely diced green bell pepper
1 baked potato, skin on, chopped into marble-sized pieces
1 teaspoon Worcestershire sauce
Salt and pepper, to taste

1. Heat 2 tablespoons of the butter in a heavy pan until it stops bubbling. Add the pastrami, onion, and bell pepper, and cook for about 5 minutes over medium heat.

2. Add the potato, Worcestershire sauce, and the remaining butter to the pan. Mix well. Cook for about 5 minutes per side or until very well crisped on each side. Season with salt and pepper, and serve hot.

Why Is It Called Hash?
The term hash seems to come from the French "hachet," which means to cut into small pieces. Many different types of hash are made including the classics corned beef and roast beef. You can use almost any leftover meats to make a hash, and some fish, especially smoked fish, make wonderful hashes.

Smoked Salmon and Avocado on Toast

½ an avocado, smashed
4 slices multigrain bread, toasted
Salt and pepper, to taste
¼ cup minced red onion
6 ounces smoked salmon
1 ripe tomato, sliced

The avocado makes a great substitute for the classic cream cheese in this dish.

1. Spread the avocado on 2 slices of the bread. Season with salt and pepper, and top each with the minced onion.

2. Top each with the tomato and salmon, and the remaining bread. Serve immediately.

Healthy Fat

Avocados are loaded with healthy fat. The type of fat found in avocadoes is also found in olive oil and walnuts. It is important to have fat in your diet, but it is important to vary the sources of these fats and not get them all from animal products, which are typically saturated fats. Saturated fats are unhealthier than most plant-based fats.

Granola and Yogurt Parfait

2 cups plain low-fat yogurt
2 cups low-fat granola
1 pint strawberries, washed and sliced

This is a nice and healthy way to start the day.

Simply alternate layers of yogurt, granola, and berries in a tall, clear glass until it is full. Make the top layer berries for an attractive presentation.

The Facts about Granola

Granola has been touted as a very healthy food. The facts are that "regular" granola has a very high fat content. Unfortunately, commercial granola is not only full of fat, but the fat is usually hydrogenated, which is very unhealthy. Look for low-fat granola or shop for granola in health food stores, where most are made with unhydrogenated fats.

Yogurt Cheese and Honey on Warm Pita

A very Middle Eastern breakfast, but good anywhere.

෪

2 cups plain, whole yogurt
2 pita bread rounds
4 tablespoons honey
8 ripe figs, cut in half

1. Place the yogurt in a colander lined with a coffee filter, and set over a bowl. Let drain overnight in the refrigerator. The next day, discard the water and place the yogurt cheese in a bowl.

2. Warm the pitas in a 350°F oven for 3 minutes. Spread with the yogurt cheese, drizzle with the honey, and top with the figs.

Brandy and Brown Sugar Bacon

This is a very interesting way to season bacon and makes a great breakfast side dish.

෪

½ pound sliced bacon
¼ cup light brown sugar
¼ cup brandy

1. Lay out the bacon on a baking sheet and sprinkle both sides with the brown sugar and brandy. Let marinate overnight in the refrigerator.

2. Preheat oven to 300°F.

3. Bake for about 18 minutes or until the bacon is as crispy as you like it.

Cooking Bacon
Cooking bacon in a frying pan is both messy and time-consuming. A great way to cook bacon is as described here, on a baking sheet in the oven. Another great alternative is to layer bacon between paper towels and cook it in the microwave. The fat is absorbed in the towels, and the bacon is always crisp. Experiment with different power settings until you find what works with your machine.

Smoked Ham "Pâté" on English Muffins

6 ounces smoked ham, very
thinly sliced or finely
chopped
2 tablespoons mayonnaise
2 toasted English muffins
4 slices ripe tomato
4 Perfect Poached Eggs
(page 285)

*This is a great way to use leftover ham,
but is good enough to buy ham specifically to make this dish.*

1. Place the ham and the mayo in a food processor, and blend into a smooth paste.

2. Spread the "pâté" on the English muffins, and top each with a slice of tomato and a poached egg. Serve hot.

French Toast Stuffed with Cream Cheese and Jelly

4 eggs, beaten
1 cup milk
4 slices white bread
Butter, for cooking
3 tablespoons cream cheese
3 tablespoons jam of your
choice

Use plain white bread for this version of French toast. It's just better.

1. Mix together the eggs and milk. Soak the bread in the mixture for 1 minute. Fry well on both sides in butter.

2. Spread one side of 2 slices of the French bread with the cream cheese. Top each with the jam and a slice of bread. No syrup needed here.

Butter Is Better
Butter has superior flavor over oil in many applications, especially breakfast cookery. It is the milk solids in the butter that brown when the butter is cooked and give up that rich and nutty flavor that only butter has. If you are going to be cooking over very high heat, butter is not recommended because it burns easily.

Smoky Home Fries

The trick here is cooking the potatoes halfway ahead of time.

2 large Idaho potatoes
6 slices bacon, minced
1 white onion, small diced
1 green bell pepper, small diced
2 tablespoons butter
Salt and pepper, to taste

1. Simmer the potatoes, skin on, in plenty of salted water for 10 minutes. Drain and let cool.

2. Peel the potatoes and cut into ¼-inch-thick pieces (random shapes are nice).

3. Place the bacon in a pan and cook until crispy. Remove the bacon and leave the fat in the pan. Turn the heat to medium-high and add the potatoes. Do not stir the potatoes right away. Allow them to brown well on one side before turning them.

4. Turn the potatoes over and add the onion, bell pepper, and butter. Cook for about 10 minutes or until all the potatoes are browned and the onions and peppers are soft, stirring occasionally. Add the crispy bacon and toss to mix. Season with salt and pepper, and serve.

Bell Peppers—Spicy or Not?
Green bell peppers are actually underripe red or yellow bell peppers. Many people think that red bell peppers are hot and spicy. But these peppers are actually sweeter than their green counterparts and make a great addition in many dishes for both color and flavor. Do not fear red peppers! If they are spicy, they will be advertised as such.

Green Eggs and Ham

This is not just for kids. The flavors are sophisticated and delicious.

2 tablespoons butter
4 ounces smoked ham, chopped
6 eggs, beaten
3 tablespoons store-bought pesto
Salt and pepper, to taste

1. Heat the butter in a nonstick pan until it stops bubbling. Add the ham and sauté for 1 minute.

2. Add the eggs and pesto, and cook as you would scrambled eggs. Season with salt and pepper. Serve hot on toast, or alone.

Eggselent Facts
Eggs are a great source of protein and healthy omega-3 fatty acids. The anatomy of an egg is quite interesting. The white is actually like amniotic fluid that protects the chick. The yolk is the food that the chick eats inside the shell before hatching. The little white squiggly thing on the yolk (called the chalazae) is actually what would be the chick if the egg were fertilized.

Hot Grape Nuts with Honey

This is a truly healthy and hearty breakfast. Try it on a cold morning.

3 cups Grape Nuts cereal
4 cups soy milk
3 tablespoons honey

Combine all the ingredients in a small pot and heat on low for about 6 minutes. Serve in bowls like oatmeal.

Super Soy
Soy protein is perhaps the healthiest protein on the planet, and soy milk is a great way to get some. Look for soy milks that are lower in sugar and unflavored. Japanese-style soy milks are usually much less sweet than the Chinese-style milks, which are loaded with sugar. There is no lactose in soy milk, and it is a great milk substitute for cooking and baking.

Cheddar Cheese Biscuits with Apples

Cheddar cheese and apples are a great combination anytime.

1. Preheat oven to 425°F.

2. Mix together the flour, baking soda, and salt. Add the shortening and cheese, and mix well. Add the milk slowly, mixing just until the dough holds together.

3. Knead slightly on a floured board for just a few seconds. Roll out to about ½ inch thickness and cut with a biscuit cutter. Place on a baking sheet, and bake for 15 minutes.

4. Heat the butter in a small pan until it stops bubbling. Add the apples and sauté for about 3 minutes or until soft. Serve over the warm biscuits.

Cheddar and Apples

This combination is always a winner. Try eating a sweet apple between bites of a sharp Cheddar and you will see. Another great way to enjoy this flavor combination is to have some deep-dish apple pie with a slab of Cheddar melted over the top. It sounds strange, but this is a true treat and is famous in upstate New York.

1 cup all-purpose flour
1½ teaspoons baking powder
Pinch salt
2 teaspoons vegetable
    shortening
¼ cup milk
½ cup grated Cheddar cheese
2 tablespoons butter
1 large green apple, peeled,
    cored, and sliced

Kielbasa and Eggs with Onions

1 medium-sized white onion, sliced thin
2 tablespoons butter
4 ounces kielbasa, small diced
5 eggs, beaten
Salt and pepper, to taste

Be sure to cook the onions long enough to develop their sweetness.

Cook the onion over medium heat in the butter until well browned and soft. Add the kielbasa and sauté for 2 minutes. Add the eggs, and cook as you would scrambled eggs. Season with salt and pepper, and serve with rye toast.

Scrambled Egg Secrets

The secret to fluffy scrambled eggs that are moist and not watery is to cook them over medium to low heat and constantly stir the eggs. Never add milk to scrambled eggs; this only makes them watery.

Peanut Butter and Chocolate Pancakes

½ cup sifted all-purpose flour
1 teaspoon baking powder
Pinch of salt
1 egg
½ cup milk
1 tablespoon creamy peanut butter
1 teaspoon melted butter
Butter, for cooking
½ cup chocolate morsels

Who can resist this combination of flavors?

1. Mix together the flour, baking powder, and salt. Beat the egg and add to the milk. Mix with the flour mixture. Mix the peanut butter with the melted butter and mix well. Add to the batter.

2. Melt a pat of butter in a nonstick pan or griddle. Pour ¼ cup of the batter into the pan. Heat until small bubbles form on the surface of the pancake. Sprinkle the morsels over the top, then flip the pancake. Repeat with the remaining batter. No syrup is necessary for these treats.

Appendix A:
Menu Suggestions for Various Occasions

Valentines Day
Oysters in the Nude with Three Sauces, page 16

Bacon-Wrapped Figs Stuffed with Blue Cheese, page 47

Classic Roast Prime Rib with Horseradish Sauce, page 174

Chocolate and Coffee Semifredo, page 269

New Year's Eve
Baby Potatoes with Sour Cream and Caviar, page 25

Endive, Walnut, and Blue Cheese Salad, page 56

Pan-Roasted Lobster in Brandy and Butter, page 184

Saffron Crème Brûlée, page 271

First Date
Shrimp Cocktail 101, page 14

Mustard-Crusted Filet Mignon, page 162

Chocolate Chunk Cookies with Sweet Milk Sauce, page 267

Picnic
Wild Rice Salad, page 62

Buttermilk and Mustard Fried Chicken, page 151

Roasted Peach Crisp, page 266

Big Sporting Event
Prize-Winning Chili, page 203

Dominican Rice with Sofrito and Pigeon Peas, page 228

Broiled Banana Custard with Peanut Butter Sauce, page 274

Anniversary
Crab Cakes Baltimore, page 44

Grill-Smoked Rack of Lamb with Raspberry Glaze, page 169

Apple Tart Tatin with Puff Pastry, page 275

Sweet Breakfast
"Lost Bread" (True French Toast), page 282

Brandy and Brown Sugar Bacon, page 291

Maple-Apple-Brandy-Cranberry Sauce, page 284

Savory Breakfast
Creamy Goat Cheese Scramble, page 286

Pastrami Hash, page 289

Cheddar Cheese Biscuits with Apples, page 295

Cold Breakfast
Smoked Salmon and Avocado on Toast, page 290

Granola and Yogurt Parfait, page 290

Pears Poached in White Wine and Vanilla, page 262

Italian Supper
"Frico" Cheese Crisps with Onions and Mushrooms, page 39

Tuscan Tomato and Bread Soup, page 86

Spinach Noodles with Smoked Ham, page 106

Figs Roasted with Sweet Cheese and Licorice, page 265

Cold Supper

Grilled and Chilled Asparagus in Vinaigrette, page 19

Cold Pasta with Butter Beans and Tuna, page 100

Coconut and Ice Cream Snowballs, page 278

Japanese-Style Supper

Japanese Spicy Tuna Tartar, page 15

Citrus and Sesame Soybean Salad, page 66

Miso Soup with Shrimp, page 87

Chicken Cutlet "Katzu" Style, page 152

Thanksgiving for Two

Stuffed Cornish Game Hens, page 153

Orange-Glazed Baby Brussels Sprouts with Walnuts, page 235

String Beans with Toasted Bread Crumbs, page 223

Pumpkin Gratin with Marshmallows, page 273

Latin-Style Supper

Dominican Avocado Salad, page 69

Mexican Chicken Soup, page 80

Shredded Chicken Enchilada Pie, page 138

Mexican Hot Chocolate Float, page 270

Greek-Style Supper

"Smoked" Eggplant Dip, page 22

Calamari and Rice Salad, page 70

Greek-Style Taverna Oregano and Lemon Chicken, page 139

Winter Supper

Warm Spinach Salad with Deviled Egg Croutons, page 57

Roasted Sweet Potato Soup, page 90

Slow-Cooked Beef Brisket with Teriyaki Glaze, page 164

Broiled Banana Custard with Peanut Butter Sauce, page 274

Fall Supper

Easy Spinach Soufflés with Smoked Gouda, page 35

Curried Cauliflower and Green Grape Soup, page 79

Stir-fried Blackfish with Black Bean Sauce, page 132

Baked Apples with Pecan Butter, page 263

Summer Supper

Lime and Cilantro Scented Crab Salad, page 13

Brutus Salad with Roasted Garlic Dressing, page 68

Cold Pasta with Butter Beans and Tuna, page 100

Grilled Pineapple with Caramel Ice Cream, page 264

Spring Supper

Quick-Cured Salmon with Dilled Sour Cream Sauce, page 12

Spinach Noodles with Smoked Ham, page 106

Crispy and Mustardy Roasted Rainbow Trout, page 121

Crustless Ricotta Cheesecakes, page 272

Index

THE EVERYTHING SERIES!

BUSINESS & PERSONAL FINANCE

Everything® Budgeting Book
Everything® Business Planning Book
Everything® Coaching and Mentoring Book
Everything® Fundraising Book
Everything® Get Out of Debt Book
Everything® Grant Writing Book
Everything® Home-Based Business Book
Everything® Homebuying Book, 2nd Ed.
Everything® Homeselling Book, 2nd Ed.
Everything® Investing Book, 2nd Ed.
Everything® Landlording Book
Everything® Leadership Book
Everything® Managing People Book
Everything® Negotiating Book
Everything® Online Business Book
Everything® Personal Finance Book
Everything® Personal Finance in Your 20s and 30s Book
Everything® Project Management Book
Everything® Real Estate Investing Book
Everything® Robert's Rules Book, $7.95
Everything® Selling Book
Everything® Start Your Own Business Book
Everything® Wills & Estate Planning Book

COOKING

Everything® Barbecue Cookbook
Everything® Bartender's Book, $9.95
Everything® Chinese Cookbook
Everything® Cocktail Parties and Drinks Book
Everything® College Cookbook
Everything® Cookbook
Everything® Cooking for Two Cookbook
Everything® Diabetes Cookbook
Everything® Easy Gourmet Cookbook
Everything® Fondue Cookbook
Everything® Gluten-Free Cookbook

Everything® Grilling Cookbook
Everything® Healthy Meals in Minutes Cookbook
Everything® Holiday Cookbook
Everything® Indian Cookbook
Everything® Italian Cookbook
Everything® Low-Carb Cookbook
Everything® Low-Fat High-Flavor Cookbook
Everything® Low-Salt Cookbook
Everything® Meals for a Month Cookbook
Everything® Mediterranean Cookbook
Everything® Mexican Cookbook
Everything® One-Pot Cookbook
Everything® Pasta Cookbook
Everything® Quick Meals Cookbook
Everything® Slow Cooker Cookbook
Everything® Slow Cooking for a Crowd Cookbook
Everything® Soup Cookbook
Everything® Thai Cookbook
Everything® Vegetarian Cookbook
Everything® Wine Book, 2nd Ed.

CRAFT SERIES

Everything® Crafts—Baby Scrapbooking
Everything® Crafts—Bead Your Own Jewelry
Everything® Crafts—Create Your Own Greeting Cards
Everything® Crafts—Easy Projects
Everything® Crafts—Polymer Clay for Beginners
Everything® Crafts—Rubber Stamping Made Easy
Everything® Crafts—Wedding Decorations and Keepsakes

HEALTH

Everything® Alzheimer's Book
Everything® Diabetes Book
Everything® Health Guide to Controlling Anxiety

Everything® Hypnosis Book
Everything® Low Cholesterol Book
Everything® Massage Book
Everything® Menopause Book
Everything® Nutrition Book
Everything® Reflexology Book
Everything® Stress Management Book

HISTORY

Everything® American Government Book
Everything® American History Book
Everything® Civil War Book
Everything® Irish History & Heritage Book
Everything® Middle East Book

HOBBIES & GAMES

Everything® Blackjack Strategy Book
Everything® Brain Strain Book, $9.95
Everything® Bridge Book
Everything® Candlemaking Book
Everything® Card Games Book
Everything® Card Tricks Book, $9.95
Everything® Cartooning Book
Everything® Casino Gambling Book, 2nd Ed.
Everything® Chess Basics Book
Everything® Craps Strategy Book
Everything® Crossword and Puzzle Book
Everything® Crossword Challenge Book
Everything® Cryptograms Book, $9.95
Everything® Digital Photography Book
Everything® Drawing Book
Everything® Easy Crosswords Book
Everything® Family Tree Book, 2nd Ed.
Everything® Games Book, 2nd Ed.
Everything® Knitting Book
Everything® Knots Book
Everything® Photography Book
Everything® Poker Strategy Book
Everything® Pool & Billiards Book
Everything® Quilting Book
Everything® Scrapbooking Book

All Everything® books are priced at $12.95 or $14.95, unless otherwise stated. Prices subject to change without notice.

Everything® Sewing Book
Everything® Test Your IQ Book, $9.95
Everything® Travel Crosswords Book, $9.95
Everything® Woodworking Book
Everything® Word Games Challenge Book
Everything® Word Search Book

HOME IMPROVEMENT

Everything® Feng Shui Book
Everything® Feng Shui Decluttering Book,
    $9.95
Everything® Fix-It Book
Everything® Homebuilding Book
Everything® Lawn Care Book
Everything® Organize Your Home Book

EVERYTHING®
KIDS' BOOKS

All titles are $6.95

Everything® Kids' Animal Puzzle & Activity
    Book
Everything® Kids' Baseball Book, 3rd Ed.
Everything® Kids' Bible Trivia Book
Everything® Kids' Bugs Book
Everything® Kids' Christmas Puzzle
    & Activity Book
Everything® Kids' Cookbook
Everything® Kids' Crazy Puzzles Book
Everything® Kids' Dinosaurs Book
Everything® Kids' Gross Jokes Book
Everything® Kids' Gross Puzzle and
    Activity Book
Everything® Kids' Halloween Puzzle
    & Activity Book
Everything® Kids' Hidden Pictures Book
Everything® Kids' Joke Book
Everything® Kids' Knock Knock Book
Everything® Kids' Math Puzzles Book
Everything® Kids' Mazes Book
Everything® Kids' Money Book
Everything® Kids' Nature Book
Everything® Kids' Puzzle Book
Everything® Kids' Riddles & Brain Teasers Book
Everything® Kids' Science Experiments Book
Everything® Kids' Sharks Book
Everything® Kids' Soccer Book
Everything® Kids' Travel Activity Book

KIDS' STORY BOOKS

Everything® Fairy Tales Book

LANGUAGE

Everything® Conversational Japanese Book
    (with CD), $19.95
Everything® French Phrase Book, $9.95
Everything® French Verb Book, $9.95
Everything® Inglés Book
Everything® Learning French Book
Everything® Learning German Book
Everything® Learning Italian Book
Everything® Learning Latin Book
Everything® Learning Spanish Book
Everything® Sign Language Book
Everything® Spanish Grammar Book
Everything® Spanish Practice Book
    (with CD), $19.95
Everything® Spanish Phrase Book, $9.95
Everything® Spanish Verb Book, $9.95

MUSIC

Everything® Drums Book (with CD), $19.95
Everything® Guitar Book
Everything® Home Recording Book
Everything® Playing Piano and Keyboards
    Book
Everything® Reading Music Book (with CD),
    $19.95
Everything® Rock & Blues Guitar Book
    (with CD), $19.95
Everything® Songwriting Book

NEW AGE

Everything® Astrology Book, 2nd Ed.
Everything® Dreams Book, 2nd Ed.
Everything® Ghost Book
Everything® Love Signs Book, $9.95
Everything® Numerology Book
Everything® Paganism Book
Everything® Palmistry Book
Everything® Psychic Book
Everything® Reiki Book
Everything® Tarot Book
Everything® Wicca and Witchcraft Book

PARENTING

Everything® Baby Names Book
Everything® Baby Shower Book
Everything® Baby's First Food Book
Everything® Baby's First Year Book
Everything® Birthing Book
Everything® Breastfeeding Book
Everything® Father-to-Be Book
Everything® Father's First Year Book
Everything® Get Ready for Baby Book
Everything® Get Your Baby to Sleep Book,
    $9.95
Everything® Getting Pregnant Book
Everything® Homeschooling Book
Everything® Mother's First Year Book
Everything® Parent's Guide to Children
    and Divorce
Everything® Parent's Guide to Children
    with ADD/ADHD
Everything® Parent's Guide to Children
    with Asperger's Syndrome
Everything® Parent's Guide to Children
    with Autism
Everything® Parent's Guide to Children with
    Bipolar Disorder
Everything® Parent's Guide to Children
    with Dyslexia
Everything® Parent's Guide to Positive
    Discipline
Everything® Parent's Guide to Raising a
    Successful Child
Everything® Parent's Guide to Tantrums
Everything® Parent's Guide to the Overweight
    Child
Everything® Parent's Guide to the Strong-
    Willed Child
Everything® Parenting a Teenager Book
Everything® Potty Training Book, $9.95
Everything® Pregnancy Book, 2nd Ed.
Everything® Pregnancy Fitness Book
Everything® Pregnancy Nutrition Book
Everything® Pregnancy Organizer, $15.00
Everything® Toddler Book
Everything® Tween Book
Everything® Twins, Triplets, and More Book

All Everything® books are priced at $12.95 or $14.95, unless otherwise stated. Prices subject to change without notice.

PETS

Everything® Cat Book
Everything® Dachshund Book
Everything® Dog Book
Everything® Dog Health Book
Everything® Dog Training and Tricks Book
Everything® German Shepherd Book
Everything® Golden Retriever Book
Everything® Horse Book
Everything® Horseback Riding Book
Everything® Labrador Retriever Book
Everything® Poodle Book
Everything® Pug Book
Everything® Puppy Book
Everything® Rottweiler Book
Everything® Small Dogs Book
Everything® Tropical Fish Book
Everything® Yorkshire Terrier Book

REFERENCE

Everything® Car Care Book
Everything® Classical Mythology Book
Everything® Computer Book
Everything® Divorce Book
Everything® Einstein Book
Everything® Etiquette Book, 2nd Ed.
Everything® Inventions and Patents Book
Everything® Mafia Book
Everything® Philosophy Book
Everything® Psychology Book
Everything® Shakespeare Book

RELIGION

Everything® Angels Book
Everything® Bible Book
Everything® Buddhism Book
Everything® Catholicism Book
Everything® Christianity Book
Everything® Jewish History & Heritage Book
Everything® Judaism Book
Everything® Koran Book
Everything® Prayer Book
Everything® Saints Book
Everything® Torah Book
Everything® Understanding Islam Book
Everything® World's Religions Book
Everything® Zen Book

SCHOOL & CAREERS

Everything® Alternative Careers Book
Everything® College Survival Book, 2nd Ed.
Everything® Cover Letter Book, 2nd Ed.
Everything® Get-a-Job Book
Everything® Guide to Starting and Running a Restaurant
Everything® Job Interview Book
Everything® New Teacher Book
Everything® Online Job Search Book
Everything® Paying for College Book
Everything® Practice Interview Book
Everything® Resume Book, 2nd Ed.
Everything® Study Book

SELF-HELP

Everything® Dating Book, 2nd Ed.
Everything® Great Sex Book
Everything® Kama Sutra Book
Everything® Self-Esteem Book

SPORTS & FITNESS

Everything® Fishing Book
Everything® Golf Instruction Book
Everything® Pilates Book
Everything® Running Book
Everything® Total Fitness Book
Everything® Weight Training Book
Everything® Yoga Book

TRAVEL

Everything® Family Guide to Hawaii
Everything® Family Guide to Las Vegas, 2nd Ed.
Everything® Family Guide to New York City, 2nd Ed.
Everything® Family Guide to RV Travel & Campgrounds
Everything® Family Guide to the Walt Disney World Resort®, Universal Studios®, and Greater Orlando, 4th Ed.
Everything® Family Guide to Cruise Vacations
Everything® Family Guide to the Caribbean
Everything® Family Guide to Washington D.C., 2nd Ed.
Everything® Guide to New England
Everything® Travel Guide to the Disneyland Resort®, California Adventure®, Universal Studios®, and the Anaheim Area

WEDDINGS

Everything® Bachelorette Party Book, $9.95
Everything® Bridesmaid Book, $9.95
Everything® Elopement Book, $9.95
Everything® Father of the Bride Book, $9.95
Everything® Groom Book, $9.95
Everything® Mother of the Bride Book, $9.95
Everything® Outdoor Wedding Book
Everything® Wedding Book, 3rd Ed.
Everything® Wedding Checklist, $9.95
Everything® Wedding Etiquette Book, $9.95
Everything® Wedding Organizer, $15.00
Everything® Wedding Shower Book, $9.95
Everything® Wedding Vows Book, $9.95
Everything® Weddings on a Budget Book, $9.95

WRITING

Everything® Creative Writing Book
Everything® Get Published Book
Everything® Grammar and Style Book
Everything® Guide to Writing a Book Proposal
Everything® Guide to Writing a Novel
Everything® Guide to Writing Children's Books
Everything® Guide to Writing Research Papers
Everything® Screenwriting Book
Everything® Writing Poetry Book
Everything® Writing Well Book